P9-AGF-673

james beard's
treasury of
outdoor
cooking

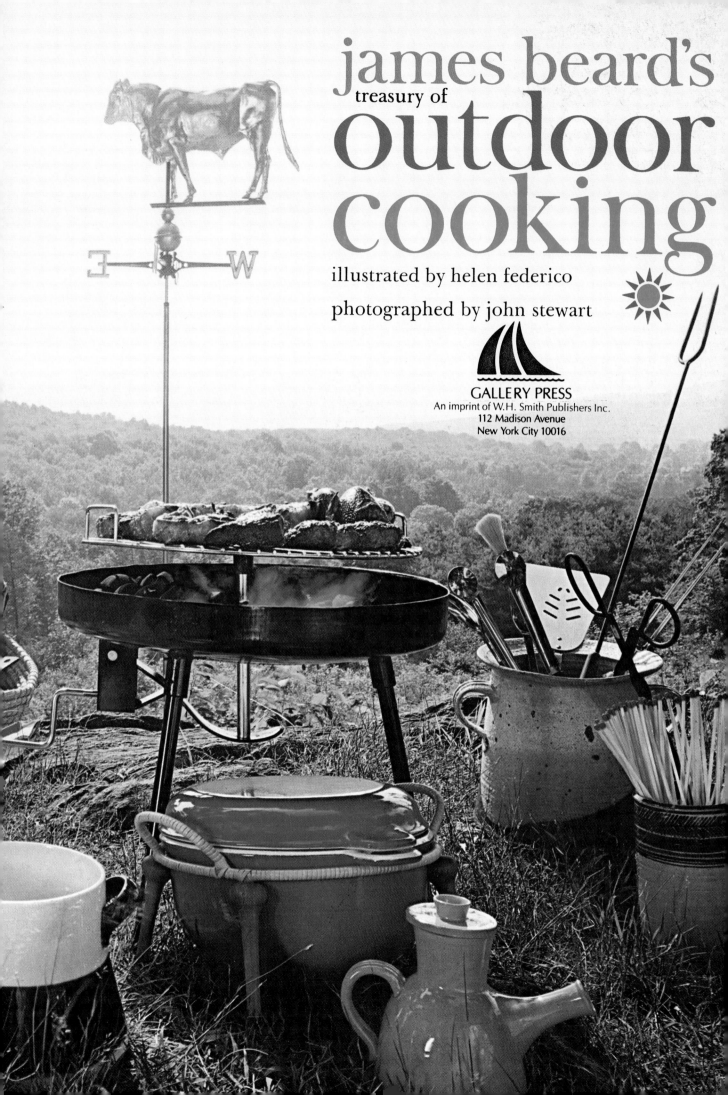

james beard's
treasury of
outdoor cooking

illustrated by helen federico

photographed by john stewart

GALLERY PRESS
An imprint of W.H. Smith Publishers Inc.
112 Madison Avenue
New York City 10016

Prepared and produced by
The Ridge Press, Inc.

Editor-in-Chief: JERRY MASON
Editor: ADOLPH SUEHSDORF
Art Director: ALBERT A. SQUILLACE
Associate Editor: RUTH BIRNKRANT
Associate Editor: EDWINA GLEN
Associate Editor: EVELYN HANNON
Associate Editor: DORIS MULLANE
Art Researcher: JOZEFA STUART
Art Associate: ALBERT KAMP

Copyright 1960 in all countries of the International Copyright Union by Western Publishing Company, Inc. and The Ridge Press, Inc.

All rights reserved. No part of this book may be reproduced or transmitted in any form or by any means, without written permission from the Publisher.

Published by Gallery Press
An imprint of W.H. Smith Publishers, Inc.
112 Madison Avenue
New York, New York 10016

Printed in the Netherlands
by Royal Smeets Offset B.V., Weert

1 2 3 4 5 6 7 8 9 10

Library of Congress Catalog
Card Number: 60–13425

ISBN 0-8317-0712-7

contents

Everywhere I go, I find a revolution in American eating—the outdoors has come into the home. A new and exciting style of open-air eating is bringing fresh delights to diners on patios and in backyards—or in dining rooms and kitchenettes. And they're available in every season of the year.

What a phenomenal change! Just twenty years ago, when I first wrote about outdoor cooking, backyard chefs were few. And their usual fare was steak or hamburger, blackened in an inferno of smoke and flame, and a great deal of beer to wash away the taste of culinary disaster. Today, in the city no less than the country, we have elevated outdoor cooking to a high art. We still have all the joys of the simplest cooking over fire, but we have added the pleasures of true international cookery. Our terraces have become second dining rooms. The kitchen stove is no longer king, but a willing partner of the grill rack, the rotisserie spit, and the fireplace. We have mingled a dozen styles of cooking—from the simplest to the most complex—to produce superb outdoor menus and meals that may be eaten and enjoyed anywhere.

As I travel about these days, I don't find it at all unusual to sit at a table indoors and find myself being served a charcoaled duckling that has been spitted over an outdoor grill, and an elaborate, kitchen-prepared rice-and-pine-nut pilaff. Or, just as excitingly, to find myself in a garden with grilled beef tenderloin with a Béarnaise sauce, potatoes Dauphinois, hot from an indoor oven, a Caesar salad, and a cheese. Such sophistication, of course, is simply a rediscovery of man's most basic style of cooking. Outdoor cookery and eating are as old as fire. Primitive man began it, and out-of-doors meals have progressed through the centuries with explorers, crusaders, missionaries, and adventurers. India, Persia, Greece, Rome, and China, all have contributed much to civilization's menu. Despite dark ages when men's bellies were as undernourished as their minds, the pleasures of the table have increased steadily—and delightfully.

America, as you might guess, also has made major contributions. The settlers who arrived here were used to a Renaissance diet. But they soon found themselves sampling strange and exotic foods of the New World—pumpkin, turkey, tomatoes. And it wasn't so long ago that pioneering Americans began discovering and acquiring new tastes as they ventured into the wilderness of the West. My own grandparents, who crossed to Oregon in a covered wagon, passed down recipes that had game, wild berries, and the green plants of plain and forest as ingredients. From them I learned to love dried apples and corn, and small bits of game impaled on sticks and roasted. By them I was introduced to vinegar pie, a practical and tasty solution to the lack of citrus fruits in winter, and to corn-meal cakes and loaves cooked on a griddle.

Now, in the 1960's, we have an inheritance of good cooking from all ages of man and a new inclination to apply them imaginatively to a pleasant mode of indoor-outdoor life. And we have all the conveniences of modern civilization to ease our task. Our spits are no longer turned by little boys on treadmills or little dogs, caged in a wheel, pursuing a morsel of meat. We have adapted the old (and often electrified it) and created the new: dehydrated foods, prepared mixes, portable ice boxes, and vacuum containers.

The time, therefore, is ripe for this book. I have constructed it simply and it is amply indexed. You should have no difficulty locating any of the hundreds of recipes and variations that interest you. The principal division of material is in terms of outdoor-cooking methods. Under each of these you will find recipes grouped according to the meat involved. Unless otherwise noted, recipes are generally calculated to serve four people. I find that appetites vary greatly, however, so you may have to adjust for your particular household. Note, too, that I have included many recipes—particularly in the section on "Outdoor Complements"—that require a stove or an oven; casseroles, breads, some vegetables, fine sauces, and so forth. This, I think you'll agree, is fitting. The day has passed when red barbecue sauce from a bottle or potato chips were adequate complements to outdoor dining. You may use with assurance any of the brand-name items I have suggested. There may be others as good, but these I have tested personally and recommend.

The taste of the outdoors lends a wonderful air of festivity and well-being to a meal. That's why I wrote this book. It's been my aim to enable you to savor this atmosphere fully, wherever you live.   *James Beard*

grilling ^{section}1

ENTRECÔTE IS PROPERLY GARNISHED WITH TOMATOES, MUSHROOMS.

Grilling was brought to perfection by the
English and transformed to an art by the French. Today
Americans are the beneficiaries of this purest of
cooking techniques for the choicest meats,
fish, and fowl. Whatever your preference—rib
roast or porterhouse, lamb leg or pork
loin, pheasant or turkey, salmon or trout—all may
be grilled to an ultimate degree of flavor
whose hallmark is a crust of exquisite brown char.

grilling beef

Thick, juicy steak on the grill is certainly one of the more usual outdoor cooking scenes in this country. It's popular, appetizing, and easy to cook, but familiarity with the types and cuts of beef is a necessary preliminary to successful broiling.

Prime is the U.S. Government designation for top-grade beef. *Choice* is only a notch below prime. Often the two may be differentiated only by the well-trained palate, and either will assure you excellent eating. *Good* beef is no more and no less than the name implies. It is quite acceptable, but for this—and certainly for all lower grades—you may have to choose recipes that compensate for lesser quality by longer cooking and tenderizing. Of course, not even the finest sauce will camouflage really poor meat. Superior beef is a rich, red color and flecked with fat. It is most savory and tender when properly aged.

The finest cuts for steaks or roasts are taken from the short loin, identified by the T- or cross-shaped bone running through it. The fillet, or tenderloin, is cut from one side of the bone, the contra-fillet—or shell—from the other. Porterhouse is the most magnificent cut from the short loin. It may be grilled in any thickness from 1½ to 3 inches. T-bone and club steaks are similar cuts from higher on the loin. The most tender cut is the fillet. It may be taken from the porterhouse for an individual serving. Or, if you are feeding a number of people, it is less expensive per pound to buy the entire tenderloin and cook it as is. You can even cut it into steaks yourself, or cut some into steaks and spit roast the remainder. Shell steaks are second only to the fillet and perfect for individual servings. (The aristocratic chateaubriand is cut diagonally from the center of the tenderloin.) Sirloin and pin-bone sirloin are both fine cuts, succulent and relatively economical for feeding a large group. They are taken from the loin end, or just above the hip, and are best for grilling when cut no less than 1½ inches thick. The English and French prefer these sirloin cuts for roasting, unlike Americans who are partial to ribs. The French call rib steaks *entre-côtes* and consider them a delicacy. As, indeed, they are, cooked either with or without the bone. They are always best when cut from the first three—or sometimes five—ribs (numbering from the loin toward the shoulder). Minute steaks are simply thin steaks, cut from the rib, sirloin, or shell. They should be pan-broiled or sautéed quickly because of their thinness.

Note: Recipes for the sauces referred to in this chapter will be found in "Outdoor Complements," beginning on page 172.

broiled sirloin steak

A sirloin, to my taste, should be at least 1½ inches thick. When you have good white coals, and the grill level registers about 350 to 375 F., sear the steak on both sides to hold in the juices. Lower the fire bed and continue cooking, turning with tongs until the proper degree of doneness is reached. If you like a charred surface, bring the coals up and flame the steak just before serving.

pin-bone sirloin steak

Excellent meat, and usually less expensive than some of the other steaks. Sometimes there is quite a bit of bone, but the meat has good flavor and texture. It slices well, too.

wedge-bone sirloin

This is merely another version of the pin bone. There is a smallish bone which may be removed easily if you want to make carving simple. While perhaps not so choice as porterhouse, it is fairly economical, and wonderful when broiled, carved carefully in thin, diagonal slices, and sauced with Béarnaise or Bordelaise.

beefsteak smothered with onions

I have a great weakness for "Beefsteak Smothered with Onions," a dish that is made for the

LAUGH KILLS LONESOME, BY CHARLES M. RUSSELL. HISTORICAL SOCIETY OF MONTANA.

outdoor grill. Use a large iron or aluminum skillet for a steak for 4. For 6 or 8, you will need 2 skillets. In each skillet, put about 3 tablespoons of beef suet and melt it over the grill. The steaks should be 1½- to 2-inch sirloins. Season with salt and pepper; rub with soft butter. Meanwhile, have another large skillet in your garden or kitchen busily sautéeing onion slices. For 4 persons, slice 4 to 6 onions. Heat 6 tablespoons butter and 2 of oil in the skillet, add the onion slices, and cook over a low heat until they soften. Season with salt and pepper. Sprinkle with 2 teaspoons sugar, and toss lightly until caramelized. Heat the steak skillet very hot. Sear steak on both sides and cook about as long as you would for grilling. When the steak is cooked, pour off all excess fat, and spoon the sautéed onions around it.

skillet steak with mushrooms

For 4 persons, sauté 1½ pounds of mushrooms in ¼ pound butter until they are delicately brown. Season with salt, pepper, 1 clove of garlic, and 2 tablespoons of chopped parsley. Arrange around steaks. Serve foil-roasted potatoes, salad, and a good red Bordeaux, perhaps a Château Cos d'Estournel.

beefsteak flamande

You have to enjoy the pungent perfume of rosemary to enjoy this recipe. Press a generous amount of fresh or dehydrated rosemary onto both sides of a 3- to 4-pound sirloin. Use the heel of your hand and press firmly. Grill to the degree of rareness you like.

Or, strew a carving board or platter with dried branches of rosemary. Grill the unseasoned steak according to your favorite method. Lay the steak on the rosemary and pour ⅓ cup warmed bourbon whiskey over it; now top with additional rosemary. Ignite, and let the rosemary burn down before serving steak.

A third way: If you have a particularly thick steak, cut a pocket in it and fill with rosemary butter made by creaming together ½ cup butter with rolled or pulverized rosemary. Broil, and when you season with salt and pepper, add a touch more of the rosemary. Add a generous amount of butter to the steak before serving. I think this particular steak asks for lyonnaise potatoes and crisp greens with a mustard dressing. Beer is an excellent accompaniment.

steak sandwiches

Any steak, properly broiled and evenly sliced, makes superb steak sandwiches. If you are cooking for wholesale lots of people, here is an easy way to serve steak. Broil either a whole tenderloin or very thick sirloin, or hip steak, to the state of rareness you prefer. Slice thin, and arrange over long strips of split, toasted, buttered French or Italian bread. Top with the other half of the bread and slice in large-sized chunks. Serve condiments.

steak in salt

Broiling a steak with a heavy crust of salt has been popular for many, many years. I'm not persuaded that this improves the flavor greatly,

but you may enjoy trying it, and certainly you won't ruin your steak. I think a wedge bone or pin bone with the bone removed is best for this method. Spread one side of the steak with English or Dijon mustard, then cover with coarse salt—Kosher salt is a natural here—about ½ inch thick. Dampen the salt, and press into the meat so that a crust is formed. Cover with a piece of absorbent paper. Turn and repeat the process on the other side. You will do best to use a basket grill, or something that holds the steak securely, for this type of broiling. Broil over fairly high heat, allowing about 12 to 14 minutes for each side. Remove the crust of salt from the outside, and place steak on a well-buttered platter to carve.

steak pizzaiola—outdoor version

Rump steak, sirloin, tenderized round, or chuck steak are all excellent here. For 4 persons, use a 3-pound steak. Season with salt and pepper. Grill the steak according to the degree of rareness you like. Meanwhile, have the following sauce ready in a skillet or saucepan: Sauté 4 chopped garlic cloves in ⅓ cup oil, and add 1 large can Italian tomatoes. Cook down to ⅓ the original amount. Season with salt, pepper, and oregano. Transfer the grilled steak to the sauce in a serving skillet and let it cook 3 to 4 minutes longer. Turn once. Carve and serve well-sauced. Because of the good sauce, I like buttered noodles with pizzaiola. With it serve a great mixed salad, including garlic croutons, and a bottle of Valpolicella. For dessert, a fine cheese.

steak with peppers

Core and cut 10 green or red peppers into sections. Heat ⅓ cup olive oil in a skillet and add 1 chopped clove of garlic and the pepper sections. Sauté, tossing occasionally until they are cooked but not mushy. Add salt and a tablespoon of wine vinegar. Surround grilled steaks with the cooked peppers. Serve French bread and a green salad with an anchovy-and-black-olive dressing, and garlic croutons.

minute steak

It is my belief that if a minute steak is sautéed in a little beef suet or butter, it is much better than if it is broiled. However, the propane grill does a wonderful job, since it is quicker than any other grill I know. Perfect food for the calorie-counter or for those who are blessed with small appetites!

steak diane

Perhaps a bit on the chi-chi side for the rugged grill, but a fine showpiece for the accomplished cook at an alfresco luncheon or dinner. Pound thin minute steaks with a meat mallet until they resemble huge scallops. Heat a griddle or large skillet on the grill. Sauté the steaks in beef fat or butter to the split second—in this case, just a little more than a quick searing on each side. Catch one end of the steak with the fork, roll in a loose roll, and keep it warm while you do the show work.

For four servings, melt 6 ounces (1½ bars) of butter in a large skillet (or electric skillet if you have an outdoor outlet). Sauté ½ cup chopped shallots or scallions lightly in the butter, add ½ teaspoon salt, and 1 teaspoon of freshly ground pepper. Add ½ cup rich stock or red wine, Dijon or English mustard, and a dash of Worcestershire. Let this cook for 2 minutes, then add the steaks. Turn quickly in the sauce and remove from heat. Pour ⅓ cup heated cognac over the meat and ignite. Serve at once with plenty of crisp French bread and a vegetable salad.

steak parpaglione

For each person, have a minute steak cut about ½ inch thick. Ask your butcher to split each steak without cutting it through. When opened up, the steaks will roughly resemble butterflies. For 4 persons, mix 1 pound finely ground beef (with a little fat in it) with 1 teaspoon salt, ½ teaspoon freshly ground black pepper, 2 table-

spoons finely chopped shallots or green onions, and 2 tablespoons finely chopped parsley. Add 1 tablespoon melted butter and mix well with your fingers. Spread ¼ of the ground-beef mixture on each steak, pressing it into the meat. Fold the steak over and press down. Grill quickly, turning with tongs and a spatula. Cover with parsley butter. You'll find that the chopped meat is just warmed through during the cooking period, giving it a deliciously fresh, spicy flavor that is an exciting complement to the steak.

glazed delmonico

Use Delmonico minute steaks or stripped sirloins for this delicious morsel. For 6 persons, you need 6 individual Delmonico steaks. On a flat platter combine 10 finely chopped garlic cloves with 3 tablespoons coarse salt. Dampen with a few drops of water and 1 to 2 teaspoons cognac. Grill the steaks very rare and remove from heat. Now increase the heat of the grill. Press each steak into the garlic-salt mixture and

return to the grill, turning the steaks quickly to glaze each side with the garlic-salt blend. Serve very hot with garlic butter.

deviled minute steak

For 4 persons, grill 4 one-inch-thick steaks—minute sirloins—over coals. When the steaks are nicely browned on the outside but rare inside press them into buttered, toasted crumbs. Return to the grill to brown. Serve with sauce Diable and water cress. French fries are traditional, but settle for sautéed potatoes. Drink a Beaujolais or a Côte du Rhône.

grilled skirt steak

Skirt is the cut in back of the flank—and as nicely flavored a cut as you will ever find. It must be skinned and prepared for grilling, after which it should be broiled quickly to a rare state. Serve with Argentine steak sauce, lyonnaise potatoes heavily laced with parsley, a good California cabernet sauvignon, and plenty of French or Syrian bread.

skirt steak oriental

Let steak stand for about 2 hours in a mixture of equal parts soy sauce, sherry, and oil, with garlic or grated ginger optional. Turn frequently. Then broil quickly over a brisk flame, not more than 8 minutes all told.

marinated steaks

A small and picturesque steak house which flourished in Los Angeles quite a while ago served fabulous steaks. I found the secret: They used top-grade beef, cut it thick, and marinated it for at least 24 hours before serving. Each portion was put in a small container and thickly covered with the following marinade: 1 chopped garlic clove, 1 teaspoon or so of lemon juice, and some good olive oil. The steaks were turned in the marinade from time to time. The next day they were broiled to a flavorful finale. Eggplant slices, brushed with the steak marinade and broiled over charcoal at the same time as the steaks, are a delicious accompaniment.

grilled porterhouse steak

A luxurious cut of beef, porterhouse is certainly one of the two best cuts to serve at a large party when you wish to have the finest of everything. Never consult your purse when buying a porterhouse. Let your conscience be smothered that day. Make sure the meat is well-aged, and have it cut 2½ to 4 inches thick. Since you will most likely be buying prime or choice beef, it will probably contain a good deal of fat. Trim excess fat before placing steak on grill. Broil until steak reaches the state of rareness you prefer. Remove it to a hot board or platter, remove the bone with a sharp knife, and carve. Slice across the steak on a slight diagonal, so that each slice has some of the tenderloin and some of the sirloin. Make slices about 1 inch thick. Serve

with garlic-parsley butter, foil-roasted potatoes, a hearty salad, French bread, and a good bottle of Beaujolais.

porterhouse steak marchands de vin

For 4 persons, broil a 4- to 5-pound porterhouse until it has achieved the degree of rareness you like. Transfer the steak to a heated platter and melt a generous chunk of butter on it. Serve with a Marchands de Vin sauce, Galette potatoes, and a bottle of first-rate claret.

porterhouse steak fines herbes

For a 5-pound steak make a sauce of ½ cup melted butter combined with 2 tablespoons each of chopped chives and chopped parsley. Transfer your broiled steak to a heated platter and pour the sauce over it. Then top with 1 cup of beef-marrow slices that have been poached for 3 to 4 minutes in salted water.

porterhouse steak with mushrooms

Such a steak is always served in one of my favorite restaurants with sautéed button mushrooms which have been gathered that morning. Heap mushrooms on the next porterhouse you grill. Sauté 1½ pounds mushrooms in ¼ pound butter. Season with salt, pepper, and a touch of garlic. When the steak is broiled just the way you like it, pile mushrooms on top to combine the two delicious flavors. The classic sauce with grilled porterhouse is Béarnaise.

grilled rump steak

Europeans have long extolled the virtues of the rump steak. The meat is tender, flavorful, and well-textured. Good for Steak au Poivre.

steak au poivre

Steak au Poivre is my all-time favorite. The pepper must not be ground; it must be crushed

or cracked peppercorns. To do this, use a meat pounder, a rolling pin, or a mortar and pestle. (Spice Islands has a good cracked pepper if you are too lazy to prepare your own.) Use a sirloin, porterhouse, or flank steak. Sprinkle both sides with plenty of cracked pepper and press it into the steak with the heel of your hand. Let stand for an hour or so. After a few trials you will be better able to judge how much pepper suits your particular taste, but for a start use a good heaping tablespoon for a steak for 4. Broil and carve.

VARIATIONS:

Grill according to your favorite method. Salt well. Transfer to a hot platter, and blaze with ¼ cup cognac.

Grill according to your favorite method. Transfer to a buttered skillet, add ¼ cup red wine, and cook over a high heat until the wine cooks down. Turn the steak occasionally. Return steak to a carving board and blend 1 cup of sour cream with the skillet juices. Heat through, but do not boil. Pour over the steak and serve.

chateaubriand

Chateaubriand is a thick, diagonally cut steak from the center of the tenderloin, the most aristocratic of the beef cuts. A good chateaubriand for 2 should weigh 1½ to 2 pounds. It should be grilled over very hot, glowing coals and served very rare! At one time it was wrapped tenderly with tougher cuts of beef, then broiled in this protective coating to preserve the juices and keep the meat from searing too much. If you try it that way, wrap with thin slices of flank or rump. Béarnaise is the classic sauce.

marinated chateaubriand

Mix 1 cup of olive oil, juice of 1 lemon, 1 crushed clove of garlic, a dash of salt, and 1 teaspoon of freshly ground black pepper. Pour this over the steak, turn several times to be sure it is evenly coated, and let stand in a warm place for several hours, or even overnight. Grill as usual, omitting additional seasoning.

roquefort-broiled steak

Cream together ¼ pound butter and 1 cup Roquefort cheese. Add 1 tablespoon Worcestershire sauce and 2 tablespoons chopped chives. Grill a 3-inch-thick sirloin. Go lightly on the salt. When the steak is nicely browned on one side, turn. As it continues cooking, spread with the butter-cheese mixture. This is a little on the highly seasoned side, but there are many people who like it very much. Potatoes baked in foil, marinated cherry tomatoes, and a lusty red Burgundy—a Chambertin or a Chambolle Musigny—would be excellent.

grilled t-bone, garlic butter

Grilled T-bone steak is an immediate reminder of the West. Hearty West Coast restaurants, like the much-mourned American Oyster House in Seattle, used to serve fantastic ones. I'm certain they gave 24 ounces per person. Choose a thick T-bone. For 4 persons, it should weigh about 4 pounds, including the bone. Season to taste. Grill to your favorite degree of rareness. While the steak grills, melt ¼ pound butter in a platter to which you can transfer the steak. Rub 1 or 2 garlic cloves in 2½ teaspoons of coarse salt. Discard garlic, mix salt with 1 teaspoon each of dry and prepared mustard, and blend. When the steak is cooked, transfer to platter and spoon the sauce over it. Carve and serve the well-sauced slices with tiny new potatoes in their jackets, marinated onions, homemade bread, and butter. Drink a fine California pinot noir.

flank steak

A most misunderstood cut of meat, but excellent eating if treated well. Ask for top quality—prime or choice—and have the butcher trim it well of membrane and excess fat. Broil quickly, allowing 3 to 4 minutes per side, until steak is well browned on the outside, but still juicy red in the middle. Season to taste and carve on the diagonal in ¼-inch slices. Beer is great with flank-steak dishes.

oriental

Marinate the steak for several hours, turning it frequently, in ½ cup of sherry, ½ cup of soy sauce, 2 chopped cloves of garlic, and ¼ cup of chopped fresh ginger (or 1 teaspoon of ground ginger). Broil and carve.

southwestern

Marinate the steak for several hours, turning it frequently, in ½ cup olive oil, ½ cup of rum, 1 tablespoon chili powder, 2 finely chopped cloves of garlic, 1 teaspoon of oregano, and several dashes of Tabasco. Broil and carve.

bordelaise

Grill in your favorite manner, remove to hot plank, and top with thin slices of beef marrow which have been poached in a little boiling, salted water for about 3 to 4 minutes. Carve and serve with Bordelaise sauce.

deviled

For 4 people, use 2 cups toasted, buttered crumbs, about ¼ pound of butter, and a devil sauce made by mixing 1 cup tomato sauce, 2 tablespoons chili powder, and 1 teaspoon oregano. Grill the steaks quickly, undercooking them a little. Spread the hot steaks with butter and roll them in buttered crumbs, pressing the crumbs in. Replace on grill for crumbs to crisp.

london broil

This flank steak must be of a good grade of meat, should be cooked rare, and carved deftly in very thin, diagonal slices. Have the steak at refrigerator temperature, remove the tough outer membrane, and slash any fat around the edge. Brush with a little melted butter and broil 8 minutes over a good fire, turning once. Slice on a very long diagonal, so that the red center will be framed by an appetizing brown crust.

hanging tenderloin

This is another one of those unusual cuts that only good butchers and their favorite customers seem to get. It is a flavorful small steak—sometimes as tender as butter—that should be grilled as you would a skirt steak.

steak timer	1 inch	grilling time in minutes 1½ inches	2 inches	2½ inches	meat thermometer temperature 3 inches or more
very rare	8	8-10	14-18	20-25	120°-130°
rare	9	10-12	18-25	25-35	125°-135°
medium	12	13-15	25-32	35-40	145°-155°
well done	15-18	15-20	30-45	45-60	160°-170°

SHEPHERD'S PEACE, 13TH CENTURY FRENCH MANUSCRIPT.
PIERPONT MORGAN LIBRARY.

fillet steak

A fillet steak is the English version of a tenderloin or tournedos. To my mind, the best fillet steak should be cut about 1 to 1½ inches thick and should be grilled to a fine rareness (heated through, but very rare). Serve it in any of the following ways:

With salt, freshly ground pepper, and a large dollop of butter. *With* freshly ground black pepper and anchovy butter. *With* Béarnaise sauce. *With* Marchands de Vin sauce. *With* a nice piece of imported goose liver spread over the seasoned fillet. *With* parsley butter. *With* tarragon butter.

fillet steak à la stanley

This famous dish was arranged for the man who ate it repeatedly at Delmonico's. It is merely a grilled fillet steak served with a grilled banana —a rather interesting combination.

tournedos

This is the thickish cut of about 1 to 1½ inches —similar to a fillet steak. It is barded (wrapped) with a thin piece of suet or, occasionally, with salt pork or bacon, to keep it moist while cooking. Traditionally, this cut is sautéed instead of grilled. If you wish, you may sauté it atop your grill in a skillet instead of exposing it directly to the coals.

VARIATIONS:

Rossini: Sautéed and served on a round of fried toast, topped with a slice of foie gras and a slice of truffle, and served with a brown sauce. This makes rather spectacular outdoor eating.

Provençale: This has small bits of garlic pressed into the meat before it is grilled or sautéed. It should be seasoned with salt and freshly ground pepper, and served with a very thick, fresh tomato sauce.

Veracruzana: I had this served to me in Mexico and was pleasantly surprised to find what the canapé turned out to be: grilled pineapple. Serve grilled or sautéed tournedos on top of a pineapple slice, decorate with 3 grilled mushroom caps, and pour a sauce Diable over it.

the whole fillet

A whole fillet will weigh anywhere from 4 to 9 pounds. While expensive, this cut is considered fairly economical since there is no waste weight in bone and fat. Have the butcher trim the fillet well. If you are going to spit-roast it, ask him to tie the meat securely and fold in the thin filet mignon tip. If you are broiling the fillet whole, cut off the thin tip for another occasion.

broiled whole fillet

The whole fillet may be laid on the grill over coals, or you can put it in a basket grill, which may be easier to handle. If the meat rests on the grill itself, be sure you turn it frequently during the grilling period, because this many-sided piece of meat should be broiled to an evenness of color. The heat should not be too intense or you will get an overcharred crust before the thickest part of the fillet is properly done. A whole fillet will take 25 minutes at high temperature, 35 minutes at medium. Test with a thermometer for 120 F. internal temperature.

fillet sandwiches

Carve a grilled fillet in paper-thin slices and place them in an overlapping pattern on split loaves of French or Italian bread spread with mustard butter. Cover with the other half of the loaf (or serve them uncovered, whichever you wish) and cut into individual portions. This is an ideal way to entertain a number of people at any outdoor gathering. If you have a large grill, you can grill 2 or 3 fillets at the same time and thus carve a rather healthy number of sandwiches. Serve with condiments, shoestring potatoes or potato chips, and a huge bowl of fresh raw vegetables with a well-seasoned mayonnaise or a sour cream-herb mixture.

marinated fillets

French: Marinate fillets for 8 to 12 hours in the refrigerator in the following mixture:

½ cup oil
1½ teaspoons thyme
1 teaspoon freshly ground pepper
1½ teaspoons salt
2 cups red wine

Broil and serve with tiny peas and mushrooms, crisp bread, a good red wine, and fruit.

Oriental: Marinate fillets for 8 to 12 hours in the refrigerator in the following:

1 cup dark soy sauce
1 teaspoon Heung New Fun Spices
or Quatre Epices
½ cup vermouth
1 onion, finely sliced
2 tablespoons grated fresh or candied ginger

Broil and serve with a rice-and-pistachio nut casserole and Chinese peas sautéed in sweet —not salt—butter.

entrecôte bercy

Have the butcher cut a rib steak about 2 inches thick. Salt and pepper both sides and grill over coals until it reaches the degree of doneness you prefer. While the steak is on the grill, melt 4 tablespoons butter and mix well with 2 tablespoons chopped parsley, 1 tablespoon chopped fresh tarragon (or 1 teaspoon Spice Islands tarragon), and 2 tablespoons of finely chopped shallots. Pour on a hot platter. When steak is properly cooked, transfer to the sauce in the platter and top it with another chunk of butter. Sprinkle lightly with more chopped parsley and tarragon. I like this with Italian bread and butter, and either a green salad or a beet, onion, and egg salad. A Beaujolais seems the right wine for this luncheon or dinner.

entrecôte, marchands de vin

In the Bordeaux area of France, this is a popular way to serve good entrecôte. Have the butcher cut your steak from the first 3 ribs, about 2 ribs thick. Ask him to trim it well and French the bones. Grill the steak to the state of doneness you prefer. Transfer to a skillet with already prepared Marchands de Vin sauce, bathing the steak generously with the sauce. Serve with grilled tomatoes and sautéed mushrooms.

entrecôte gaucho

Chop enough scallions to make 2 cups. Combine with 1 cup white wine, ½ cup wine vinegar, 1½ teaspoons salt, 1½ tablespoons ground pepper. Pour over 3 to 4 individual entrecôtes and let marinate for several hours. Grill the steaks to your favorite degree of doneness. For a sauce, cook the marinade to a boil, simmer for 4 minutes, then stir in ¼ pound butter and 1 teaspoon tarragon. Serve with wheat pilaff, and thinly sliced avocado. Drink a California Barbera with this.

barbecued short ribs of beef

For 4 servings, plan on 4 pounds of beef short ribs. Sprinkle all surfaces of the short ribs with seasoned meat tenderizer. I prefer to work the tenderizer in deeply by piercing the meat with a sharp kitchen fork. Let stand 30 to 40 minutes at room temperature (or cover loosely and refrigerate overnight). Meanwhile, prepare the following sauce:

1 cup catsup
1 cup water
¼ cup wine vinegar
1 tablespoon Worcestershire
1 small onion, minced
1 clove garlic, pressed or minced
1 tablespoon brown sugar
2 tablespoons honey
2 teaspoons dry mustard
1 teaspoon chili powder

Mix the ingredients together and simmer over low heat for 20 minutes. This sauce should be kept near at hand, on the side of the grill. Set grill about 4 inches from heat. When coals are gray and shot with a ruddy glow, place ribs on grill and cook 20 to 25 minutes. Turn frequently and baste with the sauce.

chopped beef

Hamburgers—or ground beef, or chopped tenderloin, or whatever you want to call it—is still one of the more popular meats among outdoor chefs. In fact, there are many who will recommend meat no way but chopped. In my opinion, chopped beef can be a deliciously tender and flavorful meat; on the other hand, improperly

prepared, it can be as dry and uninteresting as sawdust. For best results, buy beef which is not more than 30 per cent fat. If you are serving ground beef as a steak, allow about ½ pound per person. For hamburger patties, ¼ pound per portion is ample. When forming the cakes, handle them as little as possible—just enough to make them secure. Too much kneading tends to kill the texture. Remember that chopped beef develops bacteria faster than any other meat. Consequently, the less time that elapses between refrigerator and grill, the better off you are. When you are having hamburger steaks, form the meat into oval cakes about 1½ inches thick. They look better that way, and I have found that they cook more evenly. To broil chopped meat, brush it well with butter or oil before placing on the grill. Then cook over a fairly brisk heat and turn often to sear well on the outside. I think chopped meat is best when the exterior is crisply browned and the inside is juicily tender.

hamburger steaks

Grill hamburger steak as suggested. Remove from grill and salt and pepper to taste. Serve on a hot plate with a good dollop of butter on top. Sliced onions and tomatoes, and crisp potato chips or French fries are the classic accompaniments. Serve with a selection of mustards.

hamburger steak à cheval

Season 2 pounds of ground round steak with 1 teaspoon salt, ½ teaspoon freshly ground black pepper, and 1 egg. Blend well and form into 4 thick cakes. Grill as suggested and serve on a hot platter, garnishing each hamburger steak with a fried egg and finely chopped raw onion.

steak hambourgeoise

For 4 persons, combine 2 pounds of ground beef with 3 tablespoons finely chopped onion which have been lightly sautéed in 4 tablespoons but-

ter. Season with 1 teaspoon salt, ½ teaspoon freshly ground black pepper, and ⅛ teaspoon of nutmeg. Blend in 2 eggs and mix thoroughly. Form into 4 thick, oval cakes. Brush with melted butter and grill over a fairly brisk fire. Serve on hot plates with additional sautéed onions; garnish with parsley, water cress, or sliced tomatoes.

russian hamburger steak

To 2 pounds of freshly ground round steak, add 1 tablespoon melted butter, 1 teaspoon salt, ½ teaspoon freshly ground black pepper, ⅛ teaspoon nutmeg, and 1 tablespoon grated onion. Shape into 4 thick cakes and broil. Garnish each steak with 2 tablespoons warmed sour cream and 2 tablespoons of lightly sautéed onions. Serve with sautéed potatoes and pass additional sour cream for the hamburgers.

hamburger steak with cheese

Form 2 pounds of ground round steak into 4 thick cakes and broil. When cakes have achieved the rareness you like, transfer to a hot platter on which you have finely grated 1 cup of Switzerland Swiss cheese or ripe Cheddar, blended with ½ cup butter heated almost to the boiling point. Stir the cheese and butter together thoroughly. Add hamburgers to mixture, and turn several times to coat the meat with the sauce. Sprinkle with freshly ground black pepper and serve.

herbed hamburger steak

Blend 2 pounds of ground round steak with 1 tablespoon finely cut chives, 1 tablespoon chopped fresh tarragon, or 1 teaspoon dried tarragon, 1 teaspoon salt, ½ teaspoon freshly ground black pepper, ¼ cup finely chopped parsley, and ¼ cup finely chopped green onions. Blend with 1 egg and form into 4 thick hamburger steaks. Broil. Serve with parsley butter.

hamburger steak provençale

Blend 2 pounds of ground round steak with 2 tablespoons tomato purée, 1 teaspoon salt, a dash of Tabasco, ¼ cup chopped parsley. Form into 4 thick cakes and press ½ teaspoon chopped garlic into each one. Grill and serve with a highly seasoned Provençale tomato sauce.

notes for hamburger sandwiches

The classic hamburger accompaniments are French fries, shoestring potatoes, or potato chips. I think most commercial potato chips nowadays are pretty poor. If you find some you like, by all means serve them, but heat them slightly beforehand.

A big bowl of iced raw vegetables with a good sauce is my idea of the right salad to be served, rather than the usual tremendous mixed bowl. This makes finger-eating a possibility. If you want a salad, an onion-tomato-cucumber combination does very well.

With any of these sandwiches, you will find a chilled California rosé, especially a Grenache rosé, a Beaujolais, or beer is the best drink.

Philip and Helen Brown claim that if you want a juicy hamburger you should mold it around a small or halved ice cube before grilling.

hamburgers on buns

For the average hamburger on bun, gauge about 4 ounces of meat, although you probably will find many people can eat 2 this size. Form the meat into cakes approximately the size of the buns. Broiling is considered the most acceptable method of preparing hamburgers for a crowd, but I still like them cooked on a griddle placed on top of the grill, with a little butter or beef fat. Toast and serve with mustard and whatever relish you prefer.

california hamburger

I still say that the hamburger confections that were served at the old White Spots in Los Angeles more than 30 years ago were the best ever made. The hamburgers were grilled to per-

fection, then placed on hot, well-buttered toasted buns and topped with:

A paper-thin slice of dill pickle
Thin slice of ripe tomato
Thin slice of onion
Spoonful of homemade relish
Spoonful of mayonnaise
Smear of good mustard

On the top half of the bun a crisp lettuce leaf was added, if you wished it. It was superb eating!

cheeseburgers

Cheeseburger No. 1: Grill plain hamburgers, and when you turn them place a very thin slice of Cheddar, or 1 or 2 tablespoons of grated Cheddar or Swiss cheese, atop the cooked side. This melts while the underside cooks. Place on hot buttered buns. Serve mustard and pickle.

Cheeseburger No. 2: For each person, form 2 3-ounce cakes of hamburger. Place 2 tablespoons grated sharp Cheddar (or Swiss or Fontina) atop half of the cake. Put a teaspoon of mustard on the cheese and top with another hamburger cake, pressing the edges together. Grill as usual.

Cheeseburger No. 3: Blend together 2 pounds of ground round, ½ pound grated Cheddar or Swiss cheese, 2 tablespoons finely chopped onion, 2 tablespoons tomato sauce, and a healthy dash of Tabasco. Mix well, form 4- to 6-ounce cakes, and broil as above.

other burgers

Tomatoburgers: Form ground beef into 3-ounce patties. On half of these place thin slices of ripe tomato and of onion. Salt and pepper lightly. Top with the other patty. Press the edges down firmly and broil.

Chiliburger: Combine 2 pounds of ground round with 1 teaspoon salt, 2 tablespoons sweet chili powder, 2 tablespoons tomato sauce, 3 tablespoons finely chopped onion, and ¼ cup

pine nuts. Blend in 1 egg and form into cakes. Broil. Serve with lots of Mexican chili sauce and sour cream.

Mediterranean Hamburgers: Combine 2 pounds of ground round steak, 1 teaspoon freshly ground black pepper, ¼ cup each of finely chopped onion and chopped ripe olives. Blend in 1 egg and form into cakes. Press ½ teaspoon finely chopped garlic into each one. Brush with olive oil, broil over a brisk flame, and serve with garlic-buttered buns.

individual barbecued hamburger pizzas

2 pounds ground beef, round or chuck
1 clove garlic, pressed or minced
Seasoned meat tenderizer

TOMATO SAUCE:
2 eight-ounce cans tomato sauce
½ teaspoon garlic salt
1 teaspoon sugar
½ teaspoon Italian seasoning or,
¼ teaspoon each: oregano, marjoram, thyme

2 sweet onions, thinly sliced
½ pound Italian salami,
cut in thin rounds
½ pound Mozzarella cheese, sliced
as thinly as possible
1 eight-ounce can mushrooms (stems & pieces)
½ to 1 teaspoon oregano
½ cup grated Parmesan cheese

Mix the ground beef and garlic and form meat into 6 patties. Sprinkle patties on both sides with seasoned meat tenderizer just before placing on grill. Cook 5 minutes on each side. While the second side is cooking, add remaining ingredients to the top of each patty in this order: tomato sauce, onions, salami, Mozzarella, mushrooms, oregano, and Parmesan cheese. When cheese is melted, remove from grill and serve.

hamburger rarebit

Cover 5 or 6 hamburger patties, grilled to your taste, with your favorite Welsh rarebit recipe. This can be prepared in an electric skillet beside your grill. Here is my favorite rarebit sauce:

2 tablespoons butter
1 pound grated sharp cheese
(Cheddar, Swiss, Fontina)
1 cup beer
1 egg
2 teaspoons dry mustard
Tabasco

Melt butter over hot water, add cheese, and heat until melted. Stir in beer gradually. In another pan, beat the egg slightly, and stir in mustard and Tabasco to taste. Dribble a little of the cheese mixture into the egg mixture, then stir until it becomes rarebit. Blend, but do not boil. Pour the rarebit over your hamburgers, and garnish with olives.

chuletas

Combine 2 pounds of ground beef with 2 cups each of minced parsley and minced onion. Add 2 large eggs, 1 tablespoon of salt, ½ cup of grated Parmesan cheese, ½ teaspoon of monosodium glutamate, and some freshly ground pepper. Form into balls and pat each ball on a board covered with 3 cups of dry, sifted bread crumbs. Turn patties to cover each side. If desired, patties may be oblong-shaped instead of round. Chill well. Cook on a well-greased, fine-meshed grill for not more than 3 minutes to a side. Better yet, cook in a skillet atop the grill in a small amount of butter. This superb dish comes from the kitchen of Elena Zelayeta.

steak tartare

Steak tartare is raw chopped or ground round steak, or—if you wish to be exotically elegant—hand-chopped tenderloin. Use 6 to 8 ounces of meat for each serving. Blend with salt, pepper, English mustard, finely chopped onions, capers, 1 raw egg for each person, and Worcestershire sauce. Blend together thoroughly. Form into cakes. Arrange on cold plates. Garnish with chopped parsley and additional capers. Serve with rye bread or crisp French bread. A delicious and refreshing summer dish.

steak tartare à la forum

The glamorous *Forum of the Twelve Caesars* restaurant in New York has added a fillip to this dish with 2 tablespoons of cognac and 1 or 2 tablespoons of finely chopped anchovy fillets. This innovation has proved to be a most spritely change from the usual seasoning.

tartare toasts

Either of these recipes is fine for an hors d'oeuvre or a snack. Prepare steak tartare according to one of the given recipes. Spread the mixture very thinly on crisp, hot, buttered toast and serve with cocktails.

Or spread half a piece of buttered toast with steak tartare and the other half with fresh caviar. Top with chopped raw onion and serve as a most appealing appetizer. Drink a Valpolicella, Barbera, or good ale or beer.

grilling lamb

loin lamb chops

Three things distinguish a perfectly cooked loin lamb chop: It is thick, well-browned, and its fat is crisply charred. The meat at the center, when one cuts through, must be deliciously pink. Perfection cannot be achieved with quick cooking. The chops must grill slowly and be charred at the last. If you are in doubt you can always test by cutting close to the bone with a sharp knife to see what degree of doneness the chops have reached. Salt and pepper the chops, and serve piping hot on very hot plates. Be certain that you eschew the horrors of mint jelly. Excellent served with rice and peas, or that delightful combination known as Risi Pisi. Drink beer or ale.

tarragon chops

Cream together ¼ cup butter and 2 teaspoons dried tarragon which has been soaked for 30 minutes in 2 tablespoons of white wine or vermouth. Make small incisions in the fat side of the lamb chops with a sharp knife and stuff bits of the tarragon butter in each chop. Broil and brush with tarragon butter before serving.

garlicked chops

For 6 chops, use 6 cloves chopped garlic. Combine garlic with ½ cup oil, 1 teaspoon salt, 1 teaspoon freshly ground pepper. Press both sides of the chops into the mixture and let stand several hours to allow chops to absorb the flavors. Turn once or twice during the standing period. Broil. Serve with grilled tomatoes and mushrooms, and water cress. A light red wine —a Fleurie or a California cabernet—goes well.

herbed, stuffed lamb chops

For 4 persons, blend together 6 tablespoons butter and 2 tablespoons each of chopped chives, chopped parsley, and chopped mint. Make a small pocket in each chop and stuff with some of the mixture. Broil. Serve with additional herbed butter, garlic bread, a string-bean salad. Drink a light red wine, such as a Beaujolais or a cabernet from California.

roquefort-stuffed chops

For 4 persons, blend together ¼ pound butter, ¼ pound Roquefort cheese, 2 teaspoons cognac, and a healthy dash of Worcestershire sauce. Cream very well. Cut a small pocket in 8 chops and stuff with the creamed mixture. Broil. Season to taste with salt and pepper. Serve with Roesti potatoes and a tossed salad; drink a good red Burgundy.

english lamb chops

Correctly speaking, an English chop is cut very thick across the saddle. In other words, it is 2 loin chops. More often than not you get a double-thick loin chop or a triple-thick rib chop. Sometimes a kidney is rolled into the chop—this is a matter of taste. English chops need slow cooking. They are correctly eaten rare and to achieve this they must be heated slowly. The outside must be crisply brown, the meat fairly pink, and the fat almost burned. Crisply fried or sautéed potatoes are a natural ally. Water cress, too, and ale or beer. Cheese, crisp bread, and coffee. Excellent dining!

Or serve with baked potatoes mixed with butter, cheese, and chives; cole slaw, and rye bread.

boned, tied lamb chops

One used to find these very often, but less so now. They are thick loin chops cut across the saddle, boned, and tied. Sometimes they have most of the fat removed and a piece of bacon tied or skewered around them. Or, they may have a kidney stuck into them. Broil as you would an English chop. Salt and pepper well. Serve with young white turnips cooked so they are still quite crisp, then mixed with sautéed mushrooms. Drink a rosé, well chilled.

rib chops

Rib chops don't spell outdoor glamor to me, but if they are cut to double or triple thickness, they may be prepared in any of the fashions recommended for loin chops.

shoulder chops

Shoulder chops are a more economical buy than loin chops, but not as delicious eating. Prepare them grilled or with any of the marinades given for lamb steaks.

mutton chops

Mutton is almost unknown in the United States. One occasionally gets good Canadian mutton, but it, too, is a rarity. It is heavy with fat, but delicious when well-aged. Prepare mutton chops in any of the ways you do loin lamb chops. Be careful that you do not leave too much fat or it will drip into the fire and cause a blaze.

seasoned mutton chops

For a delightful and interesting way to cook mutton chops, sprinkle them with thyme, rosemary, or tarragon, press the spices into the meat, and grill to a desired state of doneness. While cooking, the herbs impart a special flavor to the mutton. Just before the meat has finished broiling, some cooks like to sprinkle herbs incense-fashion over the fire for added savor. These chops are best served with garlic bread, a green-bean and artichoke salad topped with French dressing, and ale or stout. If you're a lover of wine, you may prefer a hearty red one—a Charbono, perhaps.

piemontese mutton chops

For a touch of the Near East on your outdoor menu, place 2 cloves of garlic, ¼ cup pine nuts, 4 tablespoons chopped parsley, 2 teaspoons chopped fresh mint, and ¼ cup butter in a bowl and mix well with mortar and pestle or other

INTERIOR OF A BUTCHER SHOP, ANONYMOUS. NEWARK MUSEUM.

heavy implement until the ingredients are crushed finely. Then make a small pocket in each of 4 chops and stuff the mixture into the opening. Broil as desired, season to taste, and serve with grilled eggplant and tomatoes, and your favorite red wine. Any ripe melon goes well for dessert.

lamb steaks

Lamb steaks cut from the leg or shoulder are succulent morsels for the grill. In fact, they are used all too seldom by the alfresco cook. Grill a 1-inch-thick lamb steak over gray coals until it is properly rare for your palate. Serve with a garlic sauce or with mustard. Grilled eggplant is a delicious accompaniment.

provençale

Marinate the steaks for 2 hours in a flat dish in which you have put finely chopped garlic cloves—2 for each steak—4 tablespoons tomato purée, and enough olive oil to cover the bottom of the dish. Sprinkle the steaks with chopped, fresh basil, about 1 tablespoon per steak, and

turn meat several times in the dish so the steaks become steeped in the mixture. Brush with the leftover marinade. Grill until crisply browned on the outside and rare inside. Serve with rice pilaff, and a corn-and-black-olive casserole. Drink a chilled rosé.

lamb steak bordelaise

Marinate the lamb steaks in salt, pepper, and enough red wine to cover the meat halfway, turning the steaks once or twice during the 2- to 3-hour marinating period. Brush with oil or butter, and grill as suggested. Serve with a sauce Bordelaise, sautéed mushrooms with garlic and parsley, French bread, and a good Bordeaux.

lamb oriental

Soak 4 lamb steaks in a mixture of ½ cup soy sauce, ½ cup red wine, ½ cup olive oil, ¼ cup grated fresh or preserved ginger, and 2 to 3 finely chopped garlic cloves for several hours. Grill the steaks, brushing them with the marinade until nicely browned. Serve with fried rice and a good bottle of chilled ale.

lamb patties

Lamb patties are ground lamb formed into cakes and usually wrapped with bacon secured with small skewers. They may be broiled in the same manner as lamb chops, but should be brushed well with butter or oil during the cooking process. Never overcook them.

garlicked lamb patties

1½ pounds ground lamb
½ cup olive oil
2 finely chopped garlic cloves
⅓ cup chopped parsley
½ teaspoon salt
½ teaspoon freshly ground black pepper

Combine all ingredients, blend, and form into 6 patties. Brush with olive oil and grill. Continue brushing with oil during the cooking. Serve with broiled mushrooms.

VARIATION:

Add ½ cup pine nuts and 1 teaspoon tarragon to the mixture.

grilled, boned leg of lamb

For this delicious, hearty lamb dish have the butcher remove all but the shank bone. Do not have him tie it. Perfect fare for broiling over a campfire, as well as over your garden grill.

philip brown's nevada lamb

Philip Brown very often used to prepare this dish near Virginia City, Nevada, and always prepared it in a basket grill. Rub the meat with salt and pepper. Insert into the leg several garlic cloves, cut in slivers. Spread it out in a basket grill. Brush with a little oil or butter and place over a medium heat. It will take, according to size, from 1 to 2 hours and should be served quite rare. Herbed tomatoes, crisp garlic bread, and beer are very pleasant accompaniments to this savory dish.

marinated leg of lamb

Stud a boned leg with garlic cloves and marinate 24 hours in a mixture of 1 cup finely chopped onion, ½ cup finely chopped parsley, 1 bay leaf, ¼ cup wine vinegar, and enough red wine to barely cover the leg. Turn lamb several times in this mixture. Before broiling, rub with salt and sprinkle with pepper. Place in a basket grill and grill as suggested for grilled, boned leg of lamb.

hawaiian lamb

Stud a boned leg with garlic and small slivers of fresh ginger. Let it soak in soy sauce for an hour. Turn several times. Broil and serve with broiled slices of pineapple brushed with butter and sprinkled with a little sugar, so that they will caramelize heavily.

barbecued breast of lamb

Choose about 4 pounds of lamb breast and make the following Chuck Wagon sauce:

1 cup catsup
1 cup water
1 small onion, minced
1 tablespoon Worcestershire
¼ cup vinegar
1 tablespoon brown sugar
1 teaspoon paprika
2 teaspoons dry mustard
1 clove garlic, minced
1 teaspoon chili powder
1 tablespoon honey

Sprinkle breast of lamb on both sides with seasoned meat tenderizer. I usually work the tenderizer in deeply with a sharp kitchen fork. Let it stand 1 hour at room temperature, or cover loosely and refrigerate overnight. Mix all the sauce ingredients together and simmer slowly in a covered saucepan for 20 to 30 minutes. When barbecuing charcoal is gray and shot with a ruddy glow, set grill 4 inches above coals. Brush lamb breast with sauce, and grill, 1 to 1½ hours, frequently turning and basting.

grilling veal

Because it is not heavily fatted, veal is the least successful meat to use on a grill. However, I find that using a propane grill and browning the chops quickly, then wrapping them in foil with seasonings and continuing the cookery on another level of the grill makes a succulent dish.

côte de veau en papillote

Select rib or loin chops 1½ to 2 inches thick and remove any excess fat. Place grill in first notch and cook the chops for 1½ minutes on each side. Remove from the grill and place each chop on a piece of foil large enough to wrap around it. Before closing the foil over the meat, top each chop with any of the following combinations:

Salt, pepper, a few leaves of tarragon (or a pinch of dried tarragon), a few sprigs of parsley, and a pat of butter or vegetable shortening.

Salt, pepper, a sliver of garlic, a few sprigs of parsley, a pat of butter or vegetable shortening.

Salt, pepper, 2 sliced mushrooms, and a pat of butter or vegetable shortening.

Brush each chop with olive oil and add salt,

pepper, ½ clove of garlic, 1 tablespoon of tomato purée, and a few cloves of basil (or a pinch of dried basil).

One thin slice of onion, 1 anchovy fillet, a pat of butter or vegetable shortening, and a dash of pepper. No salt is needed with the anchovy.

Wrap the foil around the seasoned chops and place the grate in notch 3. Grill the chops for 6 minutes on each side. Remove the cooked chops, foil and all, to serving dishes. Slit the top of each of the wrappings and spread them open slightly. Do not remove the foil entirely or you will lose the delicious juices.

veal steaks

Veal steaks are cut from the leg and are not really suitable for grilling. A veal porterhouse, however, thickly cut from the loin of veal and cooked according to any of the rules and variations given for veal chops en papillote, is a delicious dish. Sautéed potatoes, tender peas, snow peas, or green beans all go well with veal. Soave, Pouilly-Fuissé, or Pouilly-Fumé are excellent here. They must be served well-chilled.

grilling pork

Most people consider pork too rich for summer fare, but I am like the French and enjoy it during that season. It is always well to remember that pork should be well-cooked and should reach an inner temperature of about 170 F. to be eaten with impunity. In the flesh of the pig there lurks the trichinae worm which causes a most unpleasant discomfort known as trichinosis. For the outdoor cook, pork is varied, versatile, and extremely accommodating to many flavors. It should be cooked long and slowly, be pleasantly charred on the outside and juicily tender within. The best cut for my taste is the loin chop, which is to pork as porterhouse is

to beef. In this chop there is a pleasant bit of tenderloin and a goodly section of the loin. I think the chops should be cut 1 to 2 inches thick, with most of the fat trimmed away. One large or 2 medium-sized chops would certainly be considered an adequate serving.

broiled pork chops

Salt and pepper loin chops, gauging 1 or 2 to the person. Grill them very slowly over a medium heat, turning 2 or 3 times during the broiling process. They should take 20 to 25 minutes. The chops should never be eaten rare, so if you wish to give them a little more time, they won't be ruined. Serve with horseradish and sour cream, fried apple rings, mashed potatoes with plenty of butter and cream whipped into them. Follow this with a tartly dressed salad, French bread, and some cheese. The drink—well, I think rosé goes better with pork than any other wine, and it is a very pleasant summer drink. Chill it well.

pork chops with cream gravy

Add enough milk to cover pork chops and place them in the refrigerator for several hours. Remove, dry on absorbent paper, and season with salt and freshly ground pepper. Broil. Make an old-fashioned milk gravy with the liquid in which the chops have marinated. Add lots of black pepper and a little mustard. Serve these hearty chops with thinly sliced apples, sautéed in butter in your electric skillet until they are crisply browned at the edges and just soft in the center. Sprinkle with a little granulated sugar so apples will caramelize in the pan. Baked potatoes are wonderful absorbers of the milk gravy. Cucumbers with dill, and fresh berries round out a most satisfying meal.

pork chops with an orange-mustard glaze

Broil thick loin pork chops according to directions. For 6 persons, blend together ⅔ cup honey, ⅓ cup orange juice, and ⅓ cup cognac. Spread the cooking chops with mixed English mustard, and brush several times during the cooking period with the orange-honey glaze. Chops should be browned, but tender.

italian stuffed pork chops

For 6 persons, purchase 6 extra-thick loin pork chops and cut a small pocket in each one. Chop enough Italian parsley, fresh basil, and garlic to make ⅔ of a cup or slightly more. Blend with 4 or 5 tablespoons butter and stuff a small amount of this mixture into each chop. Season chops with salt and freshly ground black pepper, and broil over medium coals until they are cooked through. Chops should be pleasantly browned and tender. Garnish with any leftover herbed butter. Serve with baked rice and pine nuts, sliced tomatoes and onions, and beer.

deviled pork chops

Broil pork chops as above. When they are just done, press the chops into toasted, buttered crumbs on each side, and return to the grill to brown. Serve with sauce Diable, lyonnaise potatoes, orange-and-onion salad with a tart French dressing flavored with rosemary. Cold ale is the ideal drink.

hawaiian

Place 4 thick loin chops in a rather shallow pan and add enough soy sauce to just cover the bottom of the pan. Pour an additional tablespoonful over the top of each chop. Turn chops 2 or 3 times in a period of 2 hours so that they absorb a good deal of the soy sauce. Brown the chops very slightly, brushing with soy sauce as you go. When almost done to your liking, brush each chop with finely chopped garlic and turn once more so that the garlic cooks into each side. Serve with a sweet-sour sauce, steamed rice and sautéed mushrooms, and snow peas.

rib chops

Rib chops, cut thick, are agreeable items on the grill, but not nearly so choice as the loin cuts. They may be prepared in any way that you use for loin chops.

mushroom-stuffed rib chops

Have the butcher cut thick rib chops—1 to a person is ample—and slit a deep pocket in each. Sauté ½ pound of mushroom stems and caps in 4 tablespoons butter. When just tender, remove

from the fire and chop them exceedingly fine. Return chopped mushrooms to the butter in the pan and blend with 2 tablespoons of finely chopped parsley and 1 tablespoon finely chopped garlic. Stuff spoonfuls of this mixture into the pockets of the chops and secure the openings with toothpicks or small metal skewers. Broil, seasoning with salt and freshly ground black pepper during the cooking process.

grilled pork steaks

Pork steaks are a cut from the leg with the bone left in. They are not well-known in America, but in France, Italy, and Germany I have eaten and enjoyed them a number of times. They shouldn't be cut too thick—I would say that ½ inch is perfect. Gauge by the size of the leg from which the steaks were cut whether it is an ample por-

tion or not. Grill them over medium heat until cooked through and delicately browned on each side. This takes 15 to 20 minutes, or perhaps slightly longer. Seasoned to taste with salt and pepper. Serve with well-buttered rice, sautéed cabbage, and cinnamon-flavored applesauce.

mexican pork steaks

Brush 6 pork steaks with a little olive oil and sprinkle each one with a teaspoon of chili powder and a bit of oregano. Broil over medium coals, turning from time to time and brushing with a little chili sauce. When tender and nicely browned, serve with the sauce, hot tortillas, and marinated, sliced, raw onions. Drink a good cold beer. (One can buy a rather good Mexican chili sauce in tins; or, if you are deft at making such things, all the better.)

garlic steaks

Chop 4 large or 6 medium cloves of garlic very fine and press into 4 pork steaks. Salt and pepper them and broil slowly over a medium fire, being certain that as much of the chopped garlic as possible adheres to the steaks. When steaks have cooked through, remove to hot plates and serve with broiled pineapple slices, a green salad with a sharp dressing, and herbed, heated French bread.

pork pizzaiola

Broil 4 pork steaks according to directions. Season with salt and freshly ground black pepper. Serve with a pizzaiola sauce. Accompany with polenta. Drink a good Chianti.

pork tenderloins

Pork tenderloin is the fillet of pig and one of the most delicious bits of meat you will ever find. Since tenderloins are not very large, one person can usually eat a whole one. Caution: If cooked too dry, it will lose its delicacy.

chinese pork tenderloins

Soak 6 pork tenderloins for 1 to 2 hours in a mixture of equal quantities of sherry and soy sauce, and 1 teaspoon ground anise seed, 1 teaspoon fennel seed, a dash of cinnamon, and cloves. Broil the tenderloins slowly, turn several times and brush frequently with the marinade. Serve with Chinese red-bean sauce, steamed rice, a salad of bean sprouts, slivered water chestnuts, romaine lettuce, in an olive oil dressing seasoned with a little soy sauce.

loin of pork provençale

A 5- or 6-pound roast serves 6 persons easily. Have the butcher saw through the chine bone and trim the loin for you. Cut about 5 garlic cloves into strips and place them in the pork meat. Then rub the loin with coarse salt (the Kosher type is best), freshly ground pepper, and some thyme. Grill the loin, turning occasionally, and basting with red wine for flavor. When you have placed the meat on a hot platter, pour about 4 ounces of cognac over it and ignite. Then, skim fat and excess juices from the drip pan and pour that mixture over the pork. Serve with potatoes prepared in the manner you like best.

marinated pork tenderloins

Rub 6 pork tenderloins with salt and chopped fresh or dried tarragon. Use enough tarragon to give a coating to each tenderloin. Place in a fairly shallow dish, add heavy cream, and let the tenderloins stand, turning them once or twice during a 2-hour period. Broil over medium heat, turning them several times during the cooking process. This takes 15 to 18 minutes. Serve straight from the grill or with a tarragon-flavored cream sauce if you wish. Buttered new potatoes and sautéed tomatoes are delicious with these tender bits.

swedish pork loin with prunes

Marinate pitted dried prunes in port or sherry for about 12 hours. Make 2 long cuts almost to the bone into the fleshy part of a 4- or 5-pound pork loin and stuff with the prunes until there are 2 rows slightly overlapping. Press all together and tie the loin firmly. Rub well with salt and place on grill. Turn occasionally and baste frequently with the wine in which you have soaked the prunes. Remove loin to hot platter when done and wait about 15 minutes before cutting away twine and carving. A salad or cole slaw dressed with a half-and-half mixture of mayonnaise and sour cream flavored with dill goes nicely. The prune-flavored pork is good cold, topped with hot mustard sauce.

OCTOBER SCENE DEPICTING SLAUGHTERING OF AN OX,
16TH CENTURY FLEMISH BREVIARY. PIERPONT MORGAN LIBRARY.

grilled spareribs

When serving spareribs, gauge 1 pound per person. I have known those who could eat many more than that; simply be sure you have enough. To grill spareribs, they must be parboiled until just tender or roasted at 350 F. for 45 minutes, then drained of their fat. Now brush with butter, salt, and pepper. Broil over coals until crisp on both sides.

spareribs with honey and curry

Parboil or partially roast 5 pounds of spareribs and cut in serving pieces. Brush each one with a honey-curry mixture made by blending 1 tablespoon curry powder with 1 cup honey and a few drops of lemon juice. Grill the honeyed ribs over medium coals, brushing each side with the honey-curry mixture. Broil until the ribs are nicely browned and deliciously glazed. Serve with curry-scented rice, chutney, and sliced cucumbers in a brisk French dressing.

grilled spareribs with pineapple

Parboil or partially roast 5 pounds of spareribs and cut in serving pieces. Place in a fairly shallow pan or dish and add just enough pineapple juice to cover. Allow to marinate in the refrigerator for 24 hours. Remove from the marinade, dry on absorbent paper, and brush with butter. Broil over medium heat until crisp. Serve with sautéed pineapple fingers.

pungent spareribs

Parboil spareribs and cut in serving pieces. Blend together 1 cup melted butter, 2 finely chopped garlic cloves, 1 teaspoon rosemary, 1 teaspoon salt, 1 teaspoon freshly ground black pepper. Brush the sparerib sections with this mixture and broil over medium coals until the meat is browned and delicately tender. Brush with additional garlic butter if you wish. Serve crisp French bread, a huge green salad with croutons and a few anchovies, and beer.

grilling variety meats

10 ways to serve frankfurters

Appetizers: A spicy snack with drinks is hot frankfurters or knockwurst, cut in bite-sized pieces, skewered on a toothpick, and served with a dunking bowl of hot barbecue sauce.

Tomato: Slice several green tomatoes thickly, and shake in a paper bag with flour, salt, and pepper. Fry floured tomatoes in a skillet. Serve a grilled frankfurter atop each slice.

Texas Hots: Grill your franks, place on toasted rolls, and cover them with cooked chopped meat, chili, and chopped raw onion.

Frankfurter Stroganoff: Sauté chopped onion in butter until tender. Add tomato sauce and season to taste with salt and freshly ground black pepper. Bring to a boil, then add sour cream to taste. Add sliced, grilled frankfurters and reheat, but do not allow to boil.

Cheese Stuffing: Slit each frankfurter lengthwise, but do not cut through. Insert bits of sharp Cheddar cheese, wrap in a strip of partially cooked bacon, and fasten with a toothpick. Grill slowly to allow bacon to cook.

Cheesefurter: Place grilled franks on toasted rolls, cover with pickle relish and over all a slice of cheese. Grill until cheese has melted.

Chili: Serve grilled frankfurters with chopped green chilis and sour cream.

French: Prepare a garlic butter and add chopped chives and parsley. Spread on rolls, insert grilled frank and top with a slice of cheese. Wrap in a double thickness of aluminum foil and heat until the cheese melts. Serve with a bowl of hot barbecue sauce for dunking.

Blanket: Roll uncooked frankfurters in your favorite bread or biscuit dough, which has been cut in strips ½ inch thick and wide enough to blanket each frank from end to end. There should be an overlap at the seam. Arrange on a greased baking sheet; bake in a moderate oven.

The Works: Slice lengthwise a loaf of French bread, spread with garlic butter, and toast slightly. On the bottom half place slices of tomato, onion, and cucumber. Then add split, grilled frankfurters or knockwurst. Top with mustard-mayonnaise—unless you want to add a slice of cheese as well. Cover with the other half loaf, cut in thick chunks. Serve with radishes and green onions.

grilled deviled pig's feet, st. menehould

This great French dish is ideal outdoors. If long-cut pig's feet are available—I find they are in Chinese and Italian stores—1 to a person is ample. Otherwise, the average good appetite may require 2. Don't let your butcher split them. Roll the feet in clean rags or cheesecloth and tie each one securely. Place in a large kettle with an onion stuck with cloves, a bay leaf, a stalk of celery, 1 teaspoon of thyme, 1 tablespoon of salt, and ½ cup wine vinegar. Cover with cold water, bring to a boil, cover the pot and simmer for 3-3½ hours. Remove the pig's feet, cut each string, and remove cloth wrappings. Place in a flat pan or bowl, and pour the broth over them. Allow to cool before refrigerating. When ready to grill, remove them from the jelly formed from the broth. Roll pig's feet in toasted, buttered crumbs, pressing the crumbs in exceedingly well. Grill over a very low heat, turning often, until the feet are heated through and the crumbs nicely browned. Brush with a little butter or oil occasionally if you think they need it. Serve with sauce Diable, hot, crisp French fried potatoes, and a water-cress salad. Drink an Alsatian white wine or a Muscadet or an Almaden Grenache rosé.

grilled calves' liver steak

A steak of calves' liver, cut from 1 to 2 inches thick, makes a most desirable, grillable meat. It should be grilled to a very definite pink rareness on the inside, but nicely charred and browned on the outside. Dip the liver steaks in olive oil, or brush well with butter or bacon fat before grilling. A liver steak should take any-

A FLEMISH KITCHEN, BY DAVID TENIERS, THE YOUNGER, METROPOLITAN MUSEUM OF ART, GIFT OF WILLIAM H. WEBB, 1874.

where from 8 to 12 minutes over a medium flame. Make certain you bring up the heat the last few minutes to give it a good char. Liver steak with a Béarnaise sauce is Epicurean eating. Serve with foil-roasted potatoes or with tiny boiled new potatoes rushed from the kitchen and dripping with butter.

VARIATION:

Serve calves' liver steak with a bowl of crumbled, crisp bacon, and a good mustard sauce. Cole slaw is excellent with this.

calves' liver minute steak, lyonnaise

Broil 1-inch-thick steaks of calves' liver, 1 to a person, and serve piping hot with a mountain of sautéed onion rings on top. Garnish with strips of bacon.

marinated liver steaks

For 4 persons, marinate 4 liver steaks for 2 hours in ½ cup olive oil, ½ cup red wine, 4 finely chopped garlic cloves, 1 teaspoon freshly ground black pepper, and 1 teaspoon salt. Dry on absorbent paper and broil over medium coals, brushing with a bit of the marinade several times during the broiling process. Serve with Elena's chili-rice casserole.

swiss liver steaks

Marinate, grill, and serve with a sour-cream sauce. With this rather rich dish, I suggest a good salad and some crisp French bread.

deviled liver steaks

Broil the liver steaks to your favorite degree of rareness. Press both sides into buttered bread crumbs and return to the grill to brown. Serve with a sauce Diable.

liver steak au poivre

Press 4 liver steaks into coarsely crushed black pepper and broil over medium coals until rare on the inside and nicely charred outside. Serve with a sauce Diable and crisp, sautéed potatoes.

lamb's liver

Any of the recipes given for calves' liver may be used with lamb's liver.

baby beef liver

Baby beef liver may be prepared in any of the ways given for calves' liver, but it will be more delicate if it is treated with meat tenderizer before broiling.

kidneys

My friend, Philip Brown, who is no mean gastronome, judges a restaurant by the way its chefs cook kidneys. This little-appreciated variety meat is certainly one of the more satisfying dishes you can prepare over charcoal. Recipes for preparing lamb kidneys will be found in the section on spitting and skewering. They are better adapted to that school of grilling.

veal kidneys

Do not allow the butcher to trim all the fat from the kidneys when you buy them. Split, or cut them in thickish slices, and remove the core with a sharp knife or scissors. Brush with oil or butter and broil over medium coals. Kidneys should not cook too quickly, and will toughen if overcooked. They should be nicely browned, with the fat crispy and the center a pleasant pink color. Brush with butter, salt, and pepper, and serve with boiled potatoes with melted butter and chives.

deviled kidneys

Broil the kidneys until almost done. Brush with melted butter, paint with mustard, and press into buttered, toasted crumbs. Return to the grill and continue grilling until the kidneys are nicely browned. Serve with sauce Diable, a water-cress salad with chopped hard-boiled egg, a good bread and butter, and cold beer.

grilled kidneys

Kidneys are excellent when left in their fat and grilled over coals. Turn them several times until the fat is crisp and charred. Slice thinly and serve with mustard sauce, or with a good Dijon or English mustard. Sautéed mushrooms and a salad are fine accompaniments. Follow with apple pie and heavy cream.

beef kidneys

Young beef kidneys may be sliced and grilled, although they are better if marinated for quite a long time beforehand to reduce their strong taste. One baby beef kidney serves 2 to 3 persons. Slice the kidneys in 1-inch slices, remove the core with sharp scissors, and marinate for 3 to 4 hours in a mixture of ½ cup vinegar,

½ cup dry vermouth, 1 onion finely chopped, 2 finely chopped garlic cloves, 1 teaspoon salt, 1 teaspoon freshly ground black pepper, and 2 tablespoons of soy sauce. Remove from the marinade and grill to your preferred state of doneness. Serve with crisp French fried potatoes and a sauce Diable.

sweetbreads

Sweetbreads are very delicate and should be gently treated when grilled over charcoal. If properly presented they are unusually good. Before they are grilled all sweetbreads should be blanched like this: Add enough water to cover sweetbreads, salt generously, and pour in 1 to 2 tablespoons of vinegar. Cook very gently for 20 minutes. Drain them in cold water and peel off the membrane.

broiled sweetbreads

Dip the sweetbreads into melted butter and broil gently over medium heat so that they will brown delicately and just cook through. Brush frequently with additional melted butter, and season with salt and pepper. Serve with a traditional sauce such as hollandaise or Béarnaise. Tiny new potatoes with parsley and tarragon are fine with this, and a chilled bottle of Muscadet is extremely good.

broiled sweetbreads virginia

Broil the sweetbreads and serve them on paper-thin slices of Virginia ham. Serve with buttered, toasted crumbs, and tarragon butter.

deviled sweetbreads

Brush sweetbreads well with melted butter, roll in flour, dip into mixture of egg and milk beaten together, and roll in toasted, buttered crumbs. Broil until nicely browned on both sides. Serve with tarragon butter. Drink a nice Pouilly Fuissé with this. Follow with egg salad, and a strawberry tart for dessert.

tongue—boiled & broiled

Veal or lamb tongues are delicious when boiled until tender, skinned, and broiled over coals. Beef tongues are generally not used for grilling. Veal tongues take 2 to 4 hours to boil tender, and lamb about 1 to 2 hours. Make a court bouillon with water, enough to cover the tongues, an onion stuck with cloves, a bay leaf, 1 or 2 cloves of garlic, 1 teaspoon of rosemary, a sprig of parsley, a stalk of celery, and a cup of white-wine vinegar or a pint of white wine. Simmer the tongues until just tender, let them cool slightly, and skin. If they are veal tongues, split in half. If they are lamb tongues, leave them whole.

broiled veal tongues

Crush 2 cloves garlic and add 2 tablespoons finely chopped fresh basil, 2 tablespoons finely chopped chives, 2 tablespoons finely chopped parsley. Blend this with enough olive oil to make a paste. Brush the tongues well with butter, and grill on one side for about 15 minutes, basting once or twice with the herb mixture. Turn and repeat the process on the other side, brushing again with the herb mixture. Remove from the fire, add melted butter and the herb mixture. Serve at once.

grilled lamb tongues

Dip cooked lamb tongue in garlic-flavored, melted butter. Broil for about 10 to 15 minutes over medium coals, brushing several times with additional garlic butter. Serve either one of these tongue dishes with a corn-meal soufflé from the kitchen, a raw spinach-and-egg salad, and ale.

hearts

Veal heart may be split or sliced, then marinated in a mixture of ½ cup each of soy sauce and red wine, 2 finely chopped garlic cloves, 1 teaspoon salt, 1 teaspoon freshly ground black pepper, and a teaspoon of dried basil or 2 tablespoons fresh basil. Drain, brush with melted butter or oil, and grill over a fairly hot fire until nicely browned on the outside and rare on the inside. Serve with broiled eggplant, garlic bread, and drink a California Barbera.

broiled beef heart

Beef heart may be cut about ½ to 1 inch thick and tenderized. Brush with olive oil, and broil rather quickly until fairly rare. Serve with a lemon butter, baked potatoes, and ale.

grilling game

There are two schools of thought about venison. One says it should be eaten the day it is killed; the other that it should hang for weeks. Take your choice. My own choice is to marinate it for several days, anywhere from 2 to 6, depending on age and relative tenderness, and then cook it. (Helen Evans Brown, who is one of the great authorities on food in this country, thinks that the liver from a freshly killed deer is the most delicious part of all.) A good marinade for venison is a bottle of red wine, ½ cup wine vinegar, 1 tablespoon salt, 3 cloves, 1 teaspoon coarsely ground black pepper; onions, carrots, garlic cloves (3 of each, all thinly sliced), a bay leaf, and a bit of thyme. Let your venison steaks or chops rest in this marinade from 2 to 6 days in a cool place, turning them often.

grilled, marinated venison steaks

Remove the steaks from the preceding marinade after they have soaked for several days and dry them on absorbent paper towels. Brush well with oil, and broil as you would a beef steak of similar size and weight. You may brush the broiling steak with the marinade if you wish. Serve the steaks with crisply fried corn-meal mush or hominy grits, and thinly sliced turnips, cooked with mushrooms. Drink a Burgundy.

LITHOGRAPH BY CURRIER AND IVES. KENNEDY GALLERIES.

venison steaks smitaine

While your steaks are broiling, reduce 1½ cups of the strained marinade to ½ cup over a brisk fire. Sauté ⅓ cup finely chopped shallots or scallions in 2 tablespoons butter until they are just limp. Add the reduced marinade to them and heat through. Before it reaches the boiling point, stir in 1 cup sour cream and heat thoroughly, but don't allow it to boil. Serve with the steaks.

grilled fresh venison steaks

Be certain that the venison is tender as well as fresh. Dip the steaks in melted butter or olive oil and broil quickly over a rather brisk fire, turning once or twice to color the steaks. Serve with Marchands de Vin sauce or a Bordelaise.

broiled venison steak au poivre

Cut the venison steaks to your favorite degree of thickness. For 3 steaks crush ¼ cup black peppercorns with a rolling pin or heavy weight so that the pepper is coarsely cracked. Press an ample quantity into both sides of the venison steaks with the heel of your hand. Let stand an hour or so. Broil according to directions for lamb steak or sirloin steak until your venison achieves its proper state of rareness. Serve with a Bordelaise sauce or a sauce Poivrade, a large bowl of polenta, and a crisp salad.

venison chops

Venison chops may be prepared in any of the ways described for venison steaks, but they are really best when broiled quickly over good coals, and served with a Béarnaise sauce.

broiled rabbit

Rabbit may be broiled in several ways. You can cut it in sections and grill it in a hinged or basket grill, or you can cut it in half and broil it over charcoal. Either way is good, especially when it's well basted with a marinade of melted butter, rosemary, and lemon juice. Serve with spoon bread, peas, and vin rosé.

saddle of hare

Allow 1 saddle per person, and soak the meat for no less than 3 days in enough red-wine marinade to cover. To make the marinade add to a substantial quantity of red wine, 1 teaspoon dried thyme, 1 bay leaf, 1 sliced carrot, 1 teaspoon peppercorns, an onion studded with cloves, some sprigs of parsley, and 1 teaspoon salt. During the soaking period, turn the saddles frequently so that they will moisten evenly.

Remove saddles, dry them, and bard with pork. Rub well with butter and sear the flesh quickly on both sides. Adjust the grill to a higher level and cook for an additional 15 minutes, or until the meat is just rare. Place on a hot platter. Mix the meat drippings, ¼ cup of cognac, and 3 or 4 tablespoons gooseberry jelly, and pour the mixture over the saddles, permitting it to caramelize. For a final touch add ½ cup of sauce Poivrade per saddle, heat thoroughly, and serve with the meat.

STILL LIFE WITH A VIEW OF ANTWERP, BY JAN DAVIDSZ DE HEEM.
TOLEDO MUSEUM OF ART, GIFT OF EDWARD DRUMMOND LIBBEY, 1955.

grilling poultry and fowl

Next to hamburger and steaks, chicken is certainly the most popular meat for broiling. In fact, in many localities, I might say that it is No. 1 in popularity for outdoor grilling. I never tire of the flavor of chicken and am still amazed at the variety of seasonings which may be added to a bird without robbing it of its own distinctive flavor. For those watching calories, chicken is an ideal food. Care should be taken not to overcook chicken or it will lose some of

its delectable juiciness. White meat cooks faster than dark meat—therefore, don't sacrifice the juiciness of the white meat to achieve a second joint that shows no pink. A pink joint will do you no harm. It assures a succulent chicken and proves that the bird has not been overcooked. Broilers vary in weight from 1 pound dressed to 3½ to 4 pounds. Technically, these larger ones are not broilers, but they broil deliciously. Good trenchermen can devour a whole chicken; however, the usual portion, with the exception of tiny squab chickens, is half a bird. Have them split and ask the butcher to remove the backbone and the cartilage from the breast. Turn the wings back and rub the chicken with a damp towel or with lemon juice, and it is ready for seasoning and broiling.

For 4 persons, buy 4 chicken halves and prepare as above. Brush the bone side of the chicken very well with a mixture of ¼ cup olive oil, ¼ cup melted butter, 1 teaspoon salt, ½ teaspoon freshly ground black pepper, and ½ teaspoon paprika. Let it stand 15 to 20 minutes. Brush again, and place the chickens, bone side down, on a grill over white coals. Broil approximately 12 minutes. Now brush the skin side with the mixture and turn. Continue cooking for an additional 12 to 14 minutes, depending upon the size of your chicken. Add additional salt and pepper if needed. Serve with crisp French fried potatoes, well-onioned tossed salad, and French bread. Drink a light red wine, a pleasantly chilled white wine, or California rosé, according to your taste.

broiled deviled chicken

Have the butcher split the chicken and prepare as above. Brush well with the butter-and-oil mixture and broil. When the chicken is almost done, brush lavishly with melted butter and roll in buttered crumbs. Return to the grill to brown on both sides. Serve with a Piquant sauce or a sauce Diable, along with a hearty tossed salad and herbed French bread. A good Beaujolais is excellent with this.

herb-stuffed broilers

Chop enough mixed herbs to make 1 cup for 3 broilers. They may be parsley, chives, tarragon, and a little garlic; or parsley, chives, fresh basil, and garlic. Or parsley, chives, garlic, and fresh mint. Combine the chopped herbs with 1½ bars of butter (6 ounces) and cream thoroughly. Salt and pepper to taste, and add a few drops of

lemon juice. With your index finger, loosen the skin on the breast of 6 chicken halves, stuff each half (between skin and meat) with spoonfuls of the herb-butter mixture, and secure the skin to the flesh with a small skewer or toothpicks. Brush the bone side of the chicken with additional herbed butter and broil, bone side down, for 12 to 15 minutes according to size. Turn and brush the skin side with a little melted butter. Broil, skin side down, over low heat for another 12 to 15 minutes, again according to the size of your chicken. Serve this delectable dish with new potatoes with a single strip of peel removed, and a salad of Bibb lettuce with French dressing. Fruit and cheese for dessert. Drink a pleasant, inexpensive Bordeaux with this, a chilled Beychevelle or Talbot.

mushroom-stuffed broilers

For mushroom-stuffed broilers, see the recipe for duxelles in the section on sauces. Stuff each breast (skin loosened from meat with the index finger) with a good tablespoon of duxelles, blended with a little chopped parsley. Secure the skin to the flesh with a toothpick or small metal skewer. Broil the chicken as for herbed broiler, brushing well with melted butter before placing it on the grill, and again when it is turned to cook the skin side. With this very glamorous dish, I like Potatoes Anna rushed from the kitchen, and a crisp salad, followed by a raspberry tart and good coffee. I also like a red Chassagne-Montrachet, or, if you prefer a white wine with chicken, a white Montrachet.

broiled chicken with
rosemary butter

Combine 2 tablespoons of pounded fresh rosemary or 1½ teaspoons pounded dry rosemary leaves, with ¼ pound butter and 2 tablespoons finely chopped shallots or scallions. Rub some of this butter into the bone side of each of 4 chicken halves. Broil. When you turn the chickens, rub the skin side well with the rose-

mary butter. When the chickens are done, place them on hot plates, and add a good dollop of rosemary butter to each one. Plain boiled potatoes, and tiny French peas cooked with ham and a little onion make a fine combination.

marinated broilers, honolulu fashion

Marinate 4 broiler halves for several hours in ½ cup white wine or vermouth, ½ cup soy sauce, 2 finely chopped cloves of garlic, and 3 tablespoons grated fresh ginger or 1½ teaspoons powdered ginger. Turn chickens several times during the marinating period.

To broil: Brush the bone side of the broilers with olive oil and broil for 10 to 12 minutes. Turn, brush the skin side well with olive oil, and continue broiling until the chicken is tender. You may brush with the marinade from time to time during the broiling period if you wish. Fried rice and snow peas cooked with mushrooms make a perfect accompaniment.

marinated broilers no. 2

Marinate 4 broiler halves for several hours in ½ cup olive oil, ½ cup white wine, 2 finely chopped garlic cloves, 1 teaspoon oregano, and

2 tablespoons chili powder. Turn broilers several times during marinating period, and salt and pepper to taste. Just before broiling, sprinkle with a little additional chili powder and broil according to the preceding directions, brushing from time to time with some of the marinade. Serve with a corn fondue, a radish salad, and, if you can stand that much corn, heated tortillas with butter. For dessert, cream cheese and guava paste with crackers.

broiled chicken flambé

Rub 4 broiler halves well with butter and sprinkle with salt, pepper, and paprika. Rub in a little tarragon. For the 4 broilers you will need ¼ pound butter, salt and pepper to taste, and 1½ teaspoons dried or 2 teaspoons chopped fresh tarragon. When they are broiled, place in a large iron skillet or copper pan, which you may use as a serving dish and in which you have melted about 6 tablespoons butter. Add 1 teaspoon salt, 1 teaspoon of dried tarragon, or a tablespoon of chopped fresh tarragon. Pour ⅓ cup heated cognac over them and ignite just as you serve to your guests. Roesti potatoes and mushrooms in cream flavored with a little cognac would be excellent with this.

glazed broilers

Combine ½ cup each of strained honey and soy sauce. Add the juice of 2 lemons, 3 finely chopped garlic cloves, and 2 teaspoons of dry mustard. Blend well. Brush 4 broiler halves with olive oil and broil. Turn the broilers and paint lavishly with the honey seasoning. Turn after 5 minutes and brush again with the mixture. Continue broiling, brushing from time to time, until the chicken is cooked and the skin side is nicely glazed. You must not have these broilers too close to the coals. They may take longer to cook, but that's all right. You want a nice glaze without char. Serve barley with toasted almonds and a string-bean salad. Drink a chilled rosé, perhaps a Tavel.

turkey

Small young turkeys, split, with the backbone and breastbone removed, are superb when they are charcoal broiled. A small turkey of 4 or 5 pounds, dressed weight, will serve 4 amply, with possibly a little bit left over if appetites are not too tremendous. Brush the turkey well on the bone side with butter, and season with salt and pepper. Broil quite slowly for perhaps 20 to 25 minutes. Brush the skin side with butter, season with salt and pepper, and continue broiling, skin side up, until the turkey is cooked through. This takes another 20 minutes. Turn and brush with butter again during this time. Serve broiled turkey with a Ratatouille, and toasted French bread. Drink a hearty wine, perhaps a Chateauneuf-du-Pape or a Barbera.

broiled truffled turkey

There are two types of tinned truffles available in the market. One, the tremendous black diamonds of gastronomy which come for the most part from France; and, two, the delicately scented and flavored white truffles from Italy. The white ones have a distinctive flavor which is rather gamy and slightly reminiscent of robust herbs and are the ones used for this particular dish. For 4 persons, you need a can holding 4 to 5 white truffles. Slice them fairly thin. An hour or two before broiling a 4- to 5-pound turkey, loosen the skin over the breast and second joint with your index finger and slip as many slices of the white truffles under the skin as you can lodge there. Secure the skin to the flesh with small skewers or toothpicks.

Brush the bone side of the turkey well with a half-and-half mixture of butter and olive oil. Salt and pepper to taste. Place over a medium heat, bone side down, and broil for 25 to 28 minutes. Brush the skin side with the same mixture of oil and butter, turn the turkey and broil slowly for another 20 minutes, turning to baste with the oil-butter mixture once during that time. Continue broiling until the turkey is tender and cooked through. Serve with noodles

AROUND THE FISH, BY PAUL KLEE. COLLECTION,
THE MUSEUM OF MODERN ART, N. Y., MRS. JOHN D. ROCKEFELLER, JR. FUND.

blended with butter, Gruyère cheese, and a little cream; also with tiny string beans boiled in salt water until tender, then sautéed in butter and sprinkled with chopped, toasted almonds.

herb-stuffed turkey

Follow the directions for herb-stuffed chicken, but broil as outlined for broiling turkey.

broiled turkey steaks

Buy a large frozen turkey and have the butcher saw the bird into 1-inch steaks while it is still frozen, cutting the bird in cross-section from tail to head. Brush lavishly with a mixture of butter and olive oil, and broil slowly over medium heat. Season to taste and brush with the oil-butter mixture several times during the broiling process. It takes about 20 to 25 minutes to do each side. Serve with a Béarnaise sauce, and fresh corn pancakes (an electric skillet does a good job here). Have some crisp vegetables to nibble. Drink Julienas.

VARIATIONS:

Marinated: Marinate turkey steaks in any of the marinades given for broiling chicken. Brush with the marinade during the broiling process.

Tarragon Turkey: Brush the turkey steaks before and during broiling with a half-and-half mixture of butter and oil, combined with 2 tablespoons each of chopped parsley and chopped tarragon. Pour leftover mixture over the turkey steaks when they are served. Lyonnaise potatoes, and celery salad with a brisk mustard dressing are excellent with this.

turkey cutlets

Purchase turkey breasts in a poultry parts market, or buy a small turkey and remove the meat from the breast, saving the dark meat for a ragout or for stuffed turkey legs. Grind the raw breast meat or chop it fine with a French knife. You need around two cups of chopped turkey meat. Combine the raw chopped meat with 1½ teaspoons salt, 1 teaspoon freshly ground black pepper, 1 teaspoon fresh rosemary, ½ cup bread crumbs, 1 egg, and enough heavy cream to make a workable mixture. Form into cakes about 3 inches in diameter and ½ inch thick. Dip the cakes into melted butter, then flour, then dip again into melted butter. Broil quickly to brown both sides. Brush with melted butter during the process. Serve with Béarnaise sauce, a pea soufflé, and a spinach-and-egg salad. With this, I suggest a Pouilly-Fumé.

VARIATIONS:

You may vary the cutlets with any herbs or seasonings you wish. Delicious ones are tarragon, garlic, rosemary, shallots.

duck and gosling

Duck is not one of the popular birds for grilling; in my opinion, however, it deserves much more attention. Most people tend to overcook duck or they broil birds that are too large and too fat. For the grill, one should use young duckling only, with as little fat as possible. Estimate one-half duck per person. Rub the bone side with a little oil or butter, and broil it for about 25 minutes. Brush the skin side lightly with butter or oil and prick gently with a fork. Allow to broil for 15 to 20 minutes, or until the skin is nicely browned and crispy. Serve the duck hot and crisp, on hot plates with an onion-and-orange salad, and perhaps a barley-almond casserole. Drink a good Pommard.

Note: The fat from duck may drop into the coals and cause flames. To avoid this, move the charcoal or briquets away from the line of drippings. The heat will not decrease too much. Then bring up the firebox or increase the heat for the last few minutes of cooking.

glazed duckling

Proceed as above but brush duck during the broiling process on both sides with a mixture of ½ cup Grand Marnier, ⅔ cup honey, and 2 teaspoons dry mustard blended together. Brush often to form a glaze on both the skin and bone surface. With the glazed ducklings serve a rice pilaff and a sharply dressed green salad.

VARIATIONS:

No. 1: Brush with a half-and-half mixture of honey and concentrated frozen orange juice.

No. 2: Brush with a mixture of honey and sweet sherry in equal proportions.

No. 3: Brush with a combination of ½ cup honey, ⅓ cup soy sauce, and ⅓ cup sherry for a very effective glaze.

broiled wild duck

Wild duck is delicious cooked over the grill—the more so if it is young. Split ducks and cut out the backbone. Brush both sides with butter, and broil, bone side to the heat, for 8 to 10 minutes. Turn, broil the other side for 10 to 12 minutes or until your favorite degree of pinkness has been achieved inside. Salt and pepper to taste. If you like, blaze with cognac before serving. Tiny peas with green onions, butter, and mushrooms laced into them, crisp French bread, and a bottle of Nuits St. Georges make a perfect combination.

VARIATIONS:

Stuff a few juniper berries under the skin of wild duck before broiling. Or some thyme. Or a little leaf sage.

broiled gosling

If you are fortunate enough to know someone who raises geese, and who will let you have a young one, broil it as you would a duckling. Give it a little more time to cook, so it is fairly well done. Serve with apple slices cut paper thin and dredged in butter before being sautéed quickly to a crisp brown-edged finish. I like a casserole of white beans in the Breton manner with gosling, and a Chateauneuf-du-Pape.

broiled wild goose

Follow the rules for broiling wild duckling, but give the wild goose a little more time on the grill. Serve with sautéed apple slices and polenta. Drink a Pommard.

pheasant

Either domestic or wild pheasant is a superb dish. However, since pheasant has a tendency to dry during the cooking period, it is wise to

bard or force a little salt pork under the skin of the breast before broiling. For a young pheasant, follow the directions for broiling chicken. Serve with traditional buttered bread crumbs and fried squares of hominy grits made like this: Boil hominy grits, pour into a mold or pan, allow to cool, unmold, and cut into ½-inch slices. Dip the slices into flour and sauté.

broiled wild pheasant

Wild pheasant may be treated in the same manner as chicken. To vary it for broiling, crush juniper berries, mix with butter, and force under the breast.

hung pheasants

The English dearly love hung game, which used to be hung outdoors until it was pretty well gone, but maintained an odor and flavor inspiring praise by poets. Hung pheasant, if it will withstand the treatment, may be split, well anointed with butter and oil, and broiled in the same manner as for broiling pheasant. Serve with buttered crumbs, bread sauce, and perhaps a dish of corn au gratin. Drink a fine wine from the Medoc—a Château Latour of a very good year.

quail

In this country so many different types of birds are called quail it is hard to distinguish the bird referred to when discussing the subject in various sections of the United States. One thing that everyone agrees on, however, is that no matter what the version, quail is a small bird. Split quail down the back and wrap the breast of each with salt pork or bacon, securing with toothpicks. Broil bone side down, and turn. Take 12 to 18 minutes for the entire broiling time. Salt and pepper to taste. Place the quail on squares of buttered toast and serve with lemon butter mixed with a generous sprinkling of parsley. Hot succotash, and a large casserole of

rice with butter, chives, and a little shallot are pleasant accompaniments.

flattened quail

You may flatten quail with one blow of a cleaver so they collapse completely. The portions may then be buttered and broiled in the same manner as split quail, if you wish.

quail sautéed with white grapes

Clean and split the bird. Brown it quickly in a skillet with plenty of butter and seasoning to taste. Add ½ cup of broth made by cooking giblets in a little water flavored with an onion, or by dissolving chicken-bouillon cubes in hot water. Cover pan and let quail simmer over low heat for 8 to 10 minutes. Remove the cover and add a dash of whiskey and from ½ to 1 cup of white seedless grapes. Cover again and simmer until the quail is tender.

partridge

Of all the game birds in the world I think I most prefer the partridge one gets in France. I find the American version excellent, but somehow it never quite achieves the flavor of the French perdreau. To broil partridge, split down the back, remove the backbone, and cover each breast with a thin slice of salt pork or bacon. Broil over a medium heat for 20 to 25 minutes, brushing often with melted butter or half-and-half melted butter and olive oil. Serve with crisp French bread and a bowl of water cress with no dressing. Drink a fine Château Haut Brion. Plan on 1 partridge per person. If appetites are large, plan on 2.

broiled partridge

If you shoot the birds, you may have to pluck them—a pretty tedious job. Once plucked, however, singe, draw, and split; season the bone side with salt and pepper. Butter well. Broil under medium heat for approximately 12 minutes.

Turn, brush well with more butter, and continue broiling 12 to 15 minutes, or until tender and nicely browned.

VARIATION:

> *Partridges (1 bird per person)*
> *Butter*
> *Salt and pepper*
> *1 onion stuck with cloves*
> *Toast*
> *Dijon mustard*

Singe, clean, and draw partridges. Split and rub well with butter. Broil the well-buttered birds, skin side down, to your favorite degree of doneness. Salt and pepper to taste. Turn, baste with butter and broil until nicely browned and tender. Cook giblets until tender in the 2 cups of water, with an onion stuck with cloves. Chop giblets fine and mix with 1 tablespoon butter and a little of the broth in which they cooked. Spread slices of crisp, well-buttered toast with this giblet mixture, and place a partridge on each slice. I recommend a little Dijon mustard with the birds. And a good Vosne Romanée or a Nuits St. Georges.

broiled snipe

The snipe—and it's practically all delicious breast—should be broiled whole. Singe, clean, and draw the birds. Rub with a little thyme. Spread the entire surface with butter, and place in a basket grill or a flat grill. Broil fairly slowly, turn frequently, and brush with additional butter. Salt and pepper as you brush. A snipe should take about 20 to 25 minutes over a medium fire at a 350 F. surface temperature.

squab

Squab is one of the neglected birds. The "Rock Cornish Game Hen" has supplanted the popularity of the squab, and I cannot understand why. No small bird except a partridge has such a distinctive flavor, nor lends itself so well to so many types of cooking. One squab per person is the average but there are plenty of good trenchermen who can handle two.

broiled squab

You may split the squab down the back and press it quite flat; or you may broil the whole squab. This second method necessitates frequent turning so that the bird gets the same finish on all sides. In either case, brush well with equal parts of olive oil and butter, and salt and pepper lightly. They will take 18 to 20 minutes to broil and possibly longer. Squab is one bird which is excellent overcooked, but is often undercooked. Serve broiled squab with new potatoes smothered with butter and parsley; a tomato-cognac salad; and drink a Fleurie.

squab crapaudine

This really means a squab that looks like a frog. Flatten out the squab with a hefty blow from the flat side of a cleaver. This collapses the rib cage and breaks down the frame. Brush the birds well with an olive-oil-and-butter mixture, sprinkle with salt and pepper, and tuck a little thyme in the vent of each bird. Broil 18 to 20 minutes and serve them with a hot olive sauce. Green peas cooked with crisp bacon, then mixed with toasted almonds and flavored with just a touch of Madeira, make a good accompaniment.

deviled squab

Broil either split squab, or squab Crapaudine, as previously suggested. When the birds are just about right to serve, dip into melted butter, press into buttered crumbs, and broil a bit longer to crispen. Serve with a sauce Diable and Potatoes Anna. Drink a Hermitage from the Rhone and follow with a hearty green salad and some excellent cheese. Be sure to keep an extra bottle of wine for the cheese course.

broiled grouse, woodcock, and other birds

Follow the directions for quail, partridge, or squab for any of these small birds and you will not go wrong.

grilling fish and seafood

Without a doubt there is something "different" about a fish that has been broiled or grilled over charcoal. It seems to smack of the outdoors, to have an added something that enhances its unique flavor. Be sure to use a hinged grill so the fish will not move about and fall apart while cooking and so that it will be easy to turn. It is also wise to preheat the grill until it is hot enough to mark the fish when you place it on the grid. Another necessary procedure is that of flouring and oiling the fish, whether whole, half, fillets, or steaks, and repeating the oiling during the grilling process several times. If the steaks or fillets are without skin they will need to be brushed with the oil more often than if they are whole and unskinned. You will have to learn to become aware of the "doneness" through experience since the variations—in thickness, steak, whole, half, fillet, and so forth —are endless. There is one test that is simple and seems to work well most of the time. Insert a toothpick or fork into the fish. When the flesh flakes, the fish is done. Remember, it is almost always better to have the fish slightly undercooked than overdone. Again, I repeat, you will have to learn what each fish requires.

sesame fish

A most unusual and delightful way to prepare fish is to split it, dip in melted butter or oil, and then in sesame seeds. Then grill. The finished dish is a thing of great delicacy and subtlety, and certain to please your guests. There are many fish that can be treated in this manner—striped bass, sea bass, salmon, trout, any of the larger fish. If you are cooking a large fish, grill until it is two-thirds done. Dip it again in butter (or oil) and sesame seeds, and return to the grill to finish. A medium-cut fish steak should be cooked halfway before dipping again in the sesame seeds.

plank-roasted salmon, indian fashion

A favorite method of the Indians for cooking salmon was to split and bone it, then nail it,

skin side down, to a hardwood plank. It was seasoned with salt and pepper, buttered well, and placed at an angle to the fire, like an easel, so that it cooked fairly slowly. It was brushed from time to time with butter or oil. The salmon was done if it flaked easily when tested with a fork or a small twig. If you should undertake this dish, serve with plenty of lemon butter, foil-roasted potatoes, and cucumber strips.

foil-roasted salmon

Wrap a whole salmon in several thicknesses of foil and roast it right on the coals—or spit and roast it over the coals. Season it first with salt and pepper, a good-sized sliced onion, fresh dill, and several sprigs of parsley. Serve this with melted butter and lemon, crisp French bread, and a pea pie. With this rather rich fish, I suggest you drink beer.

flaming fish

A delightful habit that began in the Mediterranean countries and has since spread to many others is that of flaming a fish in a jacket of herbs. First grill the fish and remove it to a hot platter, or bed of rock salt, which has been covered with herbs. The more usual ones are rosemary, fennel, dill, parsley, thyme. The fish is then topped with the herbs, and about 2 or 3 ounces of alcohol, usually a cognac or rum, are poured over it and ignited. The burning herbs have a dual value; they not only excite your taste buds, they also give the fish that subtle flavor which most people find irresistible. Fish may be flamed in any size fish, whole, half—you might even try it with fillets.

barbecued swordfish steak

½ cup soy sauce
2 cloves garlic, chopped
4 tablespoons tomato sauce
2 tablespoons lemon juice
¼ cup chopped parsley

1 teaspoon finely powdered oregano
½ cup orange juice
1 teaspoon freshly ground pepper

Mix all of these ingredients together and marinate the swordfish steaks in it for at least 2 hours before grilling over charcoal. During cooking, use it as a basting sauce.

broiled dungeness crab

The Dungeness crab is peculiar to the Pacific Northwest, so it may be difficult for you to get live ones, but if they aren't available, you'll find that even the boiled variety is more than worthwhile. Clean them, removing the top shell, and crack the claws. Prepare a sauce of ½ cup of melted butter and ½ cup white wine. For added savor, you may add 2 tablespoons each of soy sauce and tomato catsup, and 1 clove garlic, well crushed; season with marjoram powder. Place the crabs bottom shell down and grill over charcoal, basting frequently with the sauce. The crabs should be turned once during cooking, and should be served piping hot. Plenty of butter and lemon, a crisp French bread (and huge bibs)—all go well. Dungeness crab is also good served cracked and cold with a mayonnaise and lemon-juice dressing.

broiled king-crab legs

The giant of all crabs, properly named "king," is wonderful grilled over glowing charcoal. The *pièce de résistance* for broiling is the center section of the leg which can be delightfully prepared in the following manner: Make a cross-shaped incision in the soft part of the shell on the underside of the crab. Then place over the coals, slit side up, and baste often with a mixture of melted butter and lemon juice. When the crab is hot and the shell is browned, serve with French fried potatoes and shredded cucumbers which have been mixed well with lots of mayonnaise and flavored with dill and onions. Drink a well-chilled white wine. A Chablis or a white pinot would be superb.

standard

beef

*"Prime," "Choice," "Good,"
are, in descending order,
guides to beef's quality*

1 Square-cut chuck: *Stews*
2 Ribs: *Roasts and steaks*
3 Short loin: *Quality steaks*
4 Sirloin: *Broiled, panfried*
5 Rump: *Braised, roasted*
6 Shank: *Soups and stews*
7 Brisket: *Braised, corned*
8 Plate: *Boiled and stewed*
9 Flank: *Broiled, boiled*
10 Round: *Ground beef, heel*

lamb

*Almost the whole lamb can
be eaten, and many of the
cuts are particularly well-
suited to outdoor cooking.*

1 Shoulder: *Roasts, chops*
2 Rack: *Crown, rack, chops*
3 Loin: *Roasts and chops*
4 Shank, Breast: *Stew meat*
5 Leg: *Whole leg of lamb.
Whole saddle of lamb (the
loins, tenderloin, part of
the ribs) is spectacular
when spitted on the grill.*

US CHO

cuts of meat

pork

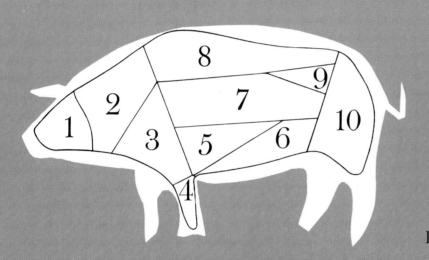

Pork is almost entirely edible, and can be served in a multitude of ways.

1 Head: *Pork headcheese*
2 Boston Butt: *Smoked*
3 Picnic: *Baked, braised*
4 Foot, Hock: *Pickled*
5 Rib Cage: *Spareribs*
6 Side: *Salt pork, bacon*
7 Loin: *Roasts and chops*
8 Back: *Fat back, lard*
9 Tenderloin: *Roasted*
10 Ham: *Baked, broiled*

veal

Veal is relatively lean, and usually needs basting with oil while cooking. Mild-flavored, it can take a good deal of seasoning.

1 Shoulder: *Roasts, steaks*
2 Arm: *Arm roast, steaks*
3 Shank: *Braised, boiled*
4 Breast: *Roasted, stewed*
5 Ribs: *Roasts and chops*
6 Loin: *Chops and steaks*
7 Rump: *Roasted, braised*
8 Whole Leg: *Roasted*

fire, fuel, and equipment

My pioneer grandparents who crossed the country in a covered wagon were expert fire builders. My mother, who loved a bonfire and, even more, loved to cook over one, could make the wettest driftwood burst into blazing glory with a deft turn of the paper and kindling. Alas, such skill as this is more or less a lost art. Nowadays there is something artificial to carry along which is quick and foolproof. Very few people ever attempt to cook over the delicious coals produced by a wood fire. Everyone cooks with charcoal briquets. Not that I have anything against briquets, but I sometimes wish for one of those great fires made with bark that has aged in the sea and drifted onto the beach to dry.

But briquets we have, and they are useful and efficient—and sometimes destructive when improperly used. By this, I mean that most people never learn to take the question of fires with ease and simplicity. To cook one poor little piece of steak, they feel that they must fill the firebox with briquets and have a raging inferno. I have seen too many 2- or 3-inch porterhouses reduced to minute steaks over improperly fired grills. It may be astounding to realize that one can cook a 5-rib roast using as few as 30 or 32 briquets, but that is all it takes if you learn how to build and care for your fire properly. It used to be necessary to start a small fire with kindling and paper to cook with briquets, but no longer. There is paint thinner; there are all sorts of lighting fluids; there are pastes that squeeze onto the briquets; and there are electric starters, all of which are quite efficient. For consistently good results when using kindling agents, I think it wise to keep a can of briquets marinating in a starter. Use a second can to help build the fire. Cut both ends out, pierce a few holes in the sides for ventilation, and place the can upright in the grill firebox. Put some of the marinated briquets into the can, stack dry briquets on top, and finish by covering with a few more saturated ones. You will need from 20 to 35 briquets for most cookery. Ignite the saturated briquets and let the fire burn briskly until all of the briquets are glowing. This

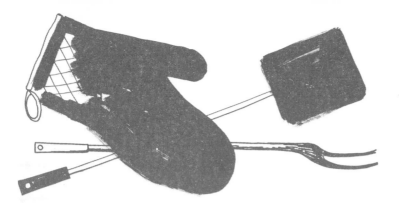

should take about 10 minutes. Then slip the can from around the stacked briquets with a pair of tongs or pliers, letting the burning coals fall freely into the firebox; then arrange them properly, so that they more or less adhere to the shape of the cooking meat.

Build the fire so that you can raise the grid without changing the distribution of the heat. If the fire is concentrated in a single area when you raise the grill, you will be left with a large, seared spot in the center of the meat while the surrounding surfaces are uncharred, or perhaps completely uncooked.

When the coals are glowing and encrusted with white ash, cooking may begin. For grilling, the surface temperature should be about 350 F.; for spit-roasting, it should be between 275 and 300 F. To be certain of the temperature of your fire, use a surface thermometer or a spit thermometer. If your spit-roasting grill does not have a separate firebox, be sure to place a pan beneath the meat to catch the drippings. The briquets must then be arranged around the pan. The pan may be makeshift—an old ice tray will do. The drip pan serves to protect the coals, and catches the delicious meat drippings which go into your sauces and bastes.

equipment

Lost with the art of building great wood fires are many simple grids and spitting contraptions. These makeshift devices, which once freely permitted savors of charcoal and seasoned woods to enhance roasting meats, have been replaced by innumerable commercial grills. Efficient and compact, the new broilers are scientifically designed to make cooking easier and to cook in almost any situation. Usually they grill foods so well that one almost forgets the charms that went with crude seaside and woodland bonfires and the art of those who cooked over them. To this day, I think the ideal device for campers and beach picnickers, where supplies of wood and driftwood are ample, is

the simple grilling rack. The cooking surface is large, it accommodates not only meats but skillets and griddles, and it travels well. It is always encouraging to me to find these gridirons still available in stores, and at very low prices.

Long ago, while watching my mother prepare for what seemed to be hordes of people, over blazing beach fires, I learned that ingenuity can be compensation enough in the world of cookery. I could see then—as I know now—that even a shortage of funds was not sufficient reason to prevent anyone from enjoying the pleasures of outdoor cooking. Commercial grills are now generally inexpensive, and the makeshift and the homemade will still cook to perfection when properly attended. The simple iron grid, left over from the cook-stove era, can be poised upon rocks piled evenly to serve as endposts and is more than adequate for grilling. Or something in the style of a Chinese *wok* may be constructed from the top of an old water tank, or other large, round, shallow pan, and surrounded with bricks and stones to steady it. It's best to fill the bottom of the *wok* with a few inches of dirt and sand to make the fire area even and to raise the level of the flame.

If your circumstances do not require it, there is no reason to trouble yourself with the makeshift. Modern methods for grilling succulent meats *are* available, and I have no objections to conveniences, particularly when they produce such palatable results. Today we seem to have as many grills as we have individual preferences for them. They may be portable, wheeled, or electric.

The most versatile are the portable grills, which adapt to both indoor and outdoor use—an important feature when a downpour suddenly sends the crowd running in search of shelter. A favorite portable of mine, and the most modern, is the Bernz-o-matic (or Ceramic Grill) which is fueled by small tubes of propane gas and produces its flame on slabs of non-flammable ceramic tile. I find it's easy to transport, safe to operate in or out of doors, and while it requires no charcoal, it lends a charcoal flavor to the food. Another grill which has excited the interest of the American hostess is the bucket portable—particularly, the little Japanese *hibachi,* a very efficient pot with a grid cover. It is centuries old in principle, dating to a period when it served for both heating and cooking, but it has been little improved upon since that time. Today, we use the hibachi for just about every conceivable grilling task, and small hibachis are even brought to table to keep foods warm. These are marvelous when you're having a luau. Unfortunately, the hibachi's cumbersome weight and shape make transporting it difficult, but the Skotch grill, a more modern version of the bucket, makes an ideal portable. The handsomely decorated, insulated pail has both grill top and cover, and it does double service, since food or briquets can be conveniently packed inside and carried to the picnic site. Another useful portable is the folding grill with its large, trough-shaped firebox, grill top, folding or removable legs, and, sometimes, even a carrying case. I like this one particularly because it is simple and light and because it provides ample cooking surface.

Outdoor cooking equipment never seems complete any more unless I see at least one of the wheeled grills. Of all these, probably the best-known is the brazier, which resembles a large, round, shallow pan, topped with a grid. These are sometimes equipped with electric spits, and all of them have adjustable fireboxes so that you are able to control the distance of food from flame. Big Boy grills, another of the wheeled variety, are also popular with many people. Certain of these models can both grill and spit foods, and some come complete with hoods, so that it is possible to use them for smoke cooking. I must admit I had my reservations about the Big Boy grills at first, but recently many improvements have been made on the early models, and I feel they should now be counted among the better pieces of cookout equipment. Not so familiar as the Big Boys and braziers are the vertical grills that cook in front of, rather

than over, the coals, and are sometimes equipped with two fireboxes, so that they can grill both sides of the food at once. Drip pans catch the fat and prevent flaring. My only objection to them is that they tend to decrease the amount of charcoal flavoring which so enhances the food. Otherwise they are most satisfactory. Probably the most luxurious pushmobile is the Bartron barbecue, a large, stainless-steel stove with two fireboxes—one for grilling and one for spitting—a hood, and shelves. It is not only convenient, but certainly most handsome. I find it makes a fine addition to the kitchen during winter months. However, it *is* large and quite expensive. Multiple-spitted, wheeled grills also are available for those who are especially fond of spit-and-skewer cookery. They have the singular advantage of being able to spit roast several meats and vegetables at the same time.

Recently, too, the Corning Glass people have developed an astounding glass material called Pyroceram, which is non-flammable, durable when exposed to temperature extremes, and holds heat so well that it does not require a high flame. It is currently being produced only in casserole shapes, but the company plans to bring out an electric skillet made entirely of Pyroceram which should be marvelous on the terrace or in the garden for any type of cooking. Pyroceram casseroles perform wonderfully when filled with live coals and used as small table grills. Food may also be frozen in them, then placed directly in the oven without defrosting. They all have removable handles. I think they are the most revolutionary pieces of equipment that have come on the market in a long time. If a base plug or outlet is accessible to your porch or patio, you'll find electrical equipment a handy supplement to your other barbecue apparatus. Electric broilers and rotisseries, such as the Town and Country Electric Grill, may be used in the garden and will do a better job of roasting than most charcoal rotisseries because they maintain an even heat and permit the spitting to be timed so perfectly that there is no chance of failure. The Town and Country will

take a 25-pound turkey, a 5-rib standing roast of beef, or almost any kind of roast you want to cook. It also has special brochettes for kebabs and a "weenie wheel" which delights the younger generation. If you like, you can broil on it too, but, for me, broiling over charcoal is much more exciting and flavorsome. In recent years, I have also noted an increasing trend to the electric skillet, another superb aid to the outdoor cook—and to the indoor cook, for that matter. It may be used for vegetables, for suki-yaki, and for auxiliary dishes of every kind. Electric deep-fat friers are also tremendous helps, particularly when you're preparing French fries or doughnuts. And there are electric cookers and saucepans, chafing dishes, and hot trays and tables. The Thermo Tray, produced by the Cornwall Corporation, can be a lifesaver. It comes in 8 different sizes and some are large enough to keep an entire feast warm. They're rugged, yet light in weight and safely watertight. I find them ideal for buffet suppers, hot hors d'oeuvres, or keeping food warm.

Aside from basic equipment, there are dozens of small items you should have on hand to make the job easier. You'll need a sturdy table or large cutting surface; tongs for turning grilled foods and for plucking potatoes and corn from the fire; a sprinkler bottle—makeshift is as good as any — for controlling the flame; pliers to tighten the holding forks on the spit and to position it; skewers, ornate or simple (the most inexpensive chopsticks do quite nicely); utensils which can be taken from the kitchen, such as drip pans, spoons, forks, and knives that can be sharply honed. You'll also need a brush for basting. If you want to go primitive, a faggot of herb or a husk of corn will do, but I prefer a long-handled pastry brush. Never use cotton swabs or mops. Asbestos gloves and canvas or leather work gloves are a must. For handling charcoal or briquets, work gloves are far better than tongs, and the asbestos mitts are invaluable for work near the fire. Finally, see that you have the proper thermometers on hand. You should have both a spit thermometer, which is

attached to the spit and permits you to check the external temperature at which the meat is roasting, and a grill or meat thermometer, which can be inserted into the meat to determine internal temperatures. Unfortunately, most meat thermometers scale only from 140 to 220 F, so that it is impossible to obtain the proper rare-meat reading. Try to get the type that reads from zero to 220 F. These are usually available at laboratory supply houses. (I use one put out by Griffith Laboratories.)

Although you certainly can cook more than adequately without them, there are also a number of extras that are handy and fun. Here I suggest a peppermill, one that can be regulated to grind from coarse to fine; a salt shaker for coarse salt, since I almost always suggest Kosher salt for outdoor grilling; paper towels; pot holders; a carry-all basket of wicker or wire for cooking supplies; aprons (I think heavy white denim without fancy pictures and funny sayings is best), and carving boards. Of course, if

you can, you should purchase one or more basket grills. Once you have used them, you'll find it difficult to do without them. Made of wire, and usually shallow, flat, and hinged at the top, they are equipped with long handles for holding over the heat. The largest of them is perfect for large meat slices or foods such as fish, which are difficult to turn. There are also two smaller varieties with medium-sized and tiny grids; these are best for thin pieces of meat or poultry and for tidbits such as oysters, shrimp, scallops, and chicken livers. The newest addition to the group is a cylindrical wire basket in which whole chickens, squabs, and other small birds or roasts may be placed. It works like a spit, revolving the meat as it cooks.

Above all, however, remember that no piece of equipment, no matter how shiny or how ingenious, has ever replaced a careful and attentive cook. Get everything you think you need to do the job well—but be certain that your own skills and procedures are in working order.

The deliberate turning of a spit over,

or in front of, a fire is certainly a most delectable

way to roast a prime joint or a tender bird.

The resulting crispness of skin and juiciness of

flesh is inviting to the eye, tantalizing

to the nose, and an unbounded joy to the palate.

SPIT-ROASTED PRIME RIBS OF BEEF ARE BEST IF ALLOWED TO COAST BEFORE SLICING.

Spit roasting is an art. And it takes some practice before you do it easily and well. To be done properly, the meat must be balanced on the spit, a difficulty which is only exaggerated by the various shapes and sizes of meats and poultry. Learning to spit one does not insure success with another. For instance, standing ribs of beef generally should be spitted diagonally through the length of the roast from one cut side to the other. Rolled rib roasts are spitted similarly, but a sirloin roast, the Franco-English favorite, is most easily balanced when spitted straight through the center. Poultry, on the other hand, is usually best balanced when the spit is run diagonally from the tail of the bird to the breastbone. Experiment. If necessary, re-spit the roast or bird several times until the weight is evenly distributed. For only this way will the meat rotate freely and rhythmically, and cook slowly to perfection. Thus, before placing the meat over the fire, check to see that you have achieved the proper balance by resting the spit on the tips of your fingers. The spitted meat should revolve away from you.

A well-practiced cook may decide when meat is done by intuition and experience, but if this seems too imprecise, use a spit thermometer or meat thermometer. Try not to rely on cooking charts. They fail to account for the many variables of wind, outside temperature, quality of meat, evenness of cooking, and become a hindrance rather than a help.

Remember, meat continues to cook—sometimes for as long as 15 or 20 minutes—after being removed from the heat. Before carving, allow the meat to coast (remain) on the spit for several minutes until the juices settle.

There are any number of devices to use for spit roasting, and all cook equally well. One of the oldest is the hand-propelled spit which is inserted in a heavy, oval-shaped container of glazed pottery and set in front of the fire. The pottery glaze reflects the heat and allows the meat to cook slowly. Drippings are caught in the container-bowl, to be used later as the base for sauce. Another type long in use is the revolving spit, hung vertically in front of the fire. A pan is placed below to catch the drippings. Modern electric rotisseries, charcoal spits, and rotisserie attachments to stoves have made few changes and little improvement on these older, more dramatic methods, but they are handsome to look at and do the job effectively.

Though the image of a whole animal or bird, or succulent ribs of meat, spit roasting over the fire seems a symbol of ancient cuisines, probably the first real step in this direction was the discovery that a skewer or stick could be used to roast chunks or cubes of meat over flame. Undoubtedly, it proved as much a delight in the world of primitive cooks as it does now in the realm of the outdoor chef. Today, however, the sticks have been replaced by elegantly fashioned skewers which roast both meat and vegetables over scientifically prepared fires. Moreover, authors no longer refer to the method as skewer cooking, but as "Kebab," where the recipe is attributed to the Near East; as "Shashlik," when referring to a Russian variation, and to foods "en brochette," when cooked in French style. As with spit roasting, skewering may be done in front of, or over, the fire and in any number of broilers and grills. While just as exciting for guests, it requires less practice, a little less attention.

Note: Recipes for sauces referred to in this chapter will be found in "Outdoor Complements," beginning on page 172.

sirloin of beef

Sirloin, with or without bone, is a fine cut of beef and far more economical than the prime ribs. Unfortunately, it's often difficult in this day of packaged meat to find a butcher who will cut a good sirloin roast. Under these circumstances, prime ribs might well be a safer bet and more available. But once you find a *sympathique* butcher, heap favors and congratulations on his head, and order as you will.

to roast a sirloin

Gauge a pound of meat per person and a little extra. Have the roast trimmed of excess fat and score the outside fat. Rub with salt and freshly ground black pepper. I think that herbs and seasonings, such as garlic, detract rather than enhance the honest, homely flavor of good beef. Spit the roast accurately. Attach the spitted meat to the grill and start cooking! Your fire should be a bed of ash-covered coals—briquets or charcoal. Arrange the coals so that fat does not drip into the fire and cause a conflagration. Gauge about 15 minutes per pound for rare, 17 minutes per pound for medium. Your internal temperature is 125 F. for rare. Serve your roast sirloin in thin slices. A horseradish sauce, mustard sauce (or just freshly grated, unadorned horseradish), foil-wrapped potatoes with butter, chopped chives, and parsley—all go very well with this.

prime ribs

A good rib roast is well-aged, cut from prime or choice beef, and nicely marbled with fat. It should run 4 or 5 ribs—if your spit will take it. Otherwise, a 2- or 3-rib roast will do, as long as you guard carefully against overcooking. Trim excess fat to prevent the drippings that make your fire blaze. Spit on the diagonal to achieve the best balance. Remove the roast when it reg-

isters 125 F. (very rare) and let it stand for 10 or 15 minutes before you carve. For me, 2 thin slices (English cut) have more flavor than 1 thick slab (American cut)—but be guided by your guests' preferences.

VARIATIONS:

Garlicked: Rub the surface of the roast with a peeled garlic bud and salt. Make several incisions and insert small spikes of the garlic bulb. Roast as for Prime Ribs.

Herbed: Rub rosemary leaves into the surface of the roast, plus salt and freshly ground black pepper. Roast as above and serve with rosemary butter. You may also do the same thing with dried or fresh thyme.

eye of the rib

A cut which is becoming increasingly popular. The deckle is removed and the leg and bone are left. (The same cut with bone removed is called the Spencer.) Cook as you would Prime Ribs.

VARIATIONS:

Niçoise: Rub with a bud of garlic. Serve with anchovy butter.

Spiced: Combine 2 teaspoons white pepper, 2 teaspoons salt, ¼ teaspoon clove, ¼ teaspoon nutmeg, and rub into the roast.

Perigord: Make incisions through the fleshiest part of the meat and insert truffles—as many as you can afford. Roast as for Eye of the Rib. Serve with a truffled Madeira sauce.

fillet

A whole fillet roasts perfectly if it is cooked quickly to a rare stage. If you feel that a fillet tends toward dryness, have the butcher tie the cut with a thin layer of pounded suet. If you do not bard the roast, brush it well with melted butter or, better yet, rendered beef suet, which is deliciously beefy in flavor. A fillet needs about 25 to 35 minutes total cooking time.

truffle-stuffed fillet

Bard and tie a large fillet. Make 2 incisions right through. Stuff in as many buttered truffles as possible. Balance on the spit and roast. Serve with sauce Béarnaise or sauce Perigueux, and drink a hearty red wine.

oriental

Marinate a fillet in enough soy sauce to cover it halfway. Add ½ cup grated, fresh ginger or 1 tablespoon powdered ginger, 2 crushed garlic cloves, and ½ cup sherry or Madeira. Let this marinate 4 to 6 hours, turning several times. Spit and roast rare, brushing with the marinade from time to time.

VARIATION:

Prepare an Oriental marinade. Then make a glaze with 1 cup honey, 1 cup of the marinade, ¼ cup lemon juice, and 3 tablespoons curry powder. As the fillet cooks, brush with the glaze. Serve with curried rice and chutney.

southwestern

Piqué a fillet with garlic slivers, using 4 or 5 cloves. Rub the meat with ⅓ cup olive oil mixed with 1 tablespoon salt and 2 tablespoons chili powder. Balance on spit and roast, basting or brushing with a mixture of 1 cup tomato sauce, blended with 1 tablespoon chili powder, and 1 teaspoon oregano. Serve with heated tortillas, grilled corn on the cob, and beer.

à la ficelle

This is a luscious dish, and although it can be made by cooking the fillet on a trivet in a large pot of broth, it is more fun to make it this way: Tie the fillet securely with heavy string, leaving a tag-end perhaps 2 feet long. Place makeshift endposts on either side of your fire and poise a rod between them, or you may use the spit-attachment on your grill; the point is to have some type of crossbar running above the fire. Place a large pot of broth over the grill and let it boil. Carefully lower the fillet into the liquid until completely covered with broth. The idea is to keep the fillet immersed in the broth, but not touching the bottom of the pan. Tie the string to the rod, or crossbar, and cook about 18 or 20 minutes for rare. Remove from broth, slice, and serve with coarse salt, horseradish, and sour gherkins.

chuck roast

This is a lesser cut, but one that can be pleasant—and relatively inexpensive—for a change. Tenderize the roast according to the directions on the tenderizer bottle; it makes no difference in this case whether you use flavored or unflavored. Let the roast rest in the refrigerator for 12 hours. Spit and roast as you would for prime ribs. Carve in thin, rare slices.

bottom round

When tenderized, this cut is particularly flavorful. Tenderize slowly according to directions. Spit and roast. Carve in paper-thin slices. This is especially good for beef sandwiches, with crisp French bread—split, toasted, and buttered. Try a rosemary, anchovy, or tarragon butter as your spread. And drink a well-chilled beer or a good California red wine, say, a cabernet or a pinot noir.

top round

Rolled, larded, and tenderized, this, too, can make an ideal roast. Baste the roast with the following mixture:

2 tablespoons dry mustard
⅓ cup sherry
2 tablespoons olive oil
1 tablespoon tarragon

Buttered noodles and cheese are a fine accompaniment, along with a green salad, cheese, a tray of fruits, and some light red Barolo wine from Italy.

skewered beef cubes

Beef cubes solve the problem of feeding a number of guests quickly and well. Sirloin, fillet, hip steaks are especially tender and superbly suited for skewering, but any good piece of beef may be used. It should be cut into cubes, laced on skewers, brushed with oil or melted butter. Keep the pieces well separated and broil about 6 to 8 inches above the coals, turning the meat frequently until it is nicely browned. Serve with any preferred sauce—or without, if you like— usually 1 skewer per person.

simple skewered beef—american

For 4 persons, cut 3 to 4½ pounds of fillet, sirloin, rump, or hip into 1½- to 2-inch cubes. Salt and pepper and arrange the cubes on 4 metal skewers. Brush with oil or melted butter. Cook over medium coals, turning and brushing often so that the meat achieves an evenness of cooking and browning. Serve on very hot plates with hashed-brown potatoes.

greek

4 pounds beef
½ cup lemon juice
1 tablespoon thyme
½ cup olive oil
1 tablespoon salt

Marinate the beef for 2 hours in a mixture of the other ingredients. Skewer the beef, broil, brushing with the marinade. Serve this with a Béarnaise sauce.

italian

4 pounds cubed beef
1 cup olive oil
1 teaspoon oregano
1 tablespoon salt
½ cup chopped Italian parsley

Marinate the beef for 2 hours in a mixture of the other ingredients. Skewer the beef, broil,

brushing with the marinade. Serve with finely cut Italian white truffles (canned). Risotto would be delicious, and a Valpolicella.

south american

4 pounds beef sirloin cut in cubes
6 large onions, finely chopped
½ cup vinegar
1 cup white wine
½ tablespoon oregano

Marinate cubes in oregano, onion, wine, and vinegar for 2 to 3 hours. Skewer. Brush with oil or butter. Heat ½ pound butter, add the marinade, salt, and freshly ground pepper to taste. Heat to boiling and simmer 5 minutes, then add an extra ½ cup white wine and ¼ cup chopped parsley. Broil meat and serve with the heated marinade. Wonderful when served with black beans and rice.

french

4 pounds cubed beef
1 pint red wine
1 tablespoon thyme
1 bay leaf
1 cup olive oil
1 tablespoon salt
1 tablespoon freshly ground black pepper
1 cup chopped shallots or green onions

Marinate the beef for 2 hours in a mixture of the other ingredients. Skewer the beef. Bring marinade to a boil and simmer for 5 minutes. Add ¼ pound of butter. Broil skewered meat, brushing frequently with marinade. Serve with hot, reduced marinade and sautéed mushrooms, and a green salad of your choice.

russian

Skewer the beef with whole, white onions. Brush with melted butter. Broil, and salt and pepper to taste. Serve with kasha, broiled tomatoes, and a sour-cream sauce.

middle eastern

3 pounds beef cubes, 1½ inches in size
3 cloves of garlic, finely chopped
½ cup lemon juice
2 tablespoons curry powder
½ cup olive oil

Marinate the beef for 2 hours in a mixture of the other ingredients. Broil, brushing often with the marinade. When almost cooked, sprinkle with additional curry powder. Serve with rice—and watermelon for dessert.

japanese

3 pounds of cubed beef
1 cup Japanese soy sauce
3 cloves garlic
½ cup sherry

Marinate the beef for 12 hours in a mixture of the other ingredients. Arrange beef on skewers, alternating with green pepper. Broil, basting with the marinade. Serve with rice.

VARIATION:

When partially cooked, press in sesame seeds and continue cooking until beef is done to the degree you prefer.

polynesian beef

4 to 5 pounds of cubed steak
1½ cups soy sauce
½ cup honey
½ cup sweet sherry
1 tablespoon curry powder
1 teaspoon salt
½ teaspoon cinnamon
¼ teaspoon ground clove
1 tablespoon candied ginger
or 2 tablespoons fresh ginger
3 garlic cloves, finely chopped

Marinate the beef for 2 hours in a mixture of the other ingredients. Skewer the beef and broil, brushing with the marinade. Serve on heaping plates of baked rice with pistachio nuts.

ancient roman

Although beef was not a dish frequently encountered in ancient Rome, it was served occasionally—probably skewered on swords, flavored with rosemary carried to the capital from all sections of the Empire, and served with the wonderful wines of Gaul. Here, translated into modern terms, is a surviving Roman beef recipe. If you have no swords, use skewers. And serve a contemporary wine, which, incidentally, after some two thousand years of refinement in vintners' techniques, will be better than anything the Caesars got from Gaul!

Marinate 4 to 5 pounds of cubed beef for several hours in enough red wine to cover, 1 tablespoon of salt, and 1 teaspoon of crushed black pepper. Remove the beef and roll in fresh or dried rosemary. Place on skewers, alternating the meat with mushroom caps and onions. Then broil. When ready, flame with cognac and serve with asparagus.

barbecued skewered steak

Marinate cubes of beefsteak in your favorite barbecue sauce. Skewer beef cubes, being certain they do not touch, so they will cook on all sides. Broil slowly and brush from time to time with barbecue sauce. Serve at once with more hot sauce, buns, a vegetable salad, and beer.

skewered beef with garnishes

Vegetables are delicious with beef on skewers. Here are several combinations, proved and certain to please:

Mushroom Caps: More complementary to beef than any other flavor. Dip large caps in melted butter and alternate with beef cubes. Be certain to brush with butter while cooking.

Green Pepper: Strips or squares of green pepper alternated with beef are excellent.

Onions: Small, parboiled, whole onions (or raw, if you like them) can be strung alternately with the meat. Brush with melted butter. Season with salt and pepper.

Tomatoes: One of the classic seasonings for skewer cookery. Choose tomatoes not too ripe and brush with butter. The Italian plum tomato or a medium-sized table tomato is good. Large varieties should be cut into wedges before broiling.

combinations

You may use any 2 or 3 or all of these on your skewers. *For example:* mushroom cap, beef, tomato, beef, onion, beef, pepper, beef, mushroom cap.

filet mignon en brochette

Filets mignon are the tiny ends of the long fillet, triangular in shape and quite thin. They are best when cut bite-size, skewered, and grilled.

VARIATIONS:

Marinated Filet Mignon: For 1 pound of filet mignon bits, mix together 1½ teaspoons salt, 1 teaspoon thyme, ½ cup olive oil, 12 grinds from the pepper grinder, and enough red wine to just cover the meat. Let it stand for several hours before stringing on skewers and broiling.

Filet Sandwiches: Spread Dijon mustard or English mustard on pieces of filet mignon, skewer them, broil and serve with rolls, buns, or bread spread with anchovy butter.

Note: For cocktail parties use small skewers that hold 1 or 2 small pieces of filet.

lamb

spitted lamb

Of all the meats for spitting, lamb is certainly the choicest. When properly grilled, crisp, well-cooked lamb is superb. The Shish Kebab of the Near Eastern countries is a great treat if well seasoned and well cooked. It has several variations, all of them toothsome and savory. Thyme, garlic, and rosemary are the perfect herbs to use with lamb.

whole baby lamb

If you have a sizable grill, you can cook a whole lamb or kid easily. If not, you can go primitive. Build a fire and spit the animal on a wooden spit made from a branch, and place on the forked sticks. Tie the legs to the spit so there is balance and ease of turning. If you stuff the lamb, sew it up carefully. A whole lamb should take about 2½-3 hours. Brush well from time to time with oil and butter. Cook until the meat is delicately brown and tender when tested with a fork. To carve, remove legs and shoulders, and either cut through the saddle or split it into 2 pieces. Serve very hot on heated plates—no currant or mint jelly, please! Just tiny potatoes and a pleasant Beaujolais.

VARIATIONS:

Sherry Sauce: Baste the lamb with equal quantities of melted butter and sherry. Be certain you have a drip pan so that you catch the sauce. Serve with the kidney, liver, and heart sautéed in butter, sliced, and combined with the sauce.

Or, brush with oregano and salt. Stud with garlic. Baste with olive oil. Serve with couscous.

A la Grecque: Rub with salt, sage, and lemon. Stud with garlic. Baste with equal quantities lemon juice, oil, and white wine.

haedum sive agnum tarpeianum

Though difficult to find at times, a whole lamb is delicate, tender, and excellent eating. It has a taste different from the slightly older meat one usually encounters and is a most exciting food experience. I firmly believe that baby lamb should be cooked crisp on the outside and just to the point where the pink disappears on the inside. Marcus Gabius Apicius, one of ancient Rome's great epicures, gives us this rather unusual recipe for a whole lamb or kid:

Antequam coquatur, ornatus consuitur. Piper, rutam, satureiam, cepam, thymum modicum. Et liquamine collues haedum, macerabis in furno in patella, quae oleum habeat. Cum percoxerit, perfundes in patella impensam, teres satureiam, cepam, rutam, dactylos, liquamen, vinum, caroenum, oleum, cum bene duxerit impensam, in disco pones, piper asperges et inferes.

kid or lamb à la tarpeius

Before cooking, tie or truss the animal. Moisten the lamb meat with *liquamen* (broth) to which you have added crushed pepper, rue, savory, onion, and a little thyme. Place in the oven (Roman ovens were always the open-hearth type, similar to our grills) in a shallow pan containing oil and cook until tender. When done, pour a mixture of crushed savory, onion, rue, dates, broth, wine, *caroenum* (reduced wine), and oil into the pan. When this is well thickened, put all in round dish, sprinkle with pepper, and serve.

capretto (baby goat)

Young kid is a delicious morsel, but it has little fat and I feel it is best to brush it well and often with olive or salad oil. This oil may be made more aromatic by the addition of any of several herbs. Those most agreeable are oregano, thyme, tarragon, fresh sage, garlic.

capretto italian

Clean the kid well. Rub the interior with lemon, then with garlic. Chop the liver and heart very thin and sauté quickly in butter. Salt and pepper, and reserve. Rub interior again this time with garlic-flavored oil. Tie the legs, spit the kid, and secure it to the spit. Roast, allowing about 1½-2 hours, brushing well with oil scented with garlic and oregano. Put the chopped liver and heart in the drippings pan and season with 2 tablespoons chopped onion and 2 of chopped parsley. Use this as a sauce with the kid. Delicious served with broccoli amandine and rice.

capretto grecque

Prepare as for Capretto Italian, baste with equal quantities of lemon juice and olive oil with a scent of wild thyme. Serve with rice pilaff and Aïoli sauce.

leg of lamb

Leg of lamb is one of the world's popular dishes. The trouble is that most people overcook it! Once you've tried it rare, I think you will find it so good you will never again cook it to the dismal gray-brown that diners see much too often. Rare lamb is achieved in 1 to 1½ hours and registers 140 F. on a meat thermometer.

leg of lamb française

Puncture the flesh with a very sharp knife and insert small pieces of garlic. Rub the leg with salt and pepper. Brush with melted butter and

AS DONER KEBAB COOKS SLOWLY BEFORE COALS, CHEF SLICES TIDBITS FROM ITS SIDES.

balance on the spit. Continue brushing with melted butter during the cooking process. Since this is made in the French manner, the lamb should be quite rare. Roast to 140 F., or about 1½ hours. Serve with garlic-and-tomato sauce and white beans. Drink a cabernet.

shoulder of lamb

To cook perfectly and carve easily, this cut should be boned and rolled. It has excellent flavor, is somewhat cheaper in price than leg or rack of lamb, but is slightly fatter. Have the butcher bone, roll, and tie the shoulder. Rub it well with salt, pepper, a touch of garlic, and rosemary. You might sprinkle some of the latter on the lamb before it is rolled. Press the seasonings in well so they do not fall off during the cooking. Allow the flavor to penetrate for about an hour, then insert a meat thermometer and balance the lamb on the spit. Roast until the dial reads 140 F. This will give you a pink and rare roast, which is just right. Delicious with beans Bretonne. Try a good Bordeaux.

rack of lamb

Rub the rack with salt, pepper, and fresh thyme, if available. If not, use dried, but be a bit more sparing as its aroma is quite pronounced and you will not want to overpower the delicate flavor of the lamb. Let the rack stand for an hour or so to allow the flavors to penetrate. Tie it firmly and balance on the spit. Roast for about 30 minutes, or until a meat thermometer inserted in the fleshy part reads 140 F. Serve with crispy potatoes fried in suet or goose fat.

saddle of lamb

An entire saddle is a wonderful dish to present to a group of hungry diners. One of the nicest ways to prepare it is to crush 2 or 3 cloves of garlic in about ⅔ cup of soy sauce, add salt and pepper, and rub this well into the entire saddle.

Reserve a bit for basting. Balance the saddle carefully on the spit and roast, following the directions given for rack and shoulder of lamb. Serve with a purée of potatoes and French peas.

mock venison

This is a roast of mutton that, properly prepared, achieves the excellent flavor of good venison without the toughness that venison sometimes has. Allow the mutton to soak for 2 days in a game marinade of 2 cups of red wine, the juice of 1 orange and 2 lemons, 1 large onion peeled and sliced, 8 crushed peppercorns, a sprig of thyme, 1 teaspoon of oregano, 2 carrots cut in quarters, a few celery leaves, 1 bay leaf, 2 cloves of chopped garlic, ¼ cup of wine vinegar, and ½ cup of olive or peanut oil. Salt to taste. When ready to cook, remove the mutton from the marinade and arrange on the spit. Roast just to the rare stage, using marinade to baste. Skim the fat from the drippings, then add any marinade that remains, plus 1 teaspoon mustard, 1½ teaspoons of freshly ground pepper, and salt to taste. Bring this to a boil, then allow to simmer gently for 5 minutes. Thicken with beurre manié. Serve the sauce with your mutton, and accompany with potatoes, mashed turnips, and cole slaw. Drink a red wine.

shish kebab

There are enough versions of Shish Kebab to satisfy any taste in existence. There are various spellings as well—Chiche Kepap, Tschish Kebob, and at least twelve others which may be found on menus from here to Hong Kong. No matter how it is spelled or what seasonings are used, Shish Kebab is one of the more succulent dishes one can encounter. Although I use leg or shoulder for the cubes of lamb (with a slight preference for the leg), one can use small chops cut from the ribs—rather thickly—and keep the bones intact. To make a rather amusing pattern, weave the small, chunky chops on the skewer with a rib design, and with various additives in between. Boned loin may also be used

for superb kebabs. All versions of Shish Kebab are the better for marinating and adding flavor before cooking over the coals. You may marinate anywhere from 2 hours to 2 days, depending on how pronounced a flavor you wish. Remove the pieces of lamb from the marinade and skewer them at least 30 minutes before you broil. This gets them to the proper temperature and tends to let some of the marinade dry. You may alternate the meat with various seasonings and additives as you lace it on the skewers. Be sure that you keep some idea of pattern and esthetic approach to the skewers, so that they will appeal to the eye as well as the nose and palate. I attended a party last summer where the hostess had made such handsome Shish Kebabs that it seemed almost wicked to eat them. A half pound of lamb usually is ample for a portion unless there are Brobdingnagian eaters in the group.

united states

Here, it seems, people most enjoy stringing the meat on skewers with different additives for flavor and color. These may be many and varied. Depending on the season, they may include:

small onions, either raw or partially cooked; onion sections; strips of green or red pepper or whole hot peppers; cubes of partially cooked potato; mushroom caps; truffles; thin slices of apple; whole small tomatoes or tomato wedges; preserved apricots or prunes, and various rum-soaked fruits.

french

For 4 persons, rub 2 to 2½ pounds of cubed lamb—cut from the leg in 2-inch cubes—with salt, pepper, and crushed garlic cloves. Marinate with enough white wine to barely cover and add 1 or 2 more garlic cloves. Lace the lamb cubes on skewers and brush well with melted butter. Broil over coals, turning several times to get an even brown on the meat. Brush with melted butter occasionally during the cooking process. This meat is best when eaten pinkly rare. Adjust the seasoning and serve at once with thinly cut potatoes, fried to a brown crispness in butter. Water cress, a pleasant light wine, and some crisp bread make a superb meal.

italian

Marinate 3½ pounds of lamb, cut from the leg in 2-inch cubes, with 3 crushed garlic cloves, 1½ teaspoons oregano, 1 teaspoon salt, 12 grinds from the peppermill, and enough olive oil to just cover the meat. Add a touch of wine vinegar, as well. Alternate the cubes of meat on a skewer with pitted olives and small sections of onion. Brush with olive oil and broil over the coals, turning often to give an even color to all sides of the meat. Serve with polenta and a piquant tomato sauce.

greek

For what is sometimes called Souvlakia, marinate 3½ pounds of lamb, cut from the leg in 2-inch cubes, with 1 large onion, finely chopped, the juice of 2 lemons, ½ cup olive oil, 1½ teaspoons salt, 12 grinds of the peppermill, ½ cup

chopped parsley, and 1½ teaspoons oregano. Marinate for 3 to 4 hours and then lace on skewers with wedges of tomato and small pieces of onion. Brush with the marinade during cooking, being sure to get a pleasant color on all sides of the meat. Serve with a rice pilaff.

VARIATION:

Another version of Souvlakia is made by marinating the cubed lamb with the ingredients above, to which are added 2 finely crushed bay leaves and 1 or 2 cloves of garlic.

doner kebab

This tidbit, which is sometimes called "the ever-revolving" kebab, is highly popular in Turkey. It is a boned leg of lamb which is secured to a spit and hung vertically in front of a bed of coals. The leg is revolved constantly—either automatically or by hand—and slices are cut from it as the meat becomes done. This technique can also be used with chicken. (The equipment with which to do this properly is not easy to come by. Revolving spits operated by clockwork are occasionally encountered in antique shops and some modern grills provide a hanging-spit attachment, but you may have to hunt a bit.)

north african

Kebabs have been known to the tribesmen of North Africa for years. They combine kebabs with what I choose to call an elaborate mutton stew, and steamed grains known to the world as couscous, making a meal which is older than time. Nomadic tribes and caravaners carried their couscousière along with them. They provided themselves with the necessary vegetables and spices and cooked couscous on fires of charcoal or dried camel dung. The simmering stew or sauce provided the steam necessary to cook the couscous grains, while the kebabs were cooked over the coals. Traditionally, the North Africans sat cross-legged on the ground and ate the steamed grain with a plentiful helping of the stew as a sauce, the kebabs for the hearty meat dish and, sometimes, a fiery hot sauce, superbly seasoned to pique dulled palates and increase the appetite. (The recipe for Couscous may be found on page 155 of the section on "Outdoor Complements.")

chopped lamb on skewers

Chopped lamb on skewers is popular all through the Near East and some of the combinations are thoroughly exciting and palate-tingling. Care should be taken to make certain that this type of dish is not overcooked, for nothing in the world—with the possible exception of a mouthful of cotton and straw—can be as uninteresting as a mouthful of overcooked chopped lamb.

skewered lamb with cherries

In the Near East and in parts of Europe, there is a type of cherry called the Morella that goes excellently with lamb. The nearest thing to the Morella generally available to us is the sour pie-cherry. These are available in tins without unnecessary sweetening.

To make the Near Eastern cherry sauce, melt ¼ pound of butter in a skillet. Add 1 tin of drained pie-cherries or 1 pound of pitted fresh cherries. Sprinkle with 1 tablespoon sugar or more, to taste, and just enough red wine to barely cover. Simmer this mixture for 5 minutes. For the kebabs, blend 1½ pounds of ground lamb with 1 teaspoon of salt and 1 teaspoon of freshly ground black pepper. Work well and, if you wish, rub in a little dried oregano or mint. Work the ground-meat mixture around skewers like long sausages and brush well with olive oil. Broil the kebabs over coals, turning carefully to brown on all sides. When they are grilled just right, serve on hot plates with the cherry sauce spooned over them. Rice is an excellent accompaniment; so are good French or Italian bread and a Beaujolais.

skewered lamb with pine nuts

2 pounds ground lamb
4 finely chopped garlic cloves
½ cup chopped parsley
½ cup pine nuts
1 teaspoon thyme
1 bay leaf, finely crushed
Olive oil
Salt
Freshly ground black pepper

Blend the ingredients, adding enough oil to make a heavy paste. Divide into fourths or sixths and mold around skewers, like a sausage, and then chill. Brush with olive oil and broil over medium coals, turning often to get an evenness of color. Brush with more olive oil as the skewered lamb cooks. Season to taste, and serve with a rice pilaff. Sliced cucumbers, or a similarly crunchy salad, will provide a nice contrast of texture. And red wine or beer are equally appropriate drinks.

viennese lamb balls

2 pounds ground lamb
½ pound pork sausage meat
3 ripe tomatoes,
peeled, seeded, and chopped
1 teaspoon thyme
1 teaspoon salt
½ teaspoon freshly ground black pepper
12 green onions, finely chopped
Mushroom caps
Sour cream
Olive oil

Blend the meats with the tomatoes, chopped onions, and seasonings, and work with enough sour cream to make a firm mixture. Mold into sausage-like pieces around skewers, making each piece about 3 inches long, and separate with 2 mushroom caps. Brush well with olive oil and broil, turning often to acquire an evenness of color. Salt to taste. Serve with broiled eggplant slices, dipped in butter, and seasoned with salt and pepper.

veal

spitted loin of veal

When brushed well with butter or oil and cooked properly, veal is an appetizing dish. But much care should be taken to see that the meat is neither overcooked nor undercooked. For spitting, have the loin of veal boned and tied, or simply tie it and place it on the spit. Balance the meat and roast it slowly over coals, continually brushing with a half-and-half mixture of melted butter and white wine. Allow about 18 to 20 minutes per pound. The meat thermometer should read 160 to 170 F. when the veal is ready to be served. Let the meat stand for 10 or 12 minutes before slicing. Serve with a cream sauce made by combining the drippings in the pan with heavy cream. Thicken the mixture with beurre manié—balls of butter and flour well-kneaded together.

VARIATIONS:

Italian: Piqué the veal with garlic slivers and anchovy fillets. Rub well with olive oil and basil. Roast over the coals and baste with more olive oil. Serve buttered noodles with garlic and grated cheese.

Viennese: Rub the veal well with salt, paprika, and butter. Spit and roast, basting with heavy cream and melted butter mixed with paprika. Serve a sauce made from the rich pan-drippings.

French: Rub the veal well with tarragon. Make tiny incisions in the meat and force in bits of tarragon and parsley. Baste with tarragon-flavored butter and white wine. Serve with crisp fried potatoes and a salad.

spitted veal—boned and rolled shoulder

Brush the shoulder of veal well with butter or oil, salt, and tarragon leaves. Spit and roast to a pinkish rareness; it will have much more flavor than if you dry it out. Brush with butter to get an even glaze. Serve with tarragon cream sauce and buttered noodles with poppy seeds.

VARIATION:

Niçoise: Piqué the veal with garlic slivers. Make several incisions and force in anchovy fillets. Brush with anchovy butter. Serve with broiled eggplant and a tomato sauce with black olives.

stuffed breast of veal

4-5 pound breast of veal
1 pound of sausage meat
1 cup bread crumbs
1 pound of ground veal
½ cup finely chopped onion
2 finely chopped garlic cloves
1 teaspoon thyme
¼ cup chopped parsley
3 eggs
1 teaspoon salt
¼ cup cognac

Have the veal cut with a pocket. Mix the other ingredients. Blend well and stuff the pocket of veal and sew securely. Brush with butter and oil and roast for 2½ hours or until tender. Awfully good cold, too.

skewered veal

Marinate for several hours before cooking in a mixture of olive or peanut oil and seasonings. Gauge about ½ to ¾ of a pound per person and cut into cubes. Grill cubes slowly, turn them often, and brush well with oil.

skewered veal, grecian-fashion

Marinate for several hours 2½ to 3 pounds veal leg, cut into 1½-inch cubes, in 1½ cups oil and the juice of 3 lemons. Arrange on skewers, alternating the pieces of veal with mushroom caps and thin slices of bacon. Grill until brown. Baste often with the marinade. Salt and pepper to taste and serve very hot. Rice and broiled eggplant slices go well.

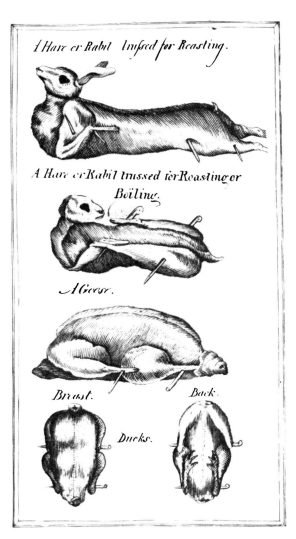

THE FRUGAL HOUSEWIFE, OR COMPLETE WOMAN COOK, PHILADELPHIA, 1802, BY SUSANNAH CARTER, RARE BOOK ROOM, NEW YORK PUBLIC LIBRARY.

turkish veal on skewers

Dust 2½ to 3 pounds cubed veal with dried thyme, salt, and pepper. Add just enough olive or other oil to cover. Give the veal about 16 to 18 grinds of a normal-sized peppermill and let the meat marinate for several hours. Place on skewers, alternating the meat cubes with 2-inch lengths of zucchini. Broil, brushing with the marinade, until well cooked and nicely browned. Season to taste and serve with rice pilaff with pine nuts.

indian veal

Most people don't realize that curry and veal are deliciously attracted to each other. If you are particularly fond of curry, use a goodly portion. Marinate for several hours:

3 pounds cubed leg of veal
1 cup olive oil
½ cup mixed lemon juice
and vinegar
2 tablespoons curry powder
2 cloves garlic, pounded
2 teaspoons turmeric
1½ teaspoons salt

Let veal stand for several hours in a marinade of the other ingredients. Arrange on skewers, alternating with cubes of eggplant and small onions. Broil slowly, basting well with the marinade. This should be served very hot with rice and grated coconut.

pork

suckling pigs

Suckling pigs run from 12 to 25 pounds and are ideal for spit roasting. Size is no deterrent, however. Very often pigs of 40 or 45 pounds are roasted on a spit over charcoal. One of the first outdoor feasts I remember was on an island in the Caribbean. A 45-pound pig was cooked on fork and stick, and for the last hour of cooking the juices dropped on a bed of plantains—a kind of Caribbean banana. The crispy, crackling skin was offered first with the drinks, then the meat and the plantains, and then a great bowl of greens. Such regal feasts are high spots in one's memory.

There is a wide selection of seasonings for suckling pigs, but first of all let us give you basic rules for roasting on a spit. Have your butcher select a pig—say, 14 to 20 pounds—and by all means leave the head and the tail on. Rub the inside with lemon juice and salt. Save giblets, unless you are stuffing the pig. Sew the stomach and spit the carcass carefully, with the legs tied together. Brush the entire surface with butter or heavy cream and roast over a medium fire, basting often with whatever seasoned baste you are using. Your pig will take from 2 to 3 hours to roast. When you transfer your pig to a carving board or platter, cut off the small hams first, then cut down through the spinal column and cleave off the chops from the ribs and from the loin. Cut the ham into small pieces so that everyone gets some of the chops and some of the ham and some of the delicious skin. Sautéed corn, roasted fresh ears of corn, lyonnaise potatoes, sautéed apple slices, apples baked in foil—all these are wonderful accompaniments to suckling pig. Drink a rosé wine or, if it is a festive occasion, champagne, which is the friendliest wine to accompany pig.

VARIATIONS:

American: Rub the pig well, inside and out, with sage, and baste with a mixture of broth, melted butter, and sage.

Mexican: Rub the pig well with oregano and chili powder. Baste with a mixture of ⅓ cup lime juice to 1 cup olive oil, seasoned with 1 tablespoon chili powder and 1 teaspoon Tabasco.

South American: You cannot find sour oranges here, so make a baste of 1 cup olive oil and ½ cup orange juice, ½ cup lemon juice, and 3 finely chopped garlic cloves. Serve with black beans and rice.

Chinese: Rub the pig inside and out with soy sauce and chopped fresh ginger. Then baste with ⅓ cup soy sauce, ½ cup honey, 1 cup sherry, ½ cup melted butter, and season with ½ teaspoon cinnamon, ¼ teaspoon cloves, and ½ teaspoon ginger.

Polynesian: Rub pig well with soy sauce and ginger and baste with a mixture of ½ lime juice and ½ olive oil. Serve with sweet-sour sauce.

Greek: Rub the pig well with thyme and lemon and finely chopped garlic. Baste with a half-and-half mixture of lemon juice and olive oil.

French: Prepare a stuffing with the liver, heart, and kidneys of the pig, chopped fine and sautéed in 4 tablespoons butter, along with ½ cup finely chopped shallots. Add 1 pound pork sausage meat and simmer for 15 minutes. Combine with 4 cups cooked rice, 2 teaspoons salt, 1 teaspoon freshly ground pepper, ¼ cup finely chopped parsley, 1 teaspoon thyme, 1 bay leaf, finely crushed, 3 eggs, and ½ cup pistachio nuts. Stuff the pig with this mixture. Sew it up very tightly, spit and roast as above, basting with a half-and-half mixture of melted butter and white wine. Serve with fried potatoes and watercress salad. Treat yourself to champagne.

Note: If you wish to make a sauce for the pig, chop the liver, heart, and kidneys very fine. Sauté ½ cup finely chopped onion in 4 tablespoons butter. Sauté chopped giblets in 4 tablespoons butter. Combine these and simmer with ½ cup white wine for 10 minutes. Gradually stir in 1½ cups heavy cream and continue stirring until the cream is well blended and just to the boiling point. Season to taste with salt and freshly ground pepper. Thicken, if you will,

CONTINUED ON PAGE 94

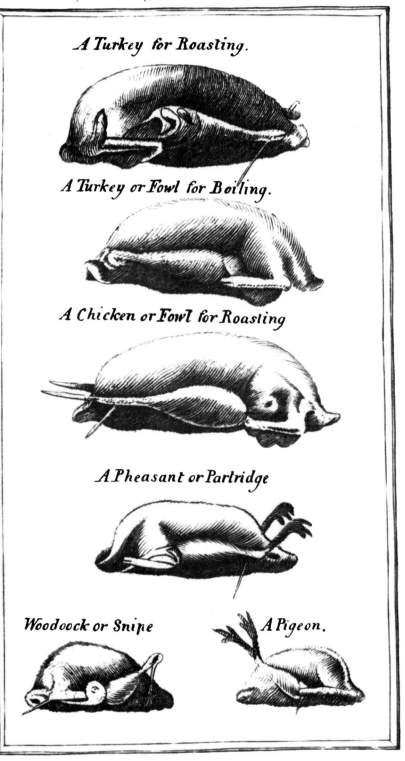

A Turkey for Roasting.

A Turkey or Fowl for Boiling.

A Chicken or Fowl for Roasting

A Pheasant or Partridge

Woodcock or Snipe

A Pigeon.

THE FRUGAL HOUSEWIFE, OR COMPLETE WOMAN COOK,
PHILADELPHIA, 1802, BY SUSANNAH CARTER,
RARE BOOK ROOM, NEW YORK PUBLIC LIBRARY.

with small balls of beurre manié. Add ¼ cup cognac and serve with rice, with mashed potatoes, or just with the pig.

loins of pork

You may roast loin of pork singly or doubly. If done doubly, both loins should be boned, fitted together, and tied so that the fat is all on the outside. As with fresh ham, pork loins should be cooked to an internal temperature of about 170 F. and you may use all sorts of seasonings for it. It slices beautifully. It is juicy and delicious. And it is a most delicate meat to serve at any time of the year. I don't believe the legend that pork is heavy meat, unfit for summer consumption.

plain loins of pork

I recommend that you use double loins here. Rub well with salt and freshly ground black pepper, and a touch of sage or thyme. Spit the loins and balance them. Roast over medium coals, being certain that the pork is thoroughly cooked through. It will need 20 to 25 minutes per pound and should be removed from the spit when it reaches an internal temperature of 170 F. Being boned, it should slice to perfection. Serve with a hot apple sauce, flavored with grated fresh horseradish or raisins heated in cognac. Good cole slaw and roasted potatoes go very well, and beer is my choice for a beverage.

boned loin oriental

Marinate a loin of pork with 1 cup soy sauce—the Chinese or Japanese soy—1 cup of sherry, 2 tablespoons chopped fresh ginger or 2 teaspoons powdered ginger, and 3 finely chopped cloves of garlic. Remove the pork from the marinade, dry with paper towels, and balance on a spit. Roast as for plain loins, basting with the marinade. About 1 hour before you remove it from the spit, brush with honey which has been mixed with a little of the marinade. Continue brushing about every 20 minutes for the final hour of cooking. This will give the loin a delicious glaze and adds tremendously to its flavor. Serve with Chinese peas cooked with butter and mushrooms, and a great bowl of steamed rice.

swedish loin of pork

It is best to use a single loin with the bone for this dish. Cut through to the meaty part of the loin two-thirds of the way to the bone. Stuff roast with pitted, dried prunes which have been soaked in sherry, port, or Madeira for several hours. Press the meat together and tie securely all along the loin. Spit, balance, and roast as for plain loins, basting with the wine in which you have soaked the prunes. Serve with a great pan of potatoes in their jackets, plenty of butter, and cucumber salad with dill dressing. Treat yourself to a fine Scandinavian beer.

norman loin of pork

You may use either a single or double loin for this. Rub it well with salt and freshly ground black pepper, a little thyme, and a touch of nutmeg. Spit and balance the meat, and roast. Baste with blended cider and apple jelly for the first 1½ hours of cooking. Serve with thinly sliced apples sautéed in butter, and foil-roasted corn. Drink apple cider.

italian herbed loin of pork

Make several slashes in either a single or double loin of pork and insert slivers of garlic. Rub the roast well with salt and freshly ground black pepper and oregano. Balance on a spit and roast over coals until the internal heat is 170 F. Serve with Risotto Milanese and, if you wish, a well-seasoned tomato sauce. Drink a good red, such as a Barolo, and have plenty of Italian bread at hand.

mexican loin of pork

Use a double loin and rub it well with chili powder. Cut gashes in the pork and insert slivers of garlic in half of them, slivers of peeled green chilis in the rest. (Green chilis are available in cans wherever Mexican food is sold.) Baste with a mixture of white wine and chili powder. Sprinkle with fresh coriander (cilantro, Chinese parsley), if it's available. Serve with toasted tortillas and frijoles refritos, and drink beer.

smoked pork loin, spitted

If your grill is long enough to accommodate an entire loin and if your guests are numerous, this is an unusual and delicious way of serving pork. It is smoked before you purchase it, and only needs to be roasted long enough to heat it through. For a baste and glaze, thin out a cup of apple sauce with any of the following: applejack, white or red wine, cognac, or rum. Balance the loin on the spit and roast. Baste frequently with the mixture. As it roasts, it will begin to take on a glaze which will be most attractive, as well as delicious, when it is served. You may add a bit of thyme to the baste, or 1 tablespoon of honey to assist in the caramelizing.

spareribs

I would venture to say that no single bit of pork is really as popular as the sparerib. Some claim that the Chinese were the first to serve barbecued spareribs, others grant the honor to the South, to the French, to practically every national group in the world. I think they have become popular through their own excellence and that no one nationality made them more popular than any other.

Whether laced on spits or broiled over coals, spareribs require slow cooking because they have a great deal of fat which must be cooked out—not burned out. Spit roasting, I think, **is**

the easiest way to cook them. If you place them on a grill, they are likely to burn and char unless you give them constant attention. Good spareribs are crisp on the outside and juicy on the inside, and easily torn from the bones. Allow at least 1 pound per person.

plain spareribs

Have the ribs left in full sides and don't let the butcher crack them. Rub well with salt and freshly ground black pepper, and a little thyme or basil. Weave in large loops on the spit. Cook over the coals for 60 to 90 minutes, so that the fat cooks out and the ribs take on a lovely brown hue. Serve them with crisp, fried potatoes and a huge lettuce-and-tomato salad tossed with a good olive oil, ripe olives, and vinegar. Beer is the ideal drink.

chinese spareribs

Marinate ribs, left in full sides, in good soy sauce to which you have added several finely chopped garlic cloves. Let them stand in this sauce for several hours, turning them often. Weave onto spits, roast, and baste from time to time with the sauce. They will cook in 1 to 1½ hours. I suggest rice as an accompaniment, with perhaps a green-pepper salad and beer.

honey-glazed spareribs

Combine ½ cup soy sauce with a cup of honey and ¼ cup lemon juice, seasoned with ½ teaspoon ground ginger, ¼ teaspoon ground cloves, and ½ teaspoon ground anise seed, if this is available. I like to add at least 1 or 2 teaspoons of dried mustard to this mixture because it gives a piquant note. Weave the spareribs onto the spit and roast them, basting from time to time with the mixture and making more if needed for a higher glaze. Serve with foil-roasted onions and foil-roasted apples.

Note: You may vary the glaze by using melted currant jelly, melted quince jelly, or puréed apricot, plum, or damson jam instead of honey. For zest, add a touch of lemon juice.

honey-orange spareribs

Combine 1 cup honey with 1 can frozen orange concentrate and ¼ cup lemon juice. Brush both sides of the spareribs with this mixture. Let them stand in the remaining mixture for several hours, turning several times. Weave onto the spits and roast, basting occasionally with the remaining marinade. Serve with charcoal-broiled eggplant slices and broiled apple rings, brushed with honey or sprinkled with sugar. A tomato salad goes very well with this.

mediterranean spareribs

Make a marinade with 3 finely chopped garlic cloves, 1 good-sized onion, also chopped fine, 1 teaspoon oregano, 1 cup of tomato sauce, 2 cups red wine, and 1 tablespoon chopped fresh basil or 2 teaspoons dried basil. Put 4 to 5 pounds of spareribs in this mixture and let them stand overnight in the refrigerator. Weave the spareribs onto a spit and roast over medium coals, brushing from time to time with the marinade. Serve with a highly seasoned tomato sauce, a salad made with crisp greens, sliced onions, quartered tomatoes, soft, black Italian olives, anchovy fillets, and a little grated Romano cheese. Use an olive-oil French dressing. Serve plenty of Valpolicella and follow with cheese and seasonal fruits.

ceylonese spareribs

In 6 tablespoons butter sauté 2 finely chopped garlic cloves and 1 large, finely chopped onion until they are golden. Add 3 peeled, seeded, and chopped ripe tomatoes, 1 cup of beef broth, 1 teaspoon salt, 1 teaspoon freshly ground black pepper, 1 teaspoon turmeric, and 2 tablespoons curry powder. Simmer for about 5 to 10 minutes. Add 1 cup white wine and let it heat through. Marinate 4 to 6 pounds of spareribs in this mixture overnight, and spit and roast the ribs over coals. Keep them moist with the marinade. Serve with rice to which you have added a bit of saffron, a cucumber salad, and chutney.

parboiled spareribs

These are much easier to cook because the ribs broil quickly and call for a minimum of watching at the grill. Place the sides of ribs in a large pan. Barely cover them with cold water, and add an onion stuck with 2 cloves, a bay leaf, a tablespoon of salt, several grinds from the peppermill, a celery top, and 1 teaspoon thyme. Bring to the boiling point and simmer about 30 to 40 minutes. Remove and cool, and cut into pieces for broiling. Serve in any of the following ways:

Brush the ribs well with butter and broil quickly over a brisk fire, brushing once or twice during cooking. They will broil in a few minutes and be crisp on the outside and juicy on the inside. Serve with a barbecue or sweet-and-sour sauce, and lentils sautéed with bacon, parsley, and onion.

Skim the water in which you have parboiled the ribs to remove all of the fat. Add several finely chopped garlic cloves, 1 cup tomato sauce, 2 tablespoons chili powder, 1 teaspoon oregano, 1 teaspoon cumin seed, and allow the ribs to marinate for several hours in this mixture. Remove from the marinade, brush with oil, and sprinkle with additional chili powder. Broil over the coals. Serve with fried rice and broiled bananas.

Brush the spareribs with a Chinese sweet-and-sour sauce and broil quickly over coals. Serve

with heated sweet-and-sour sauce, steamed rice, and a raw mushroom salad.

Dip the ribs in your favorite barbecue sauce. Broil over coals, brushing once or twice with additional sauce. Serve with broiled onion slices and foil-baked potatoes topped with sour cream and chopped bacon. With all of these dishes, I think the most harmonious drink is cold beer.

fresh ham

Fresh ham is much better on the spit if it is boned and tied. Under no circumstances should you allow the butcher to remove the skin on a fresh ham. This, to my mind, is the most delicious part. If you have a friendly butcher, he'll probably be glad to stuff the ham after he has boned it. Before spitting, the ham should be rubbed well with salt and freshly ground pepper and whatever other seasoning you wish. Allow plenty of cooking time,

because it must reach an internal temperature of 165 to 170 F. before it is safe to eat. Some people will tell you that it must be roasted to 185 or 190 F., but this will give you a very dry product. Ham is an ideal roast for a large party because it slices neatly, looks well on a plate, and can be complemented with a great many different dishes.

italian rolled and stuffed ham

My Bleecker Street butcher bones hams and stuffs them with Italian parsley, basil, a little garlic, and some ricotta cheese. Such hams are superb when they are roasted slowly and basted from time to time with a little butter, melted with a little garlic and white wine. With it, I enjoy serving buttered, homemade noodles with lots of chopped parsley and garlic, apple sauce (sometimes flavored with horseradish). Quantities of beer, crisp bread, salad, and a platter of fine cheese complete a fabulously good meal.

mexican ham

When you go to the butcher to have the ham boned, take along a little package containing 4 or 5 garlic cloves, 2 tablespoons chili powder, 1 teaspoon oregano, 1 teaspoon ground cumin, and 1 or 2 hot peppers. Ask the butcher to roll these inside the fresh ham. Again, before cooking, rub the ham well with salt, chili powder, and oregano. Spit and roast, basting occasionally with a mixture of white wine and chili powder. Serve with Elena's rice-and-chili casserole, and drink beer.

chinese ham

Marinate a rolled, boned ham with 1 cup soy sauce, 1 cup of sherry, ½ cup of honey, 6 cloves finely chopped garlic, and ¼ cup finely chopped fresh ginger—or 2 tablespoons powdered ginger. Turn the roast in this mixture several times over a period of 12 to 24 hours. Spit, and baste with the same mixture. Make additional baste if necessary. Serve with steamed rice and an orange-and-onion salad.

smoked ham

I think smoked ham does not lend itself very well to spit roasting. It takes much too long and is much better served as an appetizer. If you decide to try it anyway, use a ham that is tenderized or ready-to-eat. Remove the skin and rub the ham well with mustard and a little ground clove. Roast, basting often with sherry, Madeira, or red wine. It should take about 15 minutes per pound if it has been pre-cooked or treated. Serve it with broiled pineapple fingers, foil-roasted sweet potatoes with plenty of butter, and drink a rosé wine.

glazed ham

If you are using a ready-to-eat ham, it will require no more than a thorough heating through. If you are using the type that requires more cooking time, follow the directions for pre-cooking ham before you place it on the spit and roast it. Prepare the following glaze: Put 1 cup of apricot preserve through a sieve. Combine in a small saucepan with ½ cup dark Jamaica rum and a few tablespoons of sherry. Bring to a boil, reduce the flame, and let the sauce cook down to a very thick glaze which can be painted on the ham with a brush. Remove the ham from the spit and brush with the glaze, layer by layer, until you have built up a thick coat. Slice it the long way rather than straight down, and be prepared for wonderful eating.

canadian bacon

There is absolutely no waste with Canadian bacon, so buy only as much as you need. Insert the spit carefully, through the center, being sure that the bacon will revolve evenly. Roast over the fire until it is as well done as you like. While it is roasting, prepare the following glaze in a saucepan: heat 1 cup of pure maple syrup and the juice of 1 lemon, until it begins to boil. Reduce the flame and simmer until glaze is reduced in volume and thick enough to be painted on with a brush. Remove the bacon from the spit, place it on a platter, and brush on the glaze. Let it sit for about 10 minutes and then slice.

skewered pork

Pork cut into cubes and marinated in any of the marinades suggested for spareribs are delicious when skewered and broiled over the coals. The best cuts are from the fresh ham or loin, and you will want to use 1- to 1½-inch cubes for skewering.

american skewered pork

Marinate cubes of lean pork for 2 or 3 hours in apple juice, 1 or 2 tablespoons of oil, and salt and pepper. Thread on skewers and grill over charcoal. When finished (and re-

KITCHEN INTERIOR, BY ADRIAEN VAN NIEULANDT. METROPOLITAN MUSEUM OF ART, ROGERS FUND.

member that all pork should be very well cooked), place on a platter, pour ¼ cup warmed applejack over the skewers, and ignite.

VARIATIONS:

French: Marinate pork cubes for 2 or 3 hours in white wine, tarragon, and salt and pepper. Thread on skewers and grill.

Italian: Marinate pork cubes in olive oil, crushed garlic, salt, pepper, and 1 cup of tomato purée. Thread on skewers and grill.

South American: Marinate pork cubes in grated onion and chopped coriander. Thread on skewers and grill.

pork sates

Chop 12 scallions or green onions, 1 clove of garlic, and 3 or 4 green chilis very fine. Combine with 1 tablespoon curry powder, 1 teaspoon turmeric, 1 tablespoon chili powder, ½ cup orange juice, ¼ cup lemon juice, ½ cup soy sauce, and ½ cup of sweet sherry. Marinate 2½ to 3 pounds pork cubes in this mixture for several hours. Thread on small skewers and broil, brushing with the marinade once or twice during the broiling. Serve with fresh rolls or bread-and-butter sandwiches, so that the sates may be slipped off into a holder of bread and eaten that way.

VARIATIONS:

Apricot: Combine ½ cup soy, ½ cup puréed apricot jam, ½ cup chopped onion, 2 tablespoons vinegar, 1 teaspoon salt, ½ teaspoon ground allspice, and ½ cup sweet sherry. Marinate pork cubes in this mixture. Weave or thread on skewers and broil, basting with the marinade once or twice.

Crushed Pineapple: Combine 1 cup of crushed pineapple with ½ cup soy, 12 thinly cut scallions or green onions, ½ teaspoon freshly ground black pepper, a dash of cinnamon, a dash of ground clove, and ½ cup white wine or sherry. Remove from this marinade after a few hours and broil. Just before serving, dip each sate in sesame seeds and return to the broiler for a moment.

pork teriyaki

For teriyaki, pork should be cut into 2-inch cubes. Marinate 3 pounds of cubes in 1 cup soy sauce, 1 finely chopped garlic clove, 1½ teaspoons sugar, and ½ cup sherry. Lace the cubes on skewers and broil them slowly over charcoal. Baste several times during the broiling period. The pork for teriyaki may be cut in strips and laced on bamboo skewers. Broiling this way takes much less time.

whole pork tenderloin on skewer

Arrange whole pork tenderloins, 1 to a person, on skewers and brush well with butter seasoned with rosemary or basil. Broil slowly over a very low fire and brush occasionally with the seasoned butter. Serve with a sour-cream-and-dill sauce, and home-fried potatoes.

pork tenderloin in cubes

Alternate pieces of pork tenderloin on skewers with strips of green pepper, strips of onions, and pineapple chunks. Brush with butter, broil, and baste with soy sauce or white wine. Broil slowly to achieve good color and assure that the meat will be cooked through.

VARIATIONS:

Alternate tiny onions, mushrooms, and green pepper strips with pieces of pork tenderloin. Brush with butter and sprinkle with rosemary. Broil slowly as above.

Alternate apple wedges and onions with pieces of pork tenderloin. Brush with butter. Broil slowly and well, brushing from time to time with additional butter. Serve with a sour-cream sauce and poppy-seed noodles.

ground pork on skewers

Ground pork or sausage meat may be mixed with additional seasonings worked around skewers, and broiled over medium coals. It will take seasonings well, either thyme, sage, rosemary, or anise. A good blend is ground anise, a touch of thyme, a good deal of paprika, and a few flecks of cayenne pepper. Mold on skewers and broil slowly, brushing from time to time with butter.

VARIATIONS:

Crumble 1½ bay leaves and combine with 1 pound pork sausage meat, coarsely ground and with a minimum of fat. Add salt and freshly ground pepper and mold around skewers. Brush well with butter and broil over low heat, turning often to achieve evenness of color and thorough cooking.

Combine 1 pound of coarsely ground sausage meat with ½ teaspoon sage, ½ teaspoon salt, and ½ teaspoon freshly ground black pepper. Blend well and mold around skewers. Brush with butter and broil until well done and nicely browned.

Combine 1½ pounds coarsely ground sausage meat with 3 tablespoons olive oil, 1 tablespoon finely chopped chilis, 1 tablespoon finely chopped green pepper, 1 finely chopped hot pepper. Mold around skewers and broil.

Combine 2 pounds coarsely ground pork with ½ cup finely chopped onion and ½ cup puréed raw apple; salt and freshly ground pepper to taste. Mix well and mold around skewers. Broil until well browned and cooked through.

Serve any of these delicious pork variations either with foil-roasted potatoes and foil-roasted apples, or with green rice and a horse-radish apple sauce. Drink beer.

poultry and fowl

A pungent chicken roasting on the spit—and even the simple memory of its mouth-watering smell—has excited the appetite and inspired the poet for many centuries. For an eating experience, here is an easy and savory way to make it. Rub the outside of a roaster with butter, then rub the inside with a mixture of butter and lemon juice. Sprinkle both inside and out with salt and freshly ground pepper and truss the bird as follows: Turn the wings back so that the tips lie under the chicken; gently press the legs up toward the breast so that they will hold their shape, and tie them firmly together. Leave adequate string at both ends so you will be able to slip the string under the bird and criss-cross it around the wings. Finally, bring the ends to the front of the bird and tie to the legs. When the bird is properly trussed, it should have a symmetrical appearance. Place the bird, or birds, on the spit, carefully balancing them. If you are roasting more than one chicken, position them so that the breast of one rests against the legs of another, and alternating so that the back faces upward on one, the breast on the next. This secures the birds and permits the spit to rotate freely. Roast over a medium fire, brushing often with butter. There is really no accurate way to test when a chicken is properly done. A meat thermometer inserted into the thick part of the thigh should read 170 F. when the bird is cooked, and the leg should be fairly loose at the joint.

I like crisp-roasted chicken served with sautéed potatoes and a green salad with a vinegar-and-olive-oil dressing. For the wine, I might select a Meursault one day and settle for a light Bordeaux, say, a Château Talbot or a Château Lascombes, the next.

herbed spitted chicken

Any favorite herb will go well in this recipe. However, I think that the herb flavors most satisfactory with chicken are tarragon and rosemary. If you can get fresh herbs, so much the better. Chop enough of the fresh herbs to fill about ⅓ of a cup and combine with 6 tablespoons soft butter. With your fingers, loosen the skin over the breast of the bird and force in some of the herbed butter. Truss the bird, tying the skin of the necks securely. Place several herb sprigs inside the chicken, and balance it on the spit. Brush well with herbed butter and salt and pepper, and roast. Baste often with a mixture of equal parts herbed butter and white wine. Serve with tiny French peas, cooked with bits of onion and chopped Virginia ham, and crusty bread. Drink a red Bordeaux with this.

Note: If you are using a dry herb, such as the Spice Islands variety, you may soak ¼ cup of it in a little of the white wine for an hour and use it as you would a fresh herb.

Note: Other possible seasonings for chicken are: thyme, lemon balm, basil, and fresh sage.

spitted stuffed chicken

Prepare stuffing as follows: Sauté in 4 tablespoons butter until tender 2 garlic cloves and 2 medium-sized onions, finely chopped. Add ½ pound each of ground veal and sausage meat, 1 teaspoon thyme, ⅓ cup chopped parsley, 1 cup bread crumbs, 1 teaspoon salt, some freshly ground black pepper, 2 eggs, and additional butter, if necessary. Mix well and allow to cook for a short time. Then add ¼ cup cognac and cook a little longer. This amount will be sufficient for a fairly large chicken. Stuff the bird, sew it up, and securely truss, spit, balance it. Roast until it is crisp and the stuffing is cooked to your satisfaction.

spitted barbecued chicken

A good-sized chicken will serve about 4 people. If you want leftovers, plan for it in advance. Rub chicken inside and out with lemon juice and season with salt and freshly ground black pepper. Prepare your barbecue sauce and heat it slightly. Place the chicken properly on the

spit and roast over medium coals, basting every 15 minutes with the sauce you have chosen. Be certain that you have a pan under the chicken to collect the drippings. These, combined with the barbecue sauce, make a perfect addition to your meal. Roast the bird from 45 minutes to 1 hour. Serve with the sauce and scalloped potatoes with sweet peppers. I would suggest a pinot chardonnay or a zinfandel, depending on whether you prefer white or red wine with your chicken.

italian spitted chicken

Rub the inside of a small roaster with lemon and place a large sprig of fresh basil and some salt and freshly ground black pepper in the cavity. Chop about ¼ cup basil and blend with

an equal amount of softened butter, salt and pepper, and rub the bird well with this mixture. Spit, balance, and roast over medium coals, basting with a half-and-half mixture of melted butter and red wine and 1 tablespoon chopped basil. Serve the chicken with polenta, a salad of ripe tomatoes and black olives with cognac dressing (simply a French salad dressing in which cognac is used instead of vinegar).

spitted chicken oriental

Rub a medium-sized roasting chicken with lemon. Chop very finely 1 garlic clove and 1 canned green chili and combine with 2 tablespoons curry powder. Rub this mixture into the bird; then truss, spit, and balance. Roast over medium coals. Baste with a mixture of equal parts melted butter and chicken broth, adding 1 tablespoon curry powder for each cup of liquid. Combine pan drippings with 1 cup yogurt and an additional tablespoon of curry powder and use as gravy. Serve with chutney and very crisp, fried onion rings, and rice cooked with toasted, buttered almonds.

spitted tarragon chicken

Prepare chicken for roasting. Place ⅛ pound butter and 2 sprigs of fresh—or 1 tablespoon Spice Islands—tarragon into the cavity of the bird and sew up. Truss, spit, balance, and roast over medium coals. Baste with equal parts melted butter and white wine to which you have added another tablespoon of tarragon, some salt and freshly ground black pepper. Serve with Potatoes Anna, a salad of summer greens with a brisk French dressing, and a bottle of Beaujolais, lightly chilled.

spitted chicken flambé

Prepare a good-sized chicken for roasting. Rub the inside with butter and salt and freshly ground pepper. Truss, spit, and balance the bird. Roast over medium coals for about 45 minutes to an hour, basting with a mixture of equal parts white wine and butter. Be sure to catch all the drippings. When it is done, remove to a large carving board, pour about 2 ounces of warmed cognac over it and ignite. Use a platter or board that will catch the juices. Combine these juices with the drippings caught during the roasting period. Blend with 1 cup heavy cream and heat to the boiling point, stirring constantly. Thicken with small balls of butter and flour kneaded together. Or you may thicken the sauce with a little arrowroot. Add another dash of cognac, correct the seasoning, and serve this sauce with the chicken. With this dish I like to serve small new potatoes steamed in their jackets and a good bottle of red Burgundy, followed by seasonal fruits.

chicken squares en brochette

Bone and cut chicken breasts in 1½-inch squares. Marinate in a mixture of soy sauce and garlic for several hours. Remove from the marinade, impale on skewers, brush well with melted butter or olive oil, and broil for approximately 15 minutes. Serve with Béarnaise sauce and string beans amandine.

chicken squares polynesian

Prepare chicken squares as suggested and cover with a marinade of white wine, 2 tablespoons chutney, 2 tablespoons curry powder, 1 teaspoon Tabasco, and 1 tablespoon finely chopped hot pepper. Remove from marinade, brush with melted butter or olive oil, and broil, turning the bits of chicken often. Serve with a rice pilaff and additional chutney.

duck

Duck is a very suitable fowl for roasting—particularly outdoors on the spit. Most of the ducks available are the Long Island variety, which have a deep layer of fat beneath the skin and are therefore much better cooked slowly. To achieve crispness the skin should be pricked from time to time with a fork to allow the fat to run out. The average duck will give two generous servings.

roasted duck on a spit

Clean the duck and remove the neck. Rub the inside with lemon juice—or ½ lemon—salt, and freshly ground black pepper. Tie the legs together securely and spit the bird from the tail through the breast. Then roast duck over medium coals without basting. Prick the skin from time to time so that the fat runs out and the skin becomes crisp. If you like duck slightly on the rare side, cook it about 1 hour and 20 minutes. If you prefer it well done, allow about 20 minutes more. Salt it well before serving and be certain that your plates are very hot. Serve mashed turnips and an orange-and-onion salad.

spitted curried duck

Prepare a 4- to 5-pound duck as follows: Rub inside and out with 1 tablespoon curry powder to which you have added 2 finely chopped garlic cloves, 1 teaspoon turmeric, and ½ teaspoon Tabasco. Truss, spit, and balance. Roast over medium coals for about 1½ hours. During the last half hour of roasting, baste with a mixture of ½ cup honey, ¼ cup orange juice, ¼ cup lemon juice, and 1½ tablespoons curry powder. Prick the skin from time to time. Serve with chutney and Chinese fried rice. Drink beer.

duck with olive sauce

Season duck with salt and freshly ground black pepper and stuff with 3 or 4 juniper berries and ½ cup finely chopped green olives, and sew up the cavity. Truss, spit, and balance. Roast over medium coals for about 1½ hours. Salt and pepper well and serve with the following olive sauce: Sauté 12 finely chopped scallions in 4 tablespoons butter until just soft. Add 1 cup beef or chicken broth, and ½ cup finely sliced green olives. Cook for 2 or 3 minutes over a brisk fire. Add ¼ cup cognac and serve this sauce over the duck. Green olives heated in a little broth may be used as a garnish. Corn with finely chopped green or red peppers and toasted French rolls are good accompaniments.

duck grand marnier

Stuff duck with 6 or 8 orange sections, rub with salt and 2 tablespoons orange rind. Sew, truss, spit, and balance. Roast over medium coals, basting every 10 minutes with orange-juice concentrate. When the duck achieves a crisp skin, baste with ¼ cup of Grand Marnier. Heat another ⅓ cup of Grand Marnier, pour over roasted duck, and blaze. Serve with an orange sauce made the from drippings and additional orange juice. Add orange sections, if you wish. Serve rice with toasted almonds, and drink a good red wine.

duck with kumquats

Clean and truss duck, then place in a properly balanced position on spit. (If you are not using a spit, split the duck in half and place on grill about 6 inches from coals.) Before roasting, rub duck well with salt and pepper. When it is almost done, heat the contents of a can or jar of preserved kumquats and allow the syrup to reduce a bit. Drain off syrup and mix with a bit of soy sauce and paint duck with the mixture. Do not allow the duck to char or burn. When it is done, carve and serve surrounded with the kumquats. Pour the syrupy mixture over all.

duck with tarragon

Place 2 sprigs of fresh (or 1 tablespoon of Spice Islands) tarragon inside the duck and rub outside with salt and a little tarragon. Sew, truss, spit, and balance. Roast over medium coals, basting with a mixture of ⅔ cup white wine, ⅓ cup melted butter, 2 tablespoons chopped, fresh tarragon (or 1 tablespoon dried). Serve

with new potatoes, steamed in butter and mixed with finely chopped chives and parsley. Drink a fine Bordeaux and follow with a platter of cheese and fruit.

goose

Geese have never enjoyed the popularity they deserve in this country. This is perhaps due to the false notion that they are fat and disagreeable to the palate. Nothing could be further from the truth. In many countries, goose has long been prized as a special holiday treat, and no Christmas or New Year's Day would be complete without the traditional bird. Plump, well-fattened goose is one of the really delectable birds for spit roasting. Like duckling, it needs slow cooking and the skin must be pricked to release melted fat. Goose has a large frame and relatively little meat per pound. An 8-pound goose serves 4 to 6 persons.

spitted goose

Rub an 8- to 10-pound goose inside and out with a mixture of salt, freshly ground pepper, and thyme. Place an apple and an onion inside and sew up the bird. Truss, spit, balance, and roast the bird over medium coals for about 2 to 2½ hours. Prick the skin from time to time and baste with a little white wine and thyme mixed together. Serve your goose with foil-roasted onions and foil-roasted apples, and plenty of rye bread. Drink beer.

spitted stuffed goose

Rub the inside of an 8- to 10-pound goose with salt and thyme. Then stuff with as many pared apple halves, pitted prunes, and cooked chestnuts, all seasoned with salt and sage, as it will hold. Sew, truss, spit, and balance the goose. Roast over medium coals for about 2 to 2½ hours, or until it is crisp and tender.

Prepare a sauce as follows: Cook 4 or 5 finely chopped green onions in 4 tablespoons of butter, add a finely chopped goose liver, and cook very quickly—for about 2 minutes. Add ½ cup chicken broth, ½ cup white wine, ½ teaspoon thyme, and 2 tablespoons chopped parsley; add salt and freshly ground pepper to taste. Allow to cook very briskly for about 3 minutes, then add ½ cup heavy cream and 1 teaspoon arrowroot, and stir until the sauce thickens. Serve with marinated onion and cucumber slices. Drink a Beaujolais.

garlic-stuffed goose

Peel, and crush with a mallet, about 2 pounds of garlic. Butter the inside of an 8- to 10-pound goose and rub with salt and freshly ground black pepper. Stuff with as much garlic as you can put into it. Sew it up securely, truss, spit, and balance. Rub the skin with salt and freshly ground black pepper and roast over medium coals for 2 to 2½ hours, basting occasionally with a little white wine. Forbidding as this may sound, you will be amazed to find that it does not overpower you with garlic flavor. Serve with potatoes cooked in butter or goose fat. Add a few thinly sliced truffles, if you wish. Hot apple sauce is also good, and hot, crispy, toasted French rolls. Drink a brisk white wine.

turkey

Turkey cooked on the spit is a traditional and most delicious dish. Our ancestors prepared this South American import on a spit hung in front of the open hearth. As far as I'm concerned this method has never been improved. It is less common to see turkey spit roasted today because well-fattened birds are so hard to find. I do not recommend roasting turkey over charcoal unless you buy a plump, freshly killed bird. The eviscerated, frozen variety, which has been on a diet for weeks before it is killed and marketed, has neither much fat nor much flavor. Any type of turkey—from the tiny Beltsville to a 25- to 30-pound bird—may be spit roasted, providing your spit will accommodate it. You

tenda

Cucina per Campagna

baston di ferro sostentato da doi spedere

caldari

copia et mantili bianchi

pignato

namcela   quatro piedi con un   caldaro sopra

should gauge about 18 to 20 minutes per pound cooking time and allow about a pound per person for serving.

spitted turkey

Rub a 12- to 15-pound bird inside and out with half a lemon, then with about ¼ pound butter and some salt and pepper. Truss, spit, and balance. Roast over medium coals, basting from time to time with a mixture of equal parts melted butter and white wine. Be sure to have a shallow pan under the turkey to catch the juices. Allow the turkey to stand about 15 minutes before carving. Serve with a casserole of mushrooms and mashed turnips and make a sauce by adding some cream and a little thickening to the drippings. Drink the wine of your choice. Some prefer a white wine with turkey, but I like a red Bordeaux or a red Burgundy.

stuffed turkey

Gauge about 1 cup of stuffing per pound of turkey. One of the simplest and best stuffings is prepared this way: For a 12-pound bird sauté 1½ cups of shallots or green onions in ¼ pound of butter until just limp. Add 8 cups of grated French bread, 1 tablespoon Spice Islands tarragon (or 2 tablespoons of fresh tarragon), 2 teaspoons salt, 1 teaspoon freshly ground black pepper, and 1 cup pine nuts. Toss all the ingredients together and add another ½ to ¾ cup melted butter to bind it well. Stuff the bird lightly with this mixture, then sew, truss, spit, and balance. Roast over medium coals until it is done as you prefer. Serve with foil-roasted onions, Potatoes Anna, a green salad, and a light, red Burgundy.

truffled turkey

You may use either the white Italian truffles or the black French variety. Slice the truffles in ⅛-inch slices. With your fingers, loosen the skin over the breast and slide the truffle slices between the skin and the meat. Then place several slices inside the bird and sew securely. Rub well with a mixture of salt, freshly ground black pepper, butter, and a little thyme. Truss, spit, and balance the bird, and roast it over medium coals. Creamy mashed potatoes, sprinkled with black pepper, and a casserole of baked onions with Cheddar cheese, go nicely with this dish. Drink a Chateauneuf-du-Pape.

spitted turkey breasts

Turkey breasts may be purchased in poultry parts stores. Choose a large breast, weighing 4 or 5 pounds, and rub it well with butter, salt, freshly ground black pepper, and a little thyme. Spit, balance, and roast over medium coals, basting often with melted butter and a little thyme. Allow 15 minutes per pound. Be careful not to overcook it. It should be nicely browned and just tender. Serve with foil-roasted eggplant, a green pepper salad, and California pinot noir.

VARIATIONS:

Any of the recipes suggested for turkey (except stuffed turkey) may be applied to breast of turkey. It is delicious with herbed butter or with soy sauce—or with garlic cloves, which should be inserted into gashes made in the skin with a sharp knife.

spitted turkey hips

For those of us who like dark meat, turkey thighs and legs, seasoned to taste and spitted over charcoal, are a treat. Allow about 15 to 18 minutes per pound. A good deal of basting with melted butter is absolutely necessary. This is a very efficient and satisfactory way to serve turkey when entertaining a small group.

rolled spitted turkey

Have the butcher bone a turkey for you. Spread it with butter, sprinkle with chopped shallots or green onions, salt and pepper to taste, and enhance either with thyme, rosemary, tarragon, or sage. Roll and tie the bird securely, adjust it on the spit, and roast to an internal temperature of about 165 F. Serve with tiny creamed onions and peas, crisp, buttered toast, and a hearty white wine.

broiled, boned half-turkey

Have the butcher split a turkey in half. With a sharp boning knife and your fingers, loosen the flesh along the back bone and gradually, with the aid of a knife, push away to the wing joint. Cut through the wing joint and remove the wing at the second joint. With your fingers, push the flesh away from the thigh bone and cut through the joint. Remove the leg at the joint. Cut through, along the line of the breast, and with your finger slip the fillet away from the bone. You should now have a rather large piece of boneless turkey, plus a wing and a leg. This may be seasoned in any way you prefer. I like to brush it well with tarragon- or rosemary-flavored butter and place it in a basket grill, with skin side to the coals, and grill it for 35 to 50 minutes, depending on the size of the turkey. Turn and brush it several times with the flavored butter, and continue grilling until the turkey is tender and the skin nicely brown and crispy—about 15 to 25 minutes, according to the size of the turkey. The wing and leg may be grilled at the same time, if you wish, or may be reserved in the freezer or refrigerator, as may the second half of the turkey. Serve the broiled turkey with Béarnaise sauce, white-wine sauce, or an old-fashioned giblet sauce; with steamed rice or foil-baked potatoes, and string bean salad. For the wine, I suggest you choose a Beaujolais.

guinea hen

Guinea hen is seldom served in this country. Nevertheless, when properly prepared it is a most pleasant dish. My favorite way to serve

FROM HIGHLANDS TO LOWLANDS, WHOLE SALMON ON BLANKET OF FERNS IS SAVORY DELIGHT.

INDIAN COLLECTIONS, 17TH CENTURY. MUSEUM OF FINE ARTS, BOSTON.

guinea hen is to place an onion in the cavity of the bird, together with a slice of lemon, ½ teaspoon thyme, and a few juniper berries. Sew, truss, and spit the bird. Roast over medium coals, basting with melted butter every 10 or 15 minutes. Correct the seasoning. Drink a red Burgundy.

squab

These plump little birds are as good cold as they are hot, and for picnic fare there is nothing better in the world. Squabs weigh anywhere from 12 ounces to 1½ pounds. Choose them plump and, preferably, young. Rub them well inside and out with salt and freshly ground black pepper. Roast over medium coals for 30 to 60 minutes, basting with a mixture of equal parts melted butter and white wine. Salt well before removing from the grill. Serve at least 1 squab per person. As complements, serve rice with olive sauce, crisp, French bread, and a red Bordeaux.

russian barbecued squab

Marinate the squab for at least 12 hours, if possible, in 1 cup white wine, ½ cup olive oil, 2 teaspoons salt, 1 teaspoon freshly ground pepper, 1 cup tomato purée, 3 finely chopped garlic cloves, and 1 teaspoon oregano. Turn often. Remove from the marinade, tie, and arrange on spit. Cook over medium coals, basting often with the marinade. Allow from 45 minutes to 1 hour, but be careful neither to overcook nor undercook the bird. Now, sauté 3 tablespoons finely chopped shallots or green onions in 4 tablespoons of butter. Heat, adding the marinade not used in the basting. Let cook down to half the volume. Gradually stir in 1 cup commercial sour cream. Correct the seasoning and serve with the squab.

wild duck

Much has been written about the degree to which wild duck should be cooked. Some prefer it bloody-rare. Others like it well done. I like it best when it is spit roasted about 20 or 22 minutes. This produces neither a rare nor a well-done bird, but achieves a pleasant pinkness. Season the duck with salt, a few juniper berries, and perhaps a dash of thyme. Truss, spit, and roast the bird, basting with equal quantities of red wine and melted butter. The average person with a healthy appetite can consume 1 duck, and sometimes 1½ when they are small. I am not too fond of the currant jelly and bread sauce usually served with wild duck. Why not try it with fried lentils, or corn pudding, or corn-meal mush fried crisp?

VARIATION:

Instead of using juniper berries for seasoning, roast the ducks as suggested and when they are done, flame them with an ample quantity of gin; its juniper taste will give a subtle flavor to the birds.

Stuff each bird with an onion, wrap with some salt pork, and roast just 22 minutes. Remove the pork and blaze with cognac. Serve wild rice with sautéed mushrooms and toasted almonds with this.

Marinate your duck in a mixture of olive oil, thinly sliced raw onions, lemon juice, thyme, salt, and freshly ground black pepper. Place on spit and roast for 25 minutes. Pour on gin, cognac, or whiskey, and ignite. Bring meat closer to the flame and char for several minutes before removing it from the spit. This gives you a crisp, well-flavored bird. It is wonderful served with a casserole of peeled, sautéed apples, and a choice red Burgundy, perhaps a Volnay or a Chambertin.

wild goose

Wild geese vary in size and texture. Some are so tough they are not worth bothering with.

Others are as tender and fat as butter. If you are fortunate enough to get a good one, any of the recipes suggested for wild duck will do.

partridge

For me, there is no place like France in September, when partridge is in season. No other game bird has the delicately gamy flavor of the partridge. The American species, you'll find, is somewhat larger than the French perdreau, but very good, nevertheless.

spitted partridge

Partridge is best seasoned with juniper berries, thyme, or tarragon. Rub the bird with salt and freshly ground pepper, and butter (or you may bard with a very thin slice of salt pork). Truss, and spit on the diagonal from breast to legs, so that the partridge will cook evenly. Roast over medium coals for about 15 or 20 minutes, or until just done. Don't overcook; it will be dry and unpalatable. Chop and sauté the giblets in butter, spread them on toast, and serve with shoestring potatoes, water cress, and a pleasant red wine.

VARIATION:

Add a garlic clove and a good-sized piece of butter to each bird before sewing them. Bard with a thin sliver of salt pork and roast. Serve on a bed of sauerkraut which has cooked with juniper, garlic, and white wine for several hours. Drink a white Alsatian or Moselle—and serve some rye bread and fresh butter.

pheasant

The most important things to remember when cooking pheasant are to bard the breast well with salt pork and to be careful that it isn't cooked too long. Pheasant runs from 2 to 4 pounds. Bard it well, butter the inside lavishly, and add about 1 teaspoon of thyme and a large sprig of parsley. Truss, spit, and balance the bird. Roast over medium coals. Pheasant takes about 1 hour to cook, but you must watch it carefully. If it is too rare, it is ghastly; too well done, it is dry and stringy. The meat must be removed from the spit when it is somewhere between these extremes. I like to serve pheasant with cabbage cooked with poppy seeds. Drink a full-bodied red wine.

quail and other small birds

In America we are quite softhearted about small birds. We eat quail and snipe, but when it comes to eating larks, robins, and thrushes, we are a little reluctant. We forget that they provide the European palate with much good eating. I can remember going into shops in Florence, in Rome, and in other Italian cities and seeing great numbers of spitted thrushes and larks, with crusty slices of bread between, all done to a delicious brown and awaiting the hungry client. Quail, for some unknown reason, do not seem to arouse the Audubon in us, and we enjoy greatly this small exception to the rule. I once had a friend who could eat six quail at a sitting; on one occasion, after having devoured six for dinner, he went to the refrigerator for more! To my mind, quail are best when served in the following ways.

spitted quail

Spit 6 or 7 quail after you have barded them well with paper-thin slices of salt pork around the breast and placed a little parsley and a few juniper berries inside. Secure to the spit and roast over medium coals for about 15 minutes. Baste during that time with melted butter and white wine. You may remove the salt pork for the last few minutes of cooking to allow the birds to get more color.

mediterranean quail

Traditionally, these are wrapped in vine leaves and then—the modern touch—in parchment or foil before they are roasted in the coals. You may do this if you wish, but there is a simpler way to achieve the vine-leaf flavor. This is to wrap the grape leaves over the barding pork and spit roast as you would any other bird. Serve quail with some crisp, French-fried potatoes, water cress, and a light Bordeaux.

quail—english fashion

Remove the livers, gizzards, and hearts from your quail, and while the birds are roasting on the spit, chop the giblets rather finely and sauté them in butter. Allow about 2 tablespoons of butter for 1 bird and about 6 tablespoons for 6. Season with salt and freshly ground black pepper, and add a teaspoon or so of cognac. Spread this mixture on small pieces of well-buttered toast and serve the quail on these canapés. Accompany with crisp, fried potatoes, a brisk salad, and a good red Bordeaux or California cabernet.

tiny birds

If you are able to get larks or ortolans, you'll find them a tasty delicacy when impaled on small skewers with little strips of barding pork. Cook them over hot coals for 5 to 7 minutes. Eat with hashed-brown or creamed potatoes and drink a Rhone Valley red wine.

game

Though large and small game—deer, rabbit, and even bear—were not at all unfamiliar to our ancestors, they have certainly been supplanted in modern America by the more popular meats. But well known or not, freshly bagged game is still delicious eating, especially when simply prepared and cooked over charcoal. If the opportunity presents itself, don't waste or give away the hunter's prize. Have your butcher clean and prepare it, and if you can't eat it all at once, store some in the freezer for use later.

roast saddle of rabbit

When cooking rabbit, many people roast only the meaty section running from the haunch to the breast and save the other sections, especially the legs, for paté. A good-sized saddle, as this meaty section is commonly called, should serve two lusty appetites. Brush the meat with oil; spit and roast for 1 hour. Continue basting with olive oil and vermouth.

marinated rabbit

Cut in sections and cook in a hinged broiler. Or you may split and broil it as you would chicken. Baste with your favorite marinade. My favorite for rabbit is a combination of butter, lemon juice, and rosemary. Try a good claret with this.

spitted venison

If you have just bagged a young deer, don't miss the chance to savor its tender meat at the outdoor campsite. Try broiling the tenderloins and more tender portions of the fresh meat. In this case, you'll cook it rare.

marinated venison

Prepare your favorite red-wine marinade and soak 2 to 3 pounds of venison cubes in it for at least 24 hours. Arrange the cubes on skewers, alternating with bits of onion, tiny tomatoes, and pieces of zucchini. Broil over fairly hot coals until nicely brown, but quite rare. Serve with a Béarnaise sauce.

bear

Bear steaks, bear hams, and chopped bear meat have long been considered great delicacies by

sportsmen and connoisseurs of food. One thing to remember is that there is danger of trichinosis in bear that is served less than well done. It should be kept at a temperature of *minus* 10 F. for at least 30 days. It will then be quite safe for use in dishes which do not require thorough cooking.

saddle of bear

There is nothing better than a saddle of bear spit roasted over charcoal. Rub the meat well with salt, freshly ground black pepper, and crushed rosemary leaves; then spit and roast it to the degree of doneness you like most. I have found that when it reaches an internal temperature of 140 F., it is about right for most tastes. While the meat is cooking, baste with a mixture of red wine and olive oil. Saddle of bear is delicious served with a sauce Diable and chestnut purée with plenty of butter.

bear ham

Bear ham can be remarkably good if prepared in the following way: Have your butcher bone and tie the ham. After it has been stored at minus 10 F. for over a month, rub well with crushed bay leaf, thyme, and salt and pepper. Baste with red wine and olive oil. Roast until it reaches an internal temperature of 140 F. Serve with a mustard or Cumberland sauce.

fish and seafood

spitted whole salmon indian-fashion

The Indian guides of the Northwest and Canada very often spit a whole salmon on a fork of green spirea wood. After having blanketed the wood with ferns, they bury one end in the ground and lace the fish to the forked end. The fish is actually slow-roasted over the fire and develops a flavor somewhere between roasted and kippered salmon. The same result may be achieved today over charcoal. The salmon is cleaned and stuffed, perhaps with fresh dill or parsley, or sometimes with slices of onion or green pepper, and then sewn. It is spitted, balanced, secured with wire or cord, and roasted. It need not be basted. There is so much oil in the skin of this fish that it lubricates itself while it roasts. The skin will become crispy and almost black, and you'll discover it is a delicious part of the eating. Serve with parsley butter, small boiled potatoes, and by all means drink a brisk, dry, white wine, such as a Chablis or a good pinot chardonnay.

spitted striped bass

Striped bass is one of the more delicious of our native fish. Lace it to the spit with cord or wire, brush it well with olive oil, and roast over rather hot coals for 20 to 25 minutes, depending on its size. It is done if it flakes easily when tested with a fork or twig. Serve with plenty of lemon and melted butter, thinly sliced tomatoes and onions, and French bread. Drink a good Pouilly.

spitted tuna, sturgeon, haddock, cod, albacore, or other firm-fleshed fish

Any of these fish may be secured on a spit with wire or twine and roasted. Baste with melted butter and lemon juice, or with white wine and butter. The rules are the same for all of them. Serve with melted butter and lemon juice, or hollandaise sauce, or parsley butter—all of which go well with any of these fish. I prefer to serve plain boiled potatoes and either a green vegetable or a cucumber salad with them, and I feel that a Chablis, a Pouilly, or a good Riesling from California are the most satisfactory wines.

spitted or skewered small fish

There is no question that skewered or twigged small fish can be delicious, but most of them are really better broiled or pan-fried rather than skewered. However, if you decide to skewer, impale the fish and cook over the coals until just done. Brush well with butter while it is roasting. Be careful not to overcook fish. This is a common error. Any small fish will cook in a very short period of time—anywhere from 5 to 12 minutes, depending on the weight of the fish and on the heat.

bacon-wrapped small fish

Many people wrap strips of bacon around small fish, and secure them with toothpicks or small skewers before broiling. The wrapping tends to keep the fish moist and imparts a pleasant flavor to the skin.

bacon-stuffed fish

Clean and bone the fish, and stuff it with strips of bacon that have been partially broiled. The fish is not skewered, but impaled on twigs and smoke roasted over bonfires. Fish prepared in this manner are tasty—and the method is amusing to try, though I must confess that I think nothing can surpass a good pan-fried or broiled small fish.

multiple twigged fish

For this you have to pick triple-forked twigs. Split and bone your fish and impale them on the 3 prongs of the twig. Season with salt and pepper and broil over coals, brushing once or

twice with butter during the cooking period. Small fish should be cooked quickly.

All the preceding dishes take little time and are adaptable to any outdoor cooking. They call for fried potatoes, lemon wedges, a green salad, and a good Chablis or a Moselle wine that is very dry. Naturally, these dishes will be of more interest to campers than to guests at a cookout on the lawn.

fish cubes

The frozen, breaded cubes of fish one finds in little packages at the supermarket will not do here. Use fresh salmon, halibut, sturgeon, or tuna which has been cut into 1½-inch cubes. These can be skewered with various complements, such as stuffed or ripe olives, tiny onions, mushroom caps, and green-pepper strips. Brush with butter and broil. You may alternate any number of these in any combination with your fish squares. Serve them with rice and sautéed peppers, and drink a Sancerre.

bacon-wrapped fish cubes

Wrap fish cubes with rashers of partially cooked bacon, impale on skewers, and broil. You may also use ham instead of bacon, but be sure it is not sliced too thick and is not too fat.

polynesian fish cubes

Marinate fish cubes with equal quantities of soy sauce and sweet sherry to which you have added 1 teaspoon of curry powder for each cup of liquid. Alternate the fish cubes with mushroom caps, pineappple chunks, and strips of green pepper. Brush with the marinade and broil over the coals. Serve with an oriental sweet-sour sauce.

skewered scallops

The delicacy of scallops makes it imperative that you do not overcook them. The tiny bay scallops are extremely tender and take little more than heating through to make them perfect. The more robust sea scallops should have a longer cooking time.

grilled marinated scallops

Marinate 1½ pounds bay scallops in white wine to cover, mixed with 2 tablespoons finely chopped parsley, 1 tablespoon finely chopped tarragon, 1 teaspoon salt, and ½ teaspoon pepper. Let stand for several hours in the refrigerator. Skewer the scallops and brush them well with melted butter and broil over medium coals, turning frequently, for about 5 minutes or until they are just cooked through. Do not allow them to overcook and brush several times with melted butter during the cooking process. Serve with lemon juice and finely chopped parsley, and green rice. Drink a Muscadet.

garlicked scallops

Soak 1½ pounds bay scallops for 2 hours in enough white wine to cover. Remove from the marinating sauce, drain, and roll in a combination of finely chopped garlic and parsley. You will need about 4 garlic cloves and approximately ½ cup chopped parsley. Be sure that some of the garlic and the parsley adhere to each scallop. Skewer and broil very quickly over hot coals, brushing with melted butter to which you have added more chopped parsley and garlic. Serve with sliced tomatoes, cucumbers, and good French bread.

scallops oriental

Marinate either bay or sea scallops in a half-and-half mixture of soy sauce and sherry for 2 hours. Skewer and broil over charcoal. Brush with a half-and-half mixture of melted butter and soy sauce. Serve with rice and buttered snow peas, and drink an Alsatian Gewurtztraminer or a dry California white.

italian skewered shrimp

Slit the shells of 2 pounds of large shrimp and remove the vein. (A pair of very sharp scissors does this trick extremely well.) Place shrimp in a flat dish and add ½ cup olive oil, 1 teaspoon oregano, 2 finely cut garlic cloves, and 2 tablespoons lemon juice. Season to taste with salt and freshly ground black pepper. Allow to stand for 3 to 4 hours. Skewer the shrimp and broil over medium coals; let them brown well. Brush with the marinade several times during the broiling. Serve with a rice pilaff and drink beer.

skewered shrimp oriental

Marinate 2 pounds of large peeled shrimp in a mixture of ⅓ cup soy sauce, ⅓ cup white wine, 1 teaspoon freshly ground pepper, and ½ teaspoon ground ginger. Let stand for several hours. Skewer and broil for about 4 or 5 minutes, brushing with the marinade once during the cooking time. You may add olive oil and grated fresh ginger to this mixture. Or you may dip the shrimp in sesame seeds before broiling.

VARIATIONS:

Alternate shrimps, tiny tomatoes, and thin slices of onions on skewers. Brush with olive oil and broil.

Roll bacon strips around cleaned, raw shrimp. Skewer and broil.

Slit shrimps, stuff with anchovies, lace with bacon, and broil.

Alternate shrimp with wedges of green pepper and slices of onion. Brush with the oriental marinade and broil.

skewered lobster tails

Lobster tails may be removed from the shells and skewered, and broiled in any of the ways that have been suggested for shrimp.

stuffed lobster tails

Cut lobster tails into 1½- to 2-inch lengths. Make a slit in each one and insert a slice of water chestnut. Wrap in bacon, skewer, and broil, brushing with butter from time to time.

tarragon-flavored lobster tails

After you have removed the lobster tails from their shells, marinate them for an hour in white wine. Dip in tarragon butter, arrange on skewers, and broil, brushing from time to time with melted butter seasoned with tarragon.

skewered clams

The tender clams of the East and West Coasts lend themselves to broiling if they are well lubricated. Cook them very quickly, or they will be a complete fizzle. Clams may be wrapped in bacon, skewered, and broiled until the bacon is crisp. Or, for a variation, use ham in thin slices (and with a minimum of fat). With these clams you might drink a dry white wine and serve crisp French bread.

skewered oysters

Be careful with these. If they are overdone, you'll regret having made them. Lace the oysters on twigs or skewers, brush with butter and broil—or dip them first in melted butter, and then into a mixture of crumbled Parmesan cheese and chopped parsley before broiling.

VARIATIONS:

Take an oyster which has been dipped in melted butter and sandwich it between 2 mushroom caps. Skewer and broil, after brushing well with melted butter.

Wrap the oysters in partially cooked bacon strips and skewer and broil until the bacon is just cooked through. Or you may dip the oysters in melted butter, roll in finely chopped green onions and parsley, and skewer and broil them very quickly.

Alternate oysters on a skewer with ham and strips of green pepper, brush with butter and broil very quickly.

Finally, you might try dipping oysters in butter and alternating them on the skewer with thin slices of sausage. Broil over rather hot coals.

cooking on the top of the table

For centuries the Japanese have known that cooking at the dining table with the aid of a hibachi is both appetizing and amusing for guests and family. The hibachi, a small cast-iron or enamel pot with grid top, is an ideal grill, well designed and well ventilated. When the hibachi becomes too hot, you can regulate the fire with the draft. With other table grills it is usually necessary to spread the briquets or remove some of the charcoal to another container. Since its arrival in this country, the hibachi has enjoyed increasing popularity, and has so excited the imagination of the American hostess that innumerable variations in all sorts of new and fascinating materials have come into being. The Skotch grill was a pioneer in

THE MERRY COMPANY, BY FRANS HALS.
METROPOLITAN MUSEUM OF ART,
BEQUEST OF BENJAMIN ALTMAN, 1913.

the field and still remains one of the best all-around grills for cookouts. Pyroceram casseroles, produced by the Corning Glass people, are a recent innovation. At first, the idea of placing live coals in such a container seemed impossible to me, but it works, and with a grid placed over the top, you have a superb small broiler for the table and one, it should be noted, that is easy to clean.

To use these small grills properly requires a good eye for the amount of charcoal needed and some judgment of the time it takes to produce an even heat for cooking. Most table units are designed to burn lump charcoal; if you usually use briquets, remember that they burn longer and more intensely than lump charcoal. You will find that a maximum of 12 charcoal briquets will do a satisfactory job for almost any table grill. To start your fire, place briquets soaked in starter fluid at the bottom of a metal container and dry briquets on top. (Some barbecue units include a container, otherwise use a tin can.) Ignite, and let the fire burn for about 15 minutes before emptying the burning coals into the firebox. When using the hibachi indoors, I have found that the best way to produce glowing coals quickly is to place your briquets in one of those metal salad baskets used for shaking washed greens and set it on the electric stove over a large burner turned to high. (Be careful; don't leave them untended.)

You will find your table grill quite versatile. It will take steaks, chops, hamburgers, frankfurters, chicken, fish fillets, skewered items, and fruits, as well as traditional dishes for which it originally was intended, such as sukiyaki. You may use your hibachi as an auxiliary to a large grill, or make it the centerpiece for the preparation of an entire meal. Put it to use at cocktail parties, too, encouraging your guests to grill their own canapés on chopstick skewers.

sukiyaki

Sukiyaki can be prepared on your hibachi in either the typical Japanese sukiyaki pan or your own electric skillet. (Sukiyaki pans are readily available in Japanese specialty shops across the country.) Be sure to provide yourself with a pair of cooking chopsticks, as well. These are longer and heavier than those used for eating. With a little practice, you will find them easy to handle and extremely useful. The following recipe for sukiyaki will serve about 6.

> 1½ pounds beef sirloin, cut in strips
> 1 teaspoon sugar
> ½ cup soy sauce
> ¼ cup sherry
> 2 medium-sized onions, thinly sliced
> 1 cup sliced mushrooms
> 1 cup sliced bamboo shoots
> ½ cup sliced water chestnuts
> ½ cup beef stock
> 1½ pounds fresh spinach, well washed
> 1 cup diced white bean curd
> 6 scallions

If you wish you may add 1 package of long rice (or "rice spaghetti," as it is sometimes called). You will want a few strips of beef fat and you may need additional beef stock and soy sauce. One secret of preparing an appetizing sukiyaki is to have your ingredients beautifully arranged on a tray or a huge chop plate. The visual element plays an important role in Japanese cooking and is almost more important than the pleasure of eating what you've prepared.

Fill a bamboo or a lacquer container with steamed rice. Heat your sukiyaki pan, rub it with just enough beef fat to lubricate, then discard the remainder. Add a little of the onion and stir it about the pan well. Add the beef, which should be sliced in thin, 2- by 3-inch strips, and sear it on both sides. When it has become a nice brown, push it to one side of the pan and add the sugar, about ½ cup soy sauce, and the sherry. As it begins to bubble, add the onions, mushrooms, and bamboo shoots. Next, add the water chestnuts and the broth, keeping each addition separate in the pan. Finally add the greens and the bean curd (and the long rice, if you are using it). Let the sukiyaki bubble for a few minutes, but do not overcook it. Nothing is worse than mushy sukiyaki. Serve it in bowls or on plates with rice, garnished with shredded scallions. If you want to serve in truly oriental style, give each person a small bowl in which you have broken a raw egg, so that each diner can dip the sukiyaki from time to time.

Note: Sukiyaki may also be made with thinly sliced loin of pork. I have never been able to decide whether the beef or the pork is better, but my taste leans to the pork.

hibachi appetizer

I have found that a version of Fondue Bourguignonne makes a most pleasant cocktail snack either in or out of doors. Blend together 2½ to 3 pounds coarsely chopped beef, 2 garlic cloves, ⅓ cup finely chopped onion, 1½ teaspoons salt, 1 teaspoon freshly ground black pepper, and 1 teaspoon thyme. Form into tiny

GIRL PERFORMING THE TEA CEREMONY, BY SUIZAN MIKI. METROPOLITAN MUSEUM OF ART.

balls and chill. In the meantime prepare four sauces: 1) a Béarnaise. 2) an anchovy-mustard-butter sauce. (Chop 6 anchovy fillets rather coarsely and combine them with ½ cup of softened butter, 1½ teaspoons dry mustard, and a few drops of lemon juice. Beat very well, heap into a small serving dish, and chill.) 3) a garlic butter. (Chop and crush 2 cloves of garlic and combine with ½ cup softened butter, ½ teaspoon salt, and 1 teaspoon freshly ground black pepper. Blend and heap into a serving dish.) And 4) any uncooked barbecue sauce. Finally, to serve, soak sharpened bamboo chopsticks in water for several hours and have a goodly number of them on the table with the hibachi. Your guests may either skewer the hors d'oeuvres and grill them over charcoal or cook them in a skillet in a half-and-half combination of oil and butter. Each guest can cook the meat mixture to the degree of doneness he prefers, and dip it into the sauce of his own choosing.

polynesian steak

3 boneless strip steaks, cut thick

2 medium onions, finely chopped
1 tablespoon olive oil
1 eight-ounce can tomato sauce
1 tablespoon curry powder
1 cup beef gravy
1 dash of cinnamon
Salt to taste
1½ teaspoons cornstarch
1 cup fresh pineapple chunks
Marinade

Marinate the steaks in 1 cup of olive oil, 1 cup of Japanese soy sauce, 1 crushed garlic clove, and a dash of ginger. While the marinade is doing its work prepare the Polynesian barbecue sauce, as follows: Sauté the onions in olive oil, stir in the remaining ingredients with the exception of the cornstarch and pineapple, and bring the mixture to a boil. Blend the cornstarch with a tablespoon of water and stir into the sauce. Continue stirring until it is thick. Add the pineapple and heat through. Remove steaks from the marinade and broil them to your favorite state of doneness. Slice in diagonal slices and serve with Polynesian sauce.

Legend tells us that early French explorers of

America saw whole animals being pit roasted by the natives.

From "barbe à queue," they exclaimed, with gestures.

They meant the entrée was cooked from "head to tail."

And so, when we barbecue a steer or piglet, do we.

Pit barbecuing is probably as old as man. It is reasonable to suppose that within a few thousand years after the discovery of fire, some ancient found that it was easy to dig a pit and cook his food therein. Two systems evolved: the open pit and the closed, or covered, pit. Both called for a pit lining of heated rocks and a Stone Age foil-wrapping of leaves or fronds. Today pit roasting is little more than a relic. Occasionally, some western or middle-western city will send out an SOS for advice on how to roast a whole steer or a whole pig, but these rare exceptions simply confirm that the methods of our ancestors have become history. The most popular remaining form of pit barbecuing is the clambake, which is still practiced a great deal in New England and copied on the Pacific Coast. I think it is sometimes overrated, but it is a traditional and pleasurable form of outdoor entertainment for many people and should be included here. The very elaborate luau (which is about as far from a clambake as anything could be) has been brought home from the islands of the Pacific. Vacationers enjoy these festive occasions when they travel and like to recreate the experience in their own gardens. Although the luau has not yet achieved the general popularity of the clambake, I much prefer it. It can be as gala and colorful as you wish, and is still unusual enough to make an intriguing and distinctive party.

open-pit barbecue

The open-pit barbecue is a holdover from the days of the huge plantations and vast ranch kingdoms in the South and Southwest. Large families and community organizations gathered together for celebrations that sometimes lasted several days, and a whole steer would be butchered and barbecued for the group. It was judged that one good steer would serve a thousand guests. If the beef was to be cooked whole or in halves, a large pit was dug and huge spits erected in it. Sometimes the pit was made quite deep and a netting or grill put over it. The beef was split or cut in sections and grilled over the coals. It was mopped with barbecue sauce from time to time, and great pitchforks and picks were used to turn it. As you can see, an open-pit barbecue is not something you can easily set up in your backyard. I don't think it would be very helpful to give you any directions here for a pit roasting of this type. If you want to give a feast of such proportions, it would be wise to put yourself in the hands of one of the few large-scale barbecue artists still in existence and let him supervise the event.

ENGRAVING OF A BARBECUE AT AUGUSTA, GEORGIA, 19TH CENTURY.

closed-pit barbecue

Closed-pit barbecues are no less elaborate than open ones. If you decide, therefore, to give a simple barbecue for five hundred or a thousand people, I suggest that you start trying immediately to locate someone who can handle the job for you. On a small scale, however, the closed-pit barbecue can be quite good fun. For a start, dig a pit about 3 feet deep, 4 to 5 feet long, and 3 feet wide. Line it well with rocks. This requires a bit of work, but it's worth it. When you are ready to cook, build a wood fire and add logs gradually as it burns down. This should take 4 or 5 hours. The point is to get a great bed of coals so that the rocks heat thoroughly. Before you begin to cook, shovel out the ashes and keep them in a big can or tub. Put a layer of ferns, leaves, or corn husks on the bottom of the pit and place the meat on it. Cover the meat with more ferns or leaves, and then with the hot ashes. On top of this put a sheet of galvanized iron, or canvas, then a thick coating of earth. You can now leave the pit alone for 5 to 8 hours. Don't worry too much about the exact timing. Meat prepared this way is never rare. As a matter of fact, it is much more likely to be overdone, so don't attempt to cook the choicest prime ribs or fillets. Use chuck or round or rump. Gauge your timing, so that your guests will arrive about an hour before you plan to unveil your handiwork. Give them a few rounds of drinks and something to munch on and then stage your dramatic performance: remove the earth, the galvanized metal, the leaves or ferns, and then your work of art. Better have a good-sized pan of scalloped potatoes or a bean casserole, a hearty salad, and some French bread. As you can see, the process of digging your pit, marinating the meat (see below), placing it in the pit, waiting for it to cook, and serving it is a lengthy and fairly laborious one, so be sure you want to attempt it in the first place and prepare for the industry it involves. You will be amply rewarded.

preparing meat for closed-pit barbecue

I suggest that you choose a good-sized piece of beef and have it cut in 5- or 6-pound sections. You should estimate approximately a pound of meat per person. Marinate it in a big tub or in buckets with a mixture of red wine, vinegar, water, and olive oil to cover. Use 3 parts wine

to 1 each of vinegar, water, and oil. Season with salt, garlic, thyme, plenty of black and cayenne pepper, and chili powder, if you wish. When you are ready to put the meat in the pit, remove it from the tub and wrap in cheesecloth that has been saturated with the marinade. Then wrap each piece in aluminum foil. In this way, the meat steams in the marinade and absorbs more flavor. Beef, turkey, and pork are the only things I really recommend for this type of cooking.

the clambake

Although clambakes are traditionally held on the beach, they may be done in your backyard, as well. In either case, you will need a pit about 2 to 3 feet deep and 3 feet in diameter. Again, it must be lined with rocks—nice, smooth, oval rocks—arranged in as level a manner as possible. Build a good fire and keep it going for several hours, or until the rocks are thoroughly heated. Rake all the coals and brush off the ashes. Now work rapidly. At this point, the various ingredients should go into the pit, in sequence, as quickly as possible. Cover the hot ashes with seaweed about 6 inches deep (if you are not near the sea, substitute leaves and ferns). Cover this with a piece of wire mesh, and then layers of well-washed, soft-shelled clams. A bushel will serve 30 persons. Add a live lobster for each person. Then take your choice of sweet potatoes, white potatoes, or corn (from which the silk has been removed and the husk left); and chicken halves wrapped in foil or cooking parchment. Make a layer of your selection and cover with more seaweed, then with a piece of canvas. Weight the canvas down with large rocks. A clambake should steam for 45 minutes to 2 hours, depending on the amount you are serving. If you add chickens to your clambake, I think it is wise to broil them lightly before wrapping in foil. It is customary to eat the clams, first, served with loads of butter, then the lobster, and then the chicken. Always serve beer and great hunks of French bread.

the luau

menu

ISLANDER SHRIMP
ROAST WHOLE SEA BASS
ROAST BANANAS
SWEET POTATOES OR YAMS
LONG RICE WITH CURRY SAUCE • POI
WHOLE PIT-ROASTED PIG
COCONUT • PINEAPPLE • PRESERVED KUMQUATS
BEER

A luau is a tropical, closed-pit barbecue, and as colorful and enjoyable as any form of entertainment I know. If you want to have a thoroughly

TWO TAHITIAN WOMEN, BY PAUL GAUGUIN.
METROPOLITAN MUSEUM OF ART,
GIFT OF WILLIAM CHURCH OSBORN. 1949.

Polynesian affair, you can find tapa cloth, baby orchids, leis—all the Hawaiian trappings—in gift shops. If you're feeling really expansive, you can even hire hula dancers. The usual *pièce de résistance* of a luau is a pit-roasted whole pig. However, if you don't want to go to the trouble of digging a pit, you can substitute barbecued pork loins (see section on spit-and-skewer cooking) and barbecued spareribs with plum sauce. If you choose to do this, you can cook the long rice (noodle-like, transparent strings which may be purchased in Chinese or Japanese grocery stores) in the kitchen. It only needs to be heated briefly in hot water. Also serve a large salad of pineapple and greens with a curried French dressing. If you accompany the dinner with lots of pineapple, coconuts, rum drinks, and other Hawaiian accessories, you will retain the Polynesian effect and almost match the authentic atmosphere you get by digging a pit.

islander shrimp

1½ pounds fresh shrimp
or 2 twelve-ounce packages frozen shrimp
¼ cup lemon juice
½ teaspoon salt
1 teaspoon curry powder
⅛ teaspoon ginger
1 can (3½ ounces) flaked coconut
1 cup flour
⅔ cup milk
1 teaspoon double-action baking powder
Extra flour
Curry sauce

If you buy frozen shrimp, let them thaw before working with them. Remove the body of the shell. Leave the tail shell on to serve as a handle. Cut deeply down the back of the shrimp and remove the vein. Mix lemon juice with salt, curry powder, and ginger. Pour over shrimp, cover, and let marinate in refrigerator 4 to 6 hours. Turn in marinade once or twice. Spread coconut in a shallow pan and bake in a slow (300 F.) oven for 15 minutes, or until coco-

nut is dry. Stir a few times. Prepare batter by mixing 1 cup flour with the milk and baking powder. Stir in ¼ cup marinade drained from shrimp. Dip shrimp in extra flour, then in batter, finally in dried coconut. Fry in deep, hot fat (380 F. on deep-fat thermometer) for 3 to 5 minutes—depending on size of shrimp—or until cooked through and golden brown. Serve with curry sauce. Makes 4 to 6 servings.

whole roast bass

Marinate whole sea bass overnight in equal parts of salted water and white wine. Sprinkle with chopped onion and chopped raw tomato, and wrap in aluminum foil. Roast with the pig, unwrap, and serve.

whole spit-roasted pig

Buy your pig before you dig your pit. Pigs weigh from 50 to 85 pounds, and that means a considerable variation in length and breadth—both for pig and pit. Prepare the pit the same way you would for a closed-pit barbecue. Line it with rocks and start the fire. While the fire is burning down to ashes, heat more rocks in it. Rub the pig well with soy sauce, lemon, garlic, and white wine, and place several cloves of garlic, soy sauce, and fresh ginger inside the body cavity. With heavy tongs, pick up the extra rocks you have heated and put them inside the pig. Rake the ashes out of the fire and cover the surface with leaves (traditionally, banana leaves). Lay the pig on the leaves and surround it with foil-wrapped bananas and yams, 1 each per person. At the same time, lay in your foil-wrapped sea bass. Cover with additional leaves, seaweed, or layers of foil, and roast for about 5 hours. To serve, uncover the pit, remove the seaweed or leaves and the packages of roasting vegetables, and place the pig on a very large board or table for carving. Serve with poi (fermented taro-root paste), which is available in Chinese or Japanese groceries.

spareribs with plum sauce

4-6 pounds spareribs
1 clove garlic
1 #2 can Chinese bean sauce
1 #3 can Hoy Sin sauce
1 can plum sauce
1 teaspoon salt
1 cup sugar
1 teaspoon monosodium glutamate
1 drop red food-coloring
Olive oil

Mix all the ingredients in an electric mixer for 3 or 4 minutes at low speed. Add approximately ½ pint of olive oil, a little at a time, very slowly. This process is similar to mixing a mayonnaise, and you should try to achieve the same paste-like consistency. If you don't have an electric mixer, work by hand with a mixing bowl. When the marinade is ready, brush it on the ribs and allow them to marinate at least an hour, but preferably overnight. Before baking, brush them again with the marinade. Use your own taste and judgment to determine the thickness of the glaze. Place the ribs in a baking pan and put this inside another, larger pan half-filled with water. Bake in a slow oven for about 45 minutes. (You may also lace the spareribs on

a spit and grill them, but be sure to keep a pan under them to catch the juices.) Remove from the oven (or fire) and pour pineapple chunks and kumquats—plus juices—and the can of plum sauce over the ribs. The plum sauce is available in Oriental food shops. Replace the ribs in the oven and bake for 5 minutes.

permanent open pit

After experimenting with various kinds of pit roasting, you may decide that you want a permanent pit in your garden. If you do, make sure it is well-built; you will probably want to use it often and have it last a long time. Dig your pit about 2 feet deep, 3 feet wide, and 4 to 5 feet long. Have the bottom and sides completely lined with firebrick. The opening should be finished with a metal band. You may fit the pit with a movable grilling rack made of heavy, rust-proof metal mesh. This should be equipped with hooks so that you can adjust the distance of the rack from the firebox. Use either a wood or charcoal fire for pit cooking.

Before refrigeration, meats were preserved by smoke.

The Chinese invented the process. Imperial Rome

enjoyed bacon cured in the aromatic wood smoke of Gaul.

American colonials liked smoke flavor—and still do.

I first encountered the excitement and romance of smoke cooking as a youngster in the Northwest. I used to watch the Indians spearing the magnificent Columbia River salmon near Celilo Falls as they fought their way up the rapids each spring to spawn. Those Indians knew perfectly how to use wood flavors and fire to advantage. They gutted their catch, rubbed it with salt, impaled it on long sticks, and cooked it over dense, hot smoke. The spitted fish was tilted, easel-fashion, against a stake pounded into the ground near the fire, and slowly, as the hours passed, it cooked beautifully and became impregnated with the dark taste of fine wood smoke. This performance was one of the wonders of my childhood and I can still summon up the wonderful flavor and aroma that were part of those long-ago springs.

For the Indians, for our colonial forebears, whose smokehouses were hung with fat hams, game, and wildfowl, for Charles Lamb, whose "Dissertation Upon Roast Pig" involved smoked porker, for the Gauls who cured bacon for the Caesars, and for the Chinese, who seem to have invented the process, smoke was a food preservative. In the days before year-around refrigeration, smoke curing was about the only way one could guarantee unspoiled meat for the morrow. Today we no longer feel the sharp prod of necessity and smoking survives as a process for the sheer gastronomic pleasure it affords. It is a somewhat specialized taste, to be sure, but undeniably popular, as can be seen by the wide range of commercially prepared items available. (My Indian-style smoked fish is now marketed as "kippered salmon," and very good it is, too.) For the enthusiastic amateur, moreover, there is equipment that can be bought or built to recreate the old, home methods of smoking. If you are tempted to try it, be warned that the process is slow, complex, and laborious,

but keep in mind that the ultimate reward will be a pungent, piquant piece of meat that many people consider the epitome of good eating.

To reduce confusion, let us also define our terms. There are, in fact, two basic methods to choose between: "smoking" and "smoke cookery." The former process may utilize either hot or cold smoke and is essentially a means of preserving meat that has been marinated or dipped in brine. It employs a smoldering fire that sheds relatively little heat and travels the smoke a distance so that it has cooled somewhat before it reaches the meat. "Smoking" does not necessarily cook the meat. It simply coats and saturates it with carbon particles that cure it, thereby retarding decay. This was the method employed by our colonial ancestors in their specially built smokehouses. The meat was first "dry-cured" with salt and condiments, or "brine-cured" by soaking in a marinade of water, salt, herbs, and spices for 36 or 48 hours. Brine-cured meats were then dried. Whatever the preliminary preparations, the meat was finally smoked at low temperature for from 2 to 15 hours, depending on the amount of meat involved and the amount of marinating that had been done. Unless you have a smokehouse, it's not likely that you'll use this method.

The second process—"smoke cookery"—utilizes a hot fire and hot smoke and is intended to cook the meat as well as flavor it. Meats treated this way do not need to be marinated, although this is a matter of taste, not prescription. In either case, you start with a wood or charcoal fire, then smother it with damp wood chips or sawdust to produce a dense smoke. As the damp fuel is consumed, more must be added to keep the smoke cloud constant. The best flavor is imparted by sweet woods. Avoid resinous woods, however, such as pine. Hickory is the standard

favorite, but maple, oak, alder, or any of the fruit- or nut-tree woods are equally good. So are shredded corn cobs and grapevine trimmings. If you like, you may also sprinkle fresh or dried herbs over the burning chips to produce additional flavor accents. Soaking the chips in water for 30 minutes usually moistens them properly for a good smoky fire.

The secret of good smoke cookery, however, is in firm-handed control of the process. The size of the fire and your ability to regulate the intensity of its heat are of great importance. To maintain an even heat, you may, from time to time, have to move the fire closer to or farther away from the meat, or, if your equipment permits, adjust the damper. In the traditional Chinese oven—a large, L-shaped unit made of brick—the fire is built in the base of the L. When the walls are heated through, the fire is pushed closer to the meat hanging in the upright arm of the L with a shovel or hoe. The fire is never positioned directly under the meat; a drip pan sits there to catch the juices. The smoke, therefore, drifts horizontally along the base, turns the corner, and ascends the flue to envelop the meat.

Metal replicas of the traditional Chinese oven —mounted on wheels for convenience—can be purchased in this country, although you may have to hunt a bit or send away for them. Trader Vic, proprietor of the well-known restaurants bearing his name, has designed a modern version of the brick oven and plans for constructing it are included in one of his recent cookbooks. If you live near a Trader Vic restaurant, you might enjoy sampling some of the wide range of smoked foods on the menu.

I consider the Chinese oven best for smoking, but you can get satisfactory results from standard grills with smoke-cooking attachments—

Big Boy, for instance, offers a special hood—or from a "do-it-yourself" oven made out of a large barrel. Even an open grill will give you some smoke flavor if you simply top your fire with wet wood chips or sawdust.

Now, here is a basic marinade in which to prepare your meats for smoking. If followed carefully, it will give excellent results.

marinade

1 cup soy sauce
½ cup honey
1 cup sherry
1 teaspoon cinnamon
1 teaspoon pepper
1 teaspoon anise
½ teaspoon ground cloves
½ cup strong tea
or 1 tablespoon instant tea crystals
1 or 2 cloves garlic (optional)
A little red food coloring (optional)

If the soy flavor is too strong for you, it may be diluted, half and half, with water. Small food items need marinating only for several hours, but larger ones will taste better if soaked overnight or even for 24 hours. Appetizers such as chicken liver, rumaki, beef cubes, hamburger balls, chicken bits, sausage balls, gizzards (precooked), spareribs, and scallops will smoke cook

—at about 350 F.—in a very short time after they have been removed from the marinade. If you want a high glaze on any of these, and a more intense flavor, brush with the marinade during the cooking process. Or with a mixture of soy sauce and honey. Or soy sauce and rich, sweet sherry. One of the simplest and tastiest glazes is soy sauce mixed with the red plum sauce found in oriental food shops. If you are partial to garlic, it should be included in your marinade.

The Chinese use a variety of preparations. Fish is rubbed, dry-cured, and marinated with onion, ginger, anise, soy sauce, and yellow wine (sherry is an acceptable substitute). In the old days, they used a chicken feather to brush on the marinade during the smoking process. Chicken is smoke cooked with tea leaves. They give the bird a fine, rich color, and add to the pungent smoke flavor. (This is a good idea to keep in mind whenever you have occasion to use a soy sauce and wine marinade for chicken, however you plan to cook it.) Chinese frogs' legs are hung in pairs in the oven and cooked in smoke spiced with fennel, nutmeg, and pepper. They are rubbed from time to time with sesame oil, in part for flavor, but primarily to keep the lean flesh moist. Fennel is also used for smoke cooking kidneys, which should be trimmed of fat and soaked in wine before going into the oven. Brains, too, can be smoke cooked. Clean and blanch them, then soak in a marinade of thyme, anise, fennel, soy sauce, onion, ginger, and sherry. Incredible as it may seem, the Chinese even have a way of smoke cooking vegetables, particularly green beans, turnips, and celery.

Experiment with any of these—or with duck, chicken, squab, lamb, or beef. Choose your seasonings and proceed according to the method prescribed for your particular type of equipment. Try a fresh loin of pork, or pork chops, or your favorite breakfast sausage. Good fish for smoking are salmon, trout, whitefish, butterfish, sturgeon, shad, tuna, sablefish, or haddock. All should be marinated—or salted—before smoking.

For many people, of course, smoke cookery at home is out of the question for reasons of space, expense, or inclination. Still, there is no reason to deny yourself the pleasure of any of these great delicacies, for almost all of them are commercially prepared these days and should be available at your local markets, specialty shops, and delicatessens. Following are comments on some of the smoked meats I have found to be successful.

Prosciutto: If you entertain a great deal, a whole prosciutto is perfect. It will keep for a number of weeks and you may slice from it as needed. Also try canned prosciutto.

Ham: A basic item, and a versatile one, that is good to have on hand for all occasions. I find, however, that it is becoming increasingly difficult to get fine-flavored, well-textured hams. For the most part, they tend to be wet and uninteresting. Strangely enough, good country hams can be found here and there, and sometimes in the most surprising sections of the country. There are still excellent country hams available in Kentucky and North and South Carolina. In Pine Plains, New York, a Mr. Wilke sells exceptional hams and will even mail them. And you can still purchase good hams in Oregon, Washington, and throughout the Middle West. The best value I've found in ham lately is a Virginia ham—the Smithfield cure—which can be purchased from Thalhimers department store in Richmond, Virginia. These people have hams smoked especially for them and cook the hams themselves. They will mail them anywhere in the country. Their excellence makes them a necessity for people who entertain often. A few slices are perfect for hors d'oeuvres, or for lunch, or bits and pieces may be added to fried rice and other dishes. They make a constant auxiliary shelf. Next to the Thalhimers hams for general use, I think the Great Valley Mills hams from Pennsylvania are the most interesting. These are country hams, not the full Smithfield cure, but they are delicate and well seasoned, and simply delicious. Like most other country hams, they have to be cooked and prepared in your own kitchen, but that is really not much of a problem. Some of the canned, imported hams are quite good, too. Most of these must be refrigerated, however.

Smoked Butts and Cali Hams: I find these, and picnic hams, quite satisfactory, particularly when cooked with sherry or Madeira and served cold as a first course.

Bacon: Canadian bacon and regular bacon are both handy smoke items. Sliced and served hot or cold with toast, it makes a superb snack or hors d'oeuvre. Try it, too, served with toast, sliced tomatoes, and a good mayonnaise.

The regular bacon one finds in the shops these days is pretty poor. It is wet and flavorless, and, for my money, a dud no matter how it is served. If you have storage space, it is better to buy the country slab variety, such as Todd Virginia Bacon, and slice it yourself.

Slab bacon can be used with fruits for hors d'oeuvres, like prosciutto. I find bacon with fresh figs, or melon, or pears, or even with tiny tomatoes, to be delightful and refreshing, especially in warm weather. You may also serve a huge plate of crisp bacon with sliced turkey or chicken, sliced tomatoes, lettuce, and plenty of toast, and let guests concoct their own club sandwiches.

Poultry: Smoked turkeys and capons are now available all year around and in some places you can also purchase smoked pheasant and duck. I find these a little too smoky for my palate, but there are people who consider them among the greatest of delicacies. They are best sliced paper thin and served with pumpernickel or rye bread and butter as an hors d'oeuvre or snack. Smoked poultry combines well with fruits, too, and with eggs and salads.

Goose: This is also available smoked, and it is sensationally good, though extremely expensive. It makes a choice goody for company. Slice it thin and serve it with dark breads and salads. Or it may be served like prosciutto or even foie gras. To me, it is one of the most delightful smoked foods you can get.

Sausages: In certain parts of this country, you can find special sausage makers, and when you do, stock your cellar, or cold room, or freezer, with as much of his selection as you can carry. Otherwise, look for any of the good commercial sausages, of which there are a respectable number. In a cool place or in the refrigerator, they will keep more or less indefinitely. And they are invaluable for emergency meals or for snacks and hors d'oeuvres. Buy them whole and slice them to your needs.

Cervelat: There are many different types of this particularly fine grade of sausage on the market. It's excellent sliced, or in a salad served as an hors d'oeuvre, as the Swiss do. There is also a heavily smoked cervelat from Wisconsin which seems to be generally available.

Salami: You will find Italian, German, Hungarian, and American salami—both kosher and non-kosher—in the markets. Your choice will depend only on taste and the degree of spiciness you enjoy.

Summer Sausage: There are three kinds: cured, smoked, and heavily smoked. I enjoy its rather sour pungency.

Cotechino: A cured, rather mild-flavored Italian sausage, this requires cooking. It can be delicious hot, as an hors d'oeuvre, or with the skin removed, wrapped in bread dough, and baked and served as a luncheon dish.

Kolbasi: This Polish sausage comes in many different versions. Some have to be cooked and others are edible as is. It is well spiced and may be used hot or cold, as an hors d'oeuvre, or as an addition to many dishes.

Pepperoni: An Italian sausage, which has been dried and cured and is usually quite spicy, it is a pleasant addition to any cold platter.

Bloodwurst: This has a particular public. If you like it as I do, it is an invaluable item for your larder. It has a rich, full flavor, quite different from that of other sausages. There is also a tongue blood sausage that is delicious-looking on the serving platter because of the mosaic pattern in the meat.

Braunschweiger, Liverwurst, Goose Liver: Three extremely good additions to your list of stores, but definitely more perishable than other sausages. They will keep a week or so if refrigerated. Especially spicy and livery, they have the distinct texture one usually associates with paté. As a matter of fact, beaten with pure cream, a little garlic, cognac, and a few pistachio nuts, they will make a fine imitation paté.

Knockwurst and Frankfurters: Both wonderful for snacks, for grilling, and for a first course. You may keep them in the refrigerator for a week or so, or freeze them indefinitely.

Other Sausages: Some small smoked sausages, packed two in a plastic bag, are now imported from Holland. These may be eaten hot or cold and will keep extremely well for several weeks if refrigerated. There are several sausage varieties, too, which are lightly smoked or cured, such as the Italian mortadella, and the all-time favorite, Bologna, which comes in several thicknesses. From Pennsylvania, there is a Lebanon Bologna with an interesting, slightly sour, smoked flavor. Souse and headcheese, too, with their rather heavy jelly content, make good additions to your list of summer stores. And small pork sausages—the authentic country variety, either smoked or fresh—can be kept in the freezer for summer cooking over the coals. All of these are excellent both indoors and out.

omplementssection5

The harmony—or contrast—of tastes, textures,

and colors is the grand design of gastronomy. A meal should

have the structure of a painting: a center of interest,

perfectly framed in complementary surroundings.

appetizers and hors d'oeuvres

There is no time in the pattern of eating when tidbits and hors d'oeuvres taste quite as good as they do while you are waiting on a terrace or in a garden for a roast to cook on the spit or a chop on the grill.

If you have enough grill space, there are many delicious snacks that may be served from the grill. If there is not enough room for both snacks and a main course, you may entertain with cocktails or wine and serve a whole meal of tiny snacks, a salad, and cheese. This very often is a satisfying experience, especially if the guests can make up their own appetizing combinations and grill their own bits and pieces. If you are entertaining for cocktails, estimate 6 to 8 snacks from the grill per person—and a few extras for those with Gargantuan appetites. Before lunch or dinner, estimate 3 or 4 per person.

teriyaki

People have come to think of teriyaki as anything marinated, laced on a skewer, and broiled. This is not necessarily so, since in Japan, its land of origin, there are many such skewered and grilled dishes, and they go by a number of names. What teriyaki does mean is any meat, fowl, or fish marinated and broiled with a shiny finish or glaze. A good marinade is composed of equal parts of shoyu or soy sauce and sherry, a rather sweet variety. You may add to this chopped ginger, fresh if you can get it, or the candied kind; chopped garlic, and, if you can

find it, chopped Chinese parsley, which is the leaf of the coriander plant. (South of the border it is called cilantro.)

For teriyaki for 4 to 6 persons, you should have 1 cup each of sherry and soy sauce, 2 cloves of garlic, 1 good tablespoon (or more, if you like it very hot) of chopped fresh ginger or chopped candied ginger. You will probably not need any salt for this, since you are using soy sauce. Add 1 or more tablespoons of sugar, since this helps to achieve the desired glaze. If you are using candied ginger, reduce the sugar accordingly. Teriyaki is better marinated for 12 to 18 hours, and should be grilled over a rather brisk fire, very quickly.

Beef teriyaki can be made with thin slices of sirloin, tenderloin, or choice rump cut into pieces about 2 by 4 inches, marinated, laced on bamboo skewers, and broiled. Pork and lamb teriyakis are done in exactly the same way.

sates

Sates are similar to teriyakis but they originate in Southeast Asia and are slightly more pungent. They may be made with lamb, pork, beef, veal, preferably cubed. Prepare a marinade with ⅔ cup soy sauce, 2 tablespoons honey, ⅓ cup olive oil, ⅓ cup lime juice. Sauté 1 cup finely chopped onion and 2 finely chopped garlic cloves in 3 tablespoons olive oil until just tender. Add 1 tablespoon curry, 1 tablespoon chili powder, and 1 teaspoon of freshly ground pepper. Marinate the meat cubes for several hours. Lace 2 or 3 of them on each small skewer and broil over a brisk fire, turning several times and brushing with the marinade. Eat these by themselves or with tiny rolls or tortillas. Have available a bowl of the hot marinade so that your guests can dip the sates in it.

chicken or duck sates

Cut tiny pieces of uncooked chicken (or duck) with a sharp Chinese knife or cleaver. Marinate the pieces for several hours and lace on skewers or grill in a basket-type grill. You may alternate tiny onions, or strips of green pepper, or chunks of pineapple, or even kumquats, if you wish, with the sates. These make for a more glamorous skewer and enhance the taste.

korean sates

Make a marinade by combining 1 crushed clove of garlic, ½ cup of soy sauce, ¼ cup of sesame or peanut oil, and ¼ cup finely chopped green onions. Crush ¼ cup toasted sesame seeds with a bit of salt in a mortar or blender. Do not crush too fine. Dip thin, 1- by 2-inch slices of steak in the sesame seeds, then into the marinade and allow to sit for a few hours. Impale on skewers and broil over the coals, very slowly.

very special sates

Make a marinade by combining 1 cup finely chopped green onions with ¼ cup olive oil. Sauté very gently for 2 or 3 minutes. Add 1 tablespoon curry powder, 1 tablespoon finely chopped mango chutney, 2 teaspoons freshly ground black pepper, and cook for 3 minutes. Add ½ cup soy sauce, 2 tablespoons honey, 2 tablespoons finely chopped parsley, and ½ cup Jamaica rum. Cut 2 pounds pork loin in 1½-inch cubes, or 2 pounds sirloin steak or lamb leg in ½-inch cubes. Place in marinade for several hours. Lace on skewers, 2 or 3 cubes per person, and broil over fairly brisk coals, brushing from time to time with the marinade.

chicken & turkey on skewers

Cubes of chicken or turkey alternated with various taste accents make wonderful eating. If you are using them as hors d'oeuvres, put 2 or 3 bits on each skewer, and let your guests nibble them as they come, hot and tasty, off the grill. Handsome little Japanese skewers of varying lengths can be bought in most cities. Be sure to soak the skewers in water before threading to keep them from charring on the grill.

HERE ARE A FEW COMBINATIONS:

1. Marinate squares of raw chicken or turkey with pineapple chunks in a soy sauce and peanut-oil mixture.
2. Squares of chicken or turkey with pineapple chunks, green pepper, and chunks of ham.
3. Small cubes of chicken or turkey and pitted ripe olives.
4. Cubes of chicken or turkey and tiny marble-sized tomatoes.

grilled goodies with bacon

A wrapping of bacon adds a delectable flavor to almost any grilled hors d'oeuvres. The bacon should be partially cooked before it is wrapped around whatever you are broiling, otherwise it will not be crisp when the appetizer is heated and ready to serve. Here are a few that I have found particularly enjoyable.

Rumaki: This is a standard chicken-liver favorite with all Polynesian restaurants. It can be made many different ways, but I like best to marinate the livers in soy sauce, sometimes with a dash of curry powder, then take a slice of water chestnut for each piece of liver and wrap the two in partially cooked bacon. Skewer with toothpicks and broil over coals until the bacon is crisp and the liver cooked through. These may be prepared in advance, partially cooked in a 375 F. oven and finished off in a broiler. Serve hot mustard and soy-sauce dips with the rumaki if desired.

Chicken Livers, Plain: Sections of chicken liver,

lightly salted and peppered, wrapped in bacon, skewered and broiled, are simple yet tasty.

Calves' Liver: Cubes of calves' liver may be done the same way as chicken livers, as can turkey or duck livers. You might also try brushing the livers with a little Worcestershire sauce or a little English mustard before wrapping in bacon and broiling.

Crabmeat: Chunks of delicate crabmeat may be wrapped in bacon and skewered on bamboo or large metal skewers, and broiled over coals.

Stuffed Shrimp: Large shrimp may be split down the back with scissors, shelled, laced with strips of anchovy through the center, where you have cut out the vein. This, in turn, may be wrapped in bacon, skewered, and grilled for 3 to 5 minutes, or until the shrimp is just cooked and the bacon crisp.

Prunes: Soak for several days 1 to 2 pounds of pitted prunes in sherry or port wine to just cover. When ready to broil, remove and dry on absorbent paper towels. Wrap them in bacon, skewer, and broil till the bacon is crisp and the prunes heated through.

VARIATIONS:

You may stuff the prunes with walnut halves and about 1 teaspoon of cream cheese.

Or you may stuff the prunes with a cube of very sharp Cheddar cheese, or with 2 toasted filberts, or a slice of water chestnut, or a sliver of ham.

For the dishes that follow make a marinade of ½ cup of oil, ¼ cup of sherry, 1 teaspoon each of salt and pepper, and 2 tablespoons of chopped parsley.

Scallops: Proceed as above, marinate, wrap in bacon, thread on skewers, and broil.

Sweetbreads: Blanch and cut sweetbreads in 1-inch cubes. Marinate and grill.

Olives: Unusually good marinated, wrapped in bacon, and grilled.

Dates: Pitted dates, marinated, wrapped in

SEAFOOD LENDS ITSELF TO THE UNUSUAL FOR HORS D'OEUVRES.

bacon, and grilled are most unusual. They may be stuffed with nuts before marinating.

Avocado: Cubes of firm but ripe avocado, marinated, wrapped in bacon, and skewered and grilled are very good. Do not overcook.

Oysters: Marinate oysters, wrap in slices of bacon, thread on skewers, and grill very quickly. These must not be overcooked.

chopped-meat appetizers

Tiny balls of chopped meat or tiny hamburgers, either pan-broiled or broiled in a basket grill, are delicious with most drinks. If broiled, take care to see that they are rare.

tiny hamburgers

Mix 1 pound of chopped lean beef with a teaspoon salt, 2 tablespoons chopped onion, 1 teaspoon ground black pepper, and a dash of Worcestershire sauce. Form into tiny hamburgers, brush with butter, and grill very quickly in basket-type grill or sauté quickly in butter in a large skillet. Serve with tiny rolls or with rounds of salty rye bread.

tiny cheeseburgers

Mix 1 pound chopped round steak with ½ cup grated Cheddar or Swiss cheese, 1 teaspoon salt, 1 teaspoon prepared mustard, ½ teaspoon freshly ground black pepper. Form into tiny burgers and cook in a basket grill. Serve on rolls or toast.

tiny lamburgers with pine nuts

Mix together lightly, 1 pound of ground lamb, ½ cup coarsely chopped pine nuts, and salt and pepper. Shape into tiny burgers and grill.

chickenburgers

Grind the meat of a boned chicken in your meat grinder, using the fine blade. One chicken should yield about 2 to 3 cups. Mix with salt, pepper, a bit of tarragon, and 2 tablespoons of heavy cream to bind it together. Shape into tiny balls and grill, or sauté in melted butter.

tartare toast

Use only the finest cut of beef for this dish. Have it ground, or grind it yourself, using a very fine blade. Mix about 1½ pounds of the beef with a raw egg, salt, pepper, finely chopped raw sweet onion, and 1 tablespoon of capers. Spread it about ¼ to ½ inch thick on slices of fresh hot-buttered toast and cut into triangles or fingers. You will find that this is delicious with a very dry Martini.

corned-beef-hash patties

Here is a new idea for a grilled snack. Form canned or homemade corned-beef hash into little flat cakes, or, if you are going to do them in a pan, little balls. Grill over the fire, brushing them with butter, or sauté them in butter in a pan. Spear with toothpicks and plunge them in a bowl of chopped parsley.

anchoiade

1 pound chopped dried figs
10-12 chopped anchovy fillets
½ cup chopped pine nuts
3-4 cloves garlic
½ cup chopped parsley
Olive oil to moisten

Mix all the ingredients together, split loaves of French bread, and spread with the mixture. Wrap the loaves in foil and heat in the oven. Cut in 1½-inch slices and serve.

seafoods

Seafoods combine admirably with many ingredients to make interesting and unusual appetizers. Try some of the following—and don't be afraid to invent some of your own.

scallops

Alternate with shrimps and/or oysters. Marinate in olive oil flavored with garlic and soy sauce. Broil and then sprinkle lavishly with chopped parsley.

herb-dipped scallops

Dip in melted butter and olive oil to which you have added chopped parsley, chives, and tarragon. Broil.

sesameed scallops

Dip scallops in melted butter, then into slightly crushed sesame seeds, pressing the seeds firmly into the flesh of the scallops. Broil.

giblets

Giblets are a delicacy whose special flavors lend great piquancy to appetizers. Here are two on-the-grill specialties I have always been partial to:

gizzards

Cook for about 1½ hours, or until tender, 2 pounds of chicken gizzards in enough salted water to cover. Cool and cut away the very gristly parts. Marinate the gizzards for 2 hours in 1½ cups white wine, 2 teaspoons dehydrated tarragon, 2 tablespoons finely chopped chives, and 2 tablespoons chopped parsley. Skewer the gizzards, brush with oil, and grill very quickly over coals. Serve with thin slices of French bread.

chicken hearts

Marinate 1 pound of chicken hearts in 1 cup soy sauce, ½ cup sherry, and ½ cup finely chopped onion. Salt and pepper to taste. Skewer the hearts on bamboo or steel skewers, 3 or 4 to each skewer, brush with oil, and grill very quickly over coals, turning several times during the grilling period.

lobster rumaki

Cut lobster into 1½-inch pieces. Make a split in the center of each and insert a thin slice of water chestnut. Brush well with oil and soy sauce. Wrap in partially cooked bacon, and secure with a small skewer or toothpick. Broil until the bacon is crisp.

barbecued lobster

Soak 1½-inch pieces of lobster in your favorite barbecue sauce for several hours. Skewer them and broil quickly over coals.

marinated lobster

Marinate about 15 pieces of lobster, 1½ inches in size, in ½ cup olive oil, ¼ cup lime juice, ¼ cup finely chopped green onion, ¼ cup chopped parsley, and ¼ cup vermouth. Salt and pepper to taste. Skewer the sections and broil quickly over coals. You may vary this by wrapping the marinated lobster in strips of partially cooked bacon before grilling.

shrimp

Shrimp may be treated in exactly the same way as lobster. They may be marinated in any of the above marinades, stuffed with anchovies, water chestnuts, and so forth, and barbecued. A wrapping of bacon may also be added.

appetizers off the grill

When you go into a market today to purchase a ham—whether from your favorite corner grocer, butcher, or the huge emporiums that go by the name of "supermarket"—chances are that you will get one that has been cured by a special chemical process and "tenderized." Most hams today are precooked and do not require the long soaking or boiling that was necessary just a few short years ago. This may be all to the good as far as time and convenience are concerned, but we sacrifice much marvelous texture and flavor. Very rarely now can you find a true country ham, unless you travel about and just happen to find a farmer who cures hams the way his great-grandfather did. Even then, he probably produces just enough for his own family's consumption and it will be next to impossible to get him to part with one. The old-fashioned variety still requires the soaking and boiling necessary to get rid of the huge amount of salt required to preserve the meat in the curing process. Should you be fortunate enough to acquire one, follow the instructions usually printed on the wrapper. If you find a true farm product, be sure to ask the dealer or farmer specifically for directions.

There are other kinds of hams available, some of which are exquisite in flavor, such as the imported Polish, French, Dutch, and Czech precooked and tinned hams. The feeding of pigs in Europe, and the curing of pork, differ greatly from our methods and give each kind a unique flavor. Despite their initial high price, they are a good buy. There is no waste at all; they only need heating through, and can even be served as they come from the can. Other varieties of ham that make wonderful hors d'oeuvres are prosciutto and Westphalian ham, both very similar in appearance, curing method, and flavor. These should be sliced so thin that you can see right through them. Usually, they are served wrapped around various raw or grilled fruits.

ham on the grill

Prepare a ham according to directions on the wrapper, or if it is a precooked ham, merely wipe with a damp cloth and proceed. If you are planning to spit an entire ham, be sure to balance it on the spit carefully, or you will run into difficulties. Allow 20 minutes cooking time per pound. Another way, if you lack a spit and a motor, is to cut the ham into thick steaks and grill them directly. This will save lots of time and give you a texture quite different from that of a whole ham grilled on a spit. Here are a few ways to grill your ham:

Baste with a mixture of Jamaica rum and sherry. Glaze with apricot preserve and Jamaica rum.

Baste with Madeira, red wine, or apple cider.

Baste with bourbon and the juice from canned peaches. Heat the peaches in some reserved juice and bourbon, and serve along with the ham. Any of the above are applicable to ham slices, small ham butts, or shoulders.

canadian bacon

Use any of the above methods and recipes. Canadian bacon makes wonderful and economical eating since there is absolutely no waste. In basting you might even need to add some extra fat.

sausages

There are varieties a-plenty. The good, old-fashioned American link sausage grills beautifully on an outdoor fire, or in a pan. You can get very small ones for wonderful appetizers.

Grill tinned, precooked Vienna sausage.

Serve hot or sweet Italian sausage. Their wonderful anise flavor goes very well with drinks.

Make little, flat, sausage cakes using bulk sausage meat. You can add chopped, fresh basil, or rosemary, or thyme.

Remember that all sausage must be thoroughly cooked, so don't rush because your guests just can't wait for the next batch from the grill.

fish

Thick fish steaks of the firmer-fleshed varieties that have been marinated, grilled, and cut into cubes, make marvelous snacks. The Japanese have grilled fish—whole, in steaks, tiny, large —for thousands of years. Good fish to use in grilling are swordfish, fresh tuna, halibut, and sardines. Different marinades will give you a wide variety of flavors. Remember that these are essentially dry-fleshed fish and the marinades will need the addition of oil for lubrication. Herbs point up the flavors of fish, so use them liberally in the marinades. A much overlooked grill snack is smoked fish. Can you think of anything more delectable than a cube of smoked salmon that has been grilled over coals? Be sure that you get really thick slices if you are going to prepare salmon this way. Also, there exists a marvelous kippered salmon that lends itself to grilling. Smoked eel, white-fish, kippers, even smoked brook trout make excellent snacking out of doors. You might try dunking them as they come off the grill and are speared on toothpicks or bamboo picks. A good dunk for this would be sour cream with chopped chives or scallions.

japanese sardines

Marinate small, finger-sized sardines in soy and ginger. Skewer and grill them, and eat them whole. The bones are so tender that they won't harm you at all. Also try eel, shrimp, scallops, oysters, clams, and squid cut to bite-size and prepared in the same manner.

herbed fish steaks

Grill fish steaks until they are just about ready to come off the grill. Wrap them in half-dry, fresh sage or basil leaves and allow them to smolder for a few minutes. The herbs will impart their flavor to the steaks.

finger sandwiches

Finger sandwiches are not and should not be relegated to the tea table. They have a definite place in the scheme of outdoor dining. If they are right, they go admirably with a drink and should not be overlooked. A young turkey turning on the spit, started ahead of all the other foods, will make wonderful little sandwiches and act as a stopgap until the main dishes make their appearance.

VARIATIONS:

Shell ½ pound of walnuts. Cover the meats with stock, a bay leaf, a few celery leaves, and a slice of onion. Cook for about half an hour, drain, chop fine, and add about ½ teaspoon of salt and a dash of cayenne. Spread on slices of thin, buttered bread and cut into fingers. A beautiful complement to a drink.

Chop either ripe, green, or black olives, or a combination of all these. Mix with mayonnaise, the yolks of 2 hard-boiled eggs, and a few tablespoons of cream. Add a dash of paprika and salt, spread on buttered, thin-sliced bread, and cut into fingers.

Roast green peppers on a free corner of your grill. When the skins have charred, peel and discard them. Chop peppers fine and simmer with a bit of butter in a pan for a few minutes. Do not allow them to change color. Add salt to taste. Spread on hot or cold bread. Spread another slice of bread with cream cheese, combine the slices, and cut into finger sandwiches.

stuffed eggs

Simple to prepare, reliable, and satisfying, stuffed eggs are a pleasant addition to any hors d'oeuvres platter. Here are just a few ways to prepare them for outdoor consumption. After hard-cooking them, cool, shell, and cut into halves—either the long way or through their centers. Scoop out the centers and flavor in any of the following ways:

With Mayonnaise: Use about 2 tablespoons of mayonnaise for 6 mashed yolks. Add ½ teaspoon of mustard, 1 teaspoon of chopped chives, and 1 tablespoon of finely chopped parsley. Correct the seasoning. Heap into the whites and garnish with paprika. Chill.

With Anchovy Paste: 2 tablespoons of the paste to 6 yolks gives a good flavor. Add ½ teaspoon of onion juice and just a dash of lemon juice.

With Smoked Ham Paté: Use 1½ tablespoons Smithfield ham spread, mashed and moistened with mayonnaise, for 6 yolks. Decorate with chopped chive.

vegetable and casserole dishes

crudités

Either you love or you hate raw vegetables. I find they are as pleasant a munchable as one can possibly have in summer. By all means serve them often. I used to feel that a variety of dips was necessary for complete enjoyment of them, but now I find that either a hot dip, or a simple garlic-and-anchovy-flavored mayonnaise—homemade, of course—is quite sufficient. A well-seasoned French dressing is also very good. Other than these, nothing seems quite so good with most vegetables as coarse salt and freshly ground pepper. To be served as appetizers, the vegetables must be well washed, drained, and chilled. They should not be watery, nor should they be dry. Perhaps the best way to serve them is stacked in a large bowl of ice. Don't bring them out of the refrigerator all at once. Wrap them in wet towels and save some for second helpings. This way you won't have tired vegetables in the bowl or on your plate.

which vegetables to serve

Of the entire list of possibilities, there are probably only two or three that are not actually better served raw than cooked. Some of the very good ones are asparagus, tiny artichoke hearts, celery, fennel, carrots, cauliflower, Brussels sprouts, cucumber, Belgian endive, turnips, mushrooms, chicory, water cress, tiny tomatoes, scallions, all types of radishes, and spinach leaves. One thing is certain—celery, radishes, onions and scallions, asparagus, carrot sticks, fennel, are much better blanched in ice water for several hours. They curl and develop exquisite crispness.

potatoes baked in coals

Carefully scrub large baking potatoes and bury in the coals for 45 minutes or 1 hour, depending on size. When they can be easily pierced with a fork, they are done. Disregard the blackness of the skin as the inside will be wonderfully tender and flaky. Use lots of sweet butter.

rosin potatoes

A most wonderful outdoor way to prepare potatoes. Use a large and heavy kettle in which you melt rosin to a depth of 5 or 6 inches. When it is boiling, drop in your potatoes. They should take about 20 minutes or so to cook. Have a pile of old newspapers ready. Plop the potato in the center of a page and quickly wrap it, twisting the ends to enfold it completely. Cut through the newspaper and potato, and treat it exactly as you would a baked potato.

scalloped potatoes

2 #2 cans of potatoes
½ cup grated Parmesan cheese
½ teaspoon salt
Pepper
2 cups cream sauce
3 cups light cream
Buttered crumbs

Here is a timesaver. Slice the potatoes, mix lightly with the cheese (reserving a few tablespoonfuls). Add the salt, pepper, and the cream sauce and light cream, which have been combined. Pour into a casserole and top with buttered crumbs. Bake at 375 F. for 30 minutes. Just before taking from the oven, sprinkle the remaining cheese over the top, let it melt, and then serve.

german fried potatoes

Potatoes prepared this way just seem to be ideal outdoors. Peel and slice raw potatoes ⅛ of an inch thick, 1 good-sized potato to each person. In a large skillet heat ¼ cup of butter (or goose, chicken, or bacon fat, or lard), for each 4 potatoes, and cook over a brisk fire. Turn frequently with a wide spatula, so that

each slice comes into contact with the fat and has an opportunity to brown and become crisp. Season with salt and pepper.

potatoes fried in kidney suet

Chop beef kidney suet and try it out in a heavy skillet, being careful not to let it smoke or burn. Fry potatoes as above, carefully mixing in the little bits of crispy fat. You can do the same with bacon or chicken fat. If you use the latter be sure to add some little pieces of chicken skin for extra flavor.

lyonnaise potatoes

This wonderful way of cooking potatoes is a favorite accompaniment to beefsteak. Sauté a large sliced onion in about ⅓ cup of butter until it just begins to take on a golden color. Add 5 or 6 sliced raw potatoes and cook them until they are brown and tender. Sprinkle with ½ cup chopped parsley, and salt and freshly ground black pepper.

hashed-brown potatoes

Boil potatoes and cut them into small cubes. Sauté them in butter or beef fat, gently pressing them down into the pan with a wide spatula so they form a cake and get brown and crusty. Carefully turn them out on a flat plate with the crust on top. To do this, tip the pan gently and loosen the potatoes with the spatula. Then with a quick flip get them over and out. Season with salt and pepper to your taste.

home-fried potatoes

Boil potatoes in their jackets. Peel and slice them medium thin. Melt butter in a skillet and carefully lay in the potato slices. Sauté them slowly, turning with a spatula as they cook until they are delicately browned and crisp around the edges. Be careful not to break the slices as you turn them. Salt and pepper to taste.

roesti potatoes

Grate 4 good-sized raw potatoes. Season, form into patties, and sauté in ¼ cup of fat until the bottom is brown. Turn like a pancake to brown the other side.

potatoes hashed in cream

This is one of the really delicious and rich-tasting ways to cook potatoes. Boil potatoes and cut them into cubes. Sauté them in butter or beef fat only until they are heated through and golden. Sprinkle with a very small amount of flour, salt and pepper. Slowly pour in heavy cream to cover the bottom of the pan. Let the potatoes cook gently in the cream, watching to see that they do not scorch. Lots of paprika with this.

curried, creamed potatoes

Follow the procedure for potatoes hashed in cream, adding curry powder to your taste. Omit the paprika.

truffled potatoes

Peel medium-sized potatoes and slice—not too thinly. Wash them well, dry on paper towels, and sauté slowly in goose fat or butter. In another and smaller pan, sauté sliced truffles in butter. You will have to use canned truffles since fresh ones are practically unobtainable in this country. When the potatoes are golden and crisp, combine with the truffles. Salt and pepper sparingly, so as not to intrude on the wonderful flavor of the truffles. This is one of the simplest and yet the most elegant potato dishes known.

potatoes anna

Use a large shallow earthenware dish or, lacking this, a pie tin. Butter the dish well. Peel 4 medium potatoes and slice them quite thin. Arrange a layer of the slices on the bottom of the dish in a pattern—in a spiral if the dish is round, in rows if it is square or rectangular. In any case, be sure the pieces overlap. Season with salt and freshly ground pepper, and dot with butter. Repeat these layers until all the slices are used. Cover the top layer very liberally with butter. Bake in a 400 F. oven for 30 to 40 minutes, or until the potatoes are tender when tested with a fork or toothpick. Very carefully turn the baking dish upside down on a platter or large flat plate, so the potatoes come out in one piece, crusty side up.

galette potatoes

These potatoes are made in exactly the same way as Potatoes Anna, with the exception that they are cooked on top of the stove rather than in the oven. Peel and slice the potatoes, wash well to remove the excess starch, and arrange them in a spiral design in a skillet in which you have melted a good quantity of sweet butter. Cover and cook slowly until they are cooked through. Remove cover and increase heat for 3 or 4 minutes, then very carefully turn potatoes out on a serving platter.

potatoes dauphinois

Scald 3 cups milk and allow to stand until half-cooled. Peel and slice 4 pounds potatoes and add to milk. Mix in 1 egg, salt, pepper, and nutmeg. Grate ½ pound of Switzerland Swiss cheese and add half of it to the mixture. Rub an earthenware baking dish with garlic and butter it very well. Pour the potato mixture into this dish, dot with additional butter, and sprinkle with the remaining cheese. Bake in a 350 F. oven for about 1 hour, or until the potatoes are well cooked. This will serve 8.

richest-possible potatoes

Choose large and beautiful baking potatoes. Bake them in the usual way and scoop out the insides. Add a more than generous amount of sweet butter, salt, and freshly ground pepper. In a large skillet, melt some more butter and

add the potatoes, to which you now add still more butter and heavy cream. Heat them through, adding bits of butter and more cream so that you achieve an unbelievably rich and beautiful potato dish. Throw your calorie counter in the trash can and enjoy these stunning potatoes.

If your thrifty soul cannot bear to discard the potato skins, they may be buttered and seasoned with salt and Tabasco and crisped on a grill or in a hot oven. Serve as hors d'oeuvres.

potatoes savoyard

1 large celery root or 2 small ones, sliced
3 pounds potatoes
½ pound grated Swiss cheese
6 smoked sausages, sliced (optional)
⅔ cup butter
½ cup beef or chicken stock
Salt and pepper

Peel the potatoes and celery root and cut them into even, ⅛-inch slices. Butter an earthenware baking dish well and lay into it alternate layers of potato, sausage, cheese, and celery root, topping all with a layer of cheese. Dot with the rest of the butter and pour the stock over all. Bake in a 325 F. oven for approximately 1½ hours, or until the potatoes are tender.

elena's rice with green chilis and sour cream

1 cup raw rice
½ pound Jack cheese
2 cups sour cream
1 six-ounce can peeled green chili peppers
Salt, butter
½ cup grated cheese (optional)

Cook rice in your usual manner. (You may, if you prefer, use quick-cooking rice.) Combine it with the sour cream and salt to taste. Arrange half of the mixture in the bottom of a casserole and place on it cubes of Jack cheese wrapped in strips of the green chilis. Top with the remaining rice and dot with butter. Additional cheese can be grated over it. Heat for about 30 minutes in a 350 F. oven and bring to the table.

risotto milanese

1 cup raw long-grain rice
1 small onion
¼ cup butter
2 cups bouillon or stock, boiling hot
Pinch saffron
½ cup raw button mushrooms
1 seeded, peeled, chopped tomato
Sautéed chopped chicken livers
and/or tiny shreds of ham
Salt and pepper
Thyme or oregano
Butter

Rub the rice in a Turkish towel. Chop the onion very fine and let it get just golden in the butter, then add the rice and stir with a wooden spoon only until it begins to take on color. Add the boiling bouillon, saffron, mushrooms, tomato, and the livers and/or shredded ham. Salt and pepper to taste and add a pinch of thyme or oregano. Cover and put in a 350 F. oven for about 15 minutes, or until the liquid has been absorbed and the rice is tender. Before serving, add an egg-sized piece of butter.

rice casserole with livers

This is essentially a Risotto Milanese with the addition of chicken livers that have been sautéed in butter and added at the last moment before serving.

chinese fried rice

2 cups of cooked rice
4 strips of bacon, or an equal amount of ham
3 eggs
Soy sauce, pepper

Cut the bacon (or ham) into small bits and fry. Should the ham be very lean use an additional bit of bacon fat or oil. When crisp, remove it from the pan and add the rice. Fry for just a little while until it is lightly colored and hot through. Make a well in the center and stir in the eggs and meat bits, lightly beaten together. Bit by bit, as the eggs begin to set, incorporate the mixture into the rice. Sprinkle soy sauce over the rice and some black pepper.

green rice

Mince ½ cup each of parsley and chopped scallions and combine with ¼ cup melted butter and 4 cups of cooked rice. You may use in addition any of the following green herbs: chives, tarragon, marjoram, or basil. This goes exceptionally well with lamb, mutton, or kidneys.

pilaff

1 cup raw long-grain rice
1 small onion
¼ cup butter
2 cups bouillon or stock
Salt and pepper
Thyme or oregano
Butter

After washing the rice in cold water, rub it quite dry in a towel. Chop the onion very fine and brown it lightly in the butter. Add the rice. Fry it gently, stirring all the while until it begins to color. Add the stock, salt and pepper to taste, and a pinch of thyme or oregano. Cover and place in a moderate oven, 350 F., for about 15 or 20 minutes, or until the liquid has been absorbed and the rice is tender. Serve with additional butter on top.

persian rice

Parboil about 1½ cups of rice in 2½ cups of water until just tender. Wash well under running water in a sieve. Let it drain well. In the bottom of a heavy pot with a close-fitting lid, melt almost ¼ pound of butter. Start sprinkling the rice by handfuls, covering the bottom and building up a cone. Do not pack the rice or sprinkle too quickly. Keep the flame brisk for about 10 or 15 minutes to produce a crust. Melt another 4 tablespoons of butter and add ¼ cup water and a pinch of saffron. Sprinkle this over the cone, but do not disturb its formation. Wrap a heavy Turkish towel over the lid and cover the pot. Steam for about 45 minutes. The aroma is unbelievable—and so is the flavor.

curried rice

A variation of the rice pilaff. After you have browned the rice in butter, add curry powder, sauté a few moments more, then add broth.

rice with pine nuts and parsley

Make a pilaff as usual, but add half a cup of pine nuts and ¼ cup of chopped parsley.

indian rice

Boil rice in a large quantity of water, but do not overcook it. Drain well, place in a sieve or colander over boiling water, add ½ cup of blanched, halved almonds or peanuts, and an equal amount of currants or raisins. Cover lightly with a heavy towel and let steam for about 30 minutes, or until the rice is dry and fluffy. Watch the water in the pot and replenish if it boils away.

wild rice

This is not truly rice, but a wild grain the Indians gather by hand, which accounts for its exorbitant price. If cooked in the manner you use for rice, it usually results in a soggy mess which everybody exclaims over because it would be criminal to say that such an expensive mistake has occurred. Try this way instead. Boil enough water to cover rice with. Let stand for 5 minutes or so. Pour off and repeat the process until the rice is tender, but not mushy. You might add sweet butter and salt.

risi pisi

Cook 1½ cups of rice in your favorite way. Meanwhile, heat 2 cans of very small French peas in their own juice, drain, and add ½ cup or more of melted butter. Combine and toss the peas and rice well, sprinkle with a bit of finely chopped parsley, and serve.

kasha

1 cup of buckwheat groats
1 egg
2 cups of stock or broth
4 to 6 tablespoons of butter
Salt

Be sure to use a heavy skillet with a tight-fitting lid. Into this skillet put the groats and a raw egg. Stir over a very low flame until the groats are coated with the egg and the mixture is quite dry. Do this without burning. Add the stock or broth and salt to taste, cover and let simmer very gently for about 30 minutes, or until the groats are cooked and the broth is absorbed. Mix with the butter and serve.

barley with mushrooms

1 cup of pearl barley
1 large onion
½ pound of mushrooms
4 to 5 tablespoons of butter
2 cups of meat or chicken broth

Peel and chop the onion. With a damp cloth wipe the mushrooms and slice them. Melt the butter, and sauté the onion and mushrooms until soft. Add the barley and lightly brown it. Pour this mixture into a buttered casserole. Be sure to taste the broth for seasoning before you pour it over the barley. Add salt and pepper if needed. Pour 1 cup of liquid over the barley in the casserole and cover. Bake in a 350 F. oven for ½ hour and then uncover and add the second cup of broth. Continue baking until the liquid is absorbed and the barley is done. In place of chicken or meat broth, you may also make your own broth, using 3 bouillon cubes to 2 cups of boiling water.

VARIATIONS:

While you are baking the barley take an additional half-pound of whole mushrooms and sauté them in butter. Let them cook down until they are very rich, almost black. Mix with plenty of whole, toasted almonds and spread this mixture over the top just before serving. This dish goes particularly well with poultry and game, I find.

Cook 1 pound of gizzards until tender in water, salt and pepper, and an herb of your choice. Use the broth to finish the casserole after the preliminary steps. Slice the gizzards and mix into the barley.

couscous

One should really have a couscousière to make a good couscous, but a colander with fine holes that can fit over a large kettle will do. Couscous is two things: It is a dish originating in North Africa and it is also the name of a semolina that goes into the dish. It is made of very hard wheat and must be washed and squeezed well to remove all excess water, so it does not lump. This is placed in the top of the couscousière and hung over the mutton broth that is cooking below it. For the mutton broth:

2 pounds shoulder of lamb or mutton,
cut into cubes
3 large brown onions, diced
6-8 large tomatoes, peeled, seeded,
and quartered
1½ pounds zucchini, split and
cut into 1½-inch lengths
4 tablespoons olive oil
1 pound chick peas (The tinned variety;
dried peas take days to reconstitute)
4 carrots, sliced
4 to 5 turnips, diced
3 sweet green or red peppers
2 very hot peppers
Salt and pepper

Brown the lamb in the olive oil very quickly. Do not attempt to cook it at this stage. Add the onions and let them sauté a few minutes to get tender, then add the tomatoes and the zucchini. Cover with water and bring to a boil. Add the chick peas and let the mixture simmer very gently. Salt and pepper to taste. About 1 hour before you plan to serve, add the turnips, carrots, peppers (sweet and hot). Go easy on the last, since the sauce served with the dish is fiery. The sauce is as follows: Ground black pepper, ground coriander, oil and cayenne pepper, all blended with a little hot water.

Serve the broth in a gravy bowl for ladling over the couscous. Serve the hot sauce separately, as well—and caution your guests. It's powerful. Couscous is the traditional North African accompaniment to lamb shish kebabs and to poached chicken.

polenta

1½ cups of corn meal
3 cups of water
1 teaspoon salt

Bring the water and salt to a boil in a very heavy saucepan. Very slowly, without letting the boiling cease, pour in the corn meal. Stir with a wooden spoon so that the meal does not lump. Continue cooking and stirring until it is quite thick and smooth. Line a strainer or colander with cloth and pour the mix into it. Place over simmering water, covered, and let steam for 3 hours, or until the corn meal has become a firm loaf. Serve it cut into slices, with plenty of melted butter, salt and pepper, and, if you like, grated Parmesan cheese. This will serve 4.

VARIATIONS:

Polenta is delicious prepared as above and served with any of the many sauces that are used with spaghetti or, if you prefer, a cheese sauce. Any leftover polenta can be allowed to cool, then cut into slices and gently fried in butter or oil. Serve with grated cheese or sauce.

beans bretonne

Cook 2 cups of soaked or quick-cooking white pea beans with a bay leaf, an onion stuck with 2 cloves, salt and pepper, and a clove of garlic in water to cover. Halfway through the cooking, add ¼ cup tomato purée to the beans. Continue to cook slowly until the beans are tender but not mushy, and the liquid has thickened. Mix them with the pan juices of any roast they are to accompany. Add ½ cup chopped parsley and serve with the meat.

baked beans—but not new england

Soak a pound of pea or marrow beans overnight. In the morning, drain them, recover them with salted water, and bring to a boil. Lower the flame and let simmer until the beans are tender but not mushy. Add a bay leaf and an onion stuck with 2 cloves. Drain and save the water. In a large casserole place a layer of beans and cover with thin slices of salt pork and sliced onion. Now another layer of beans sprinkled with dry mustard. Now a layer of garlic sausage, salami, or summer sausage, another layer of sliced onions, more dry mustard, and just a bare sprinkling of brown sugar. Finally, a layer of beans which is topped with slices of salt pork. Now pour in the liquid from the beans and cook in the oven at 300 F. for 2 or 3 hours. If the beans dry out, add more water.

pinto beans

Soak 1 pint pinto beans overnight. Drain and cover with fresh water, add salt, garlic, an onion stuck with cloves, and ½ pound salt pork. Cook until the beans are tender. Drain, cook juice down to ½ original volume, and add it to beans. Correct seasoning.

beans and rice caribbean

Cook beans according to the pinto-bean recipe, and put on top of them a mound of rice which has been cooked fluffy and dry.

black beans with rum

Soak 1 pint beans overnight, drain, and cover with water and salt. Add a piece of salt pork, a bay leaf, an onion stuck with cloves, and cook until the beans are tender. Drain whatever liquid remains, add ⅓ cup of Jamaica rum, and serve with sour cream.

cognac beans

1 pound of pea beans
1 clove of garlic
1 onion
2 cloves
Bay leaf
Thyme
1 small onion, chopped
¼ cup butter
2 cups tomato purée
¼ cup minced parsley
2 teaspoons of salt
⅓ cup cognac

These beans seem to be the perfect mate for a lamb or mutton dish, or any grilled meat. Soak the beans in water to cover (or use the quick-cooking variety and follow directions to tenderize). Add garlic, the onion stuck with cloves, bay leaf, and, if you have it, a sprig of fresh thyme. If not, a pinch of dried. Simmer until just tender, drain, and reserve the liquid. Sauté the onion in butter until it is golden, add the tomato purée, parsley, salt, cognac, and 1 cup of the bean liquid. Continue simmering this mixture for 30 minutes, add to the beans, adjust the seasoning, and reheat in a casserole before you bring it to the table. This serves 8 people.

frijoles

1 pound pinto beans
Salt
½ cup lard or bacon fat

Possibly the favorite dish, not only of the Mexican, but of all of us who are aficionados of Mexican food. Frijoles seem to go well with roast pork, steaks, hamburgers, and just about any kind of grilled food. Be sure to use the Mexican variety of pink or red beans, cover them with warm water, and cook at a simmer until they are very tender, adding salt to the pot toward the end of the cooking. To achieve the true Mexican flavor, melt lard or bacon fat in an earthenware casserole, or *cazuela,* or a large and heavy skillet. Mash a few of the beans in the fat, add some liquid and more beans, mashing as you go, until you have used all the beans. Cook them to the consistency you prefer, stirring all the while. They should be somewhere between dry and moist, but not too soupy.

frijoles refritos

Melt more lard, ½ cup for each cup of frijoles cooked as above, and add the beans, cooking and stirring until the beans are very hot, the lard is absorbed, and the edges are crisp.

tipsy kidney beans

2 pounds kidney beans
1 onion, sliced
1 bay leaf
Sprig of thyme
2 stalks celery
Parsley
Ham bone or ¼ cup diced salt pork
or ¼ cup olive oil or bacon fat
Salt
Dash of Tabasco
Beurre manié
½ cup Jamaica rum
Sour cream

As the name indicates, this bean dish is prepared with spirits. Soak the beans overnight. Add additional water to cover, the onion and bay leaf, a sprig of thyme, the celery, and some parsley. Should you have a ham bone, add it. Failing that, use salt pork, olive oil, or bacon fat. Simmer gently until the beans are tender, add salt to taste and a dash of Tabasco. Drain the beans, saving the liquid, and thicken it with the beurre manié (butter and flour kneaded together). Place the beans in a casserole, discarding vegetables used for seasoning. Add rum to the liquid and pour over the beans. Bake beans in a 350 F. oven until they are very well heated. Serve very hot with ice-cold sour cream. You may vary this by topping with grated cheese and strips of bacon.

garbanzos (chick peas)

Use the precooked, canned variety for this or any other dish calling for garbanzos or chick peas, or you will find yourself spending a good day and a half just getting them to the tender stage. Drain them well and set them aside. In a skillet, fry in olive oil 1 good-sized (or 2 small) green peppers which you have seeded and cut into strips. When they are tender, add salt and pepper and the drained garbanzos. Stir all together, being sure to coat the beans with the oil. Just before you are ready to serve them, add 3 tablespoons of wine vinegar.

sautéed lentils

2 cups quick-cooking lentils
Salt
6 or 8 strips bacon
8 green onions, finely chopped
Fine-chopped parsley
Paprika

Place the lentils in a saucepan with water to cover and bring to a boil. Add 1 teaspoon salt. The moment the lentils begin to boil, reduce the heat so that they barely simmer. Be careful that the lentils remain whole and do not get mushy. Drain them. Chop the bacon and fry slowly. When the fat is melted, add the onions. Do not overcook them to the point of wilting. Add the lentils, parsley, salt to taste, and paprika. Mix well, being careful not to crush the lentils. Place a cover on the pan and cook for another 15 to 20 minutes on a very low flame. Lentils go well with a crisp salad or any dish providing a contrasting texture.

ONIONS, BY AUGUSTE RENOIR, STERLING AND FRANCINE CLARK ART INSTITUTE.

lentil casserole

2 cups of lentils
Pinch of salt
1 onion stuck with cloves
Bay leaf
4 to 6 knockwurst
Butter or bacon fat
Bacon strips
Chopped parsley

Pick over the lentils for any stones or twigs. Soak overnight in water to cover. Or you may find that the "quick-cooking" variety will serve you better if you are short of time. In either case, once the lentils have been tenderized, cover them with fresh water, add a bay leaf and an onion stuck with 2 cloves, and a pinch of salt. Bring this to a boil, lower the flame, and simmer until the lentils are barely tender. Drain and save the liquid. Throw away the onion. Cut the knockwurst in half, lengthwise, and sauté in butter or bacon fat until it is brown on both sides. Make layers in a large casserole of the lentils, the knockwurst, more lentils, etc., finishing with lentils. Pour the liquid over all and bake in a 350 F. oven for about 45 minutes. Cover the top of the casserole with strips of bacon, sprinkle with parsley, and return to the oven until the bacon is crisp.

baked hominy

2 cups hominy grits
¼ cup butter
3 eggs, very well beaten
Salt and pepper
1 cup grated cheese (optional)

Cook the grits as instructed on the box. Cool them slightly. Add the butter and eggs. After seasoning with salt and pepper, pour them into a very well-buttered casserole, being sure to dot the top with additional butter. Place in a 400 F. oven and bake until the top is brown and crispy. If you choose, you may combine the cheese with the hominy before placing in the casserole.

corn pudding

4 cups corn (about 8 large ears)
or 2 cans whole-kernel corn (drained)
3 tablespoons butter
2 tablespoons flour
3 cups milk
Salt and pepper
4 eggs, separated

A dish that traces its ancestry right back to the time of the Pilgrims and possesses a heartiness that goes well with pork, chicken, or game dishes.

of butter and bake in a 400 F. oven for 10 minutes. Then reduce the heat and bake for another 25 to 30 minutes, or until the custard is set. Serve hot, in wedges, as you would a pie. For best results chill crust for 30 minutes.

corn fondue

In an earthenware casserole which you have rubbed with a cut clove of garlic, place 2 cans of drained corn, 1 cup of sliced ripe olives, ¾ cup sliced Gruyère cheese, salt and pepper. Cover with cream and sprinkle sesame seed on top. Bake in a 350 F. oven for 20 to 30 minutes.

mexican corn

In 4 tablespoons of olive oil or butter, or a combination of both, sauté 1 large or 2 small green peppers which have been diced small. Add 2 cups of corn kernels, finely cut pimientos, and a bit of chopped onion. Cook for 5 or 6 minutes, stirring all the while, so that the vegetables are thoroughly mixed. Just before serving, add a little finely chopped parsley.

corn relish

1 cup whole kernel corn (canned or fresh)
2 tablespoons diced green pepper
1 tablespoon chopped pimiento
2 tablespoons grated onion
½ cup finely chopped celery
1 teaspoon salt
½ teaspoon black pepper
½ teaspoon dry mustard
4 tablespoons olive oil
1 tablespoon wine vinegar
A few tarragon leaves

If you are going to use fresh corn, cook 3 ears in enough cold water to cover until it boils. Allow to boil for 1 minute. Do not overcook. Cool and scrape the ears with a very sharp knife. Combine corn with green pepper, pimiento, celery, onion, salt, pepper, mustard, olive oil, and wine vinegar, in which you have soaked the tar-

Scrape the corn from the cobs with a sharp knife. Make a cream sauce with the butter, flour, and milk. Stir over moderate heat until it thickens slightly. Combine with the corn. Add salt and pepper to taste, and remove from the heat. Add the egg yolks, which have been beaten slightly. Do this gently so that the eggs do not curdle. Cool slightly and fold in the whites, which have been beaten stiff. Pour the mixture into a well-buttered soufflé or baking dish, set into another pan filled halfway with hot water, and bake at 325 F. until the custard is set—usually about 1 hour. This will serve 8.

corn quiche

Prepare a pie crust and line a pie pan with it. Drain a can of Niblet corn and cover crust with the kernels. Mix together 2 cups of rich milk—or light cream, if you wish—and 3 eggs, a pinch of salt, and a small grating of nutmeg. Lay thin slices of Swiss cheese over the corn and pour the milk and egg over this. Dot with bits

ragon leaves. Blend the mixture well and let it stand for a few hours to fuse the flavors.

eggplant and tomato casserole

1½ pounds of eggplant
1 large onion (or 2 medium)
2 medium-sized fresh tomatoes
Flour
Salt and pepper
Olive oil, or oil and butter mixed
1 teaspoon basil
½ cup fine, toasted bread crumbs
½ cup of grated Parmesan cheese

Peel and cut the eggplant and tomatoes into half-inch slices. Peel the onion and slice somewhat thinner. Dip the eggplant into seasoned flour and sauté quickly in the oil, or oil-and-butter mixture, until lightly browned on both sides. Do the same with the onion slices. Do not attempt to cook these vegetables through. Oil a casserole and make alternate layers of the eggplant, onion, and tomatoes. Season with salt, pepper, and a pinch of basil. Repeat until all the vegetables are used. Sprinkle with the bread crumbs and cheese, mix, and pour the fat from the skillet over the top. Should it seem too dry, add more oil or butter. Bake in a 350 F. oven for about 30 to 45 minutes or until it is nicely browned on top and cooked tender.

ratatouille

2 cloves garlic
1 medium eggplant
2 large onions
2 zucchini
2 green peppers
3 ripe tomatoes
¼ cup olive oil
Salt and pepper

Heat the olive oil in a large skillet. Add the garlic, chopped, and the onions which have been finely sliced. Sauté until the onion is soft. Add washed and sliced zucchini, unpeeled; peeled and sliced eggplant; seeded and sliced green peppers, all lightly floured. Cover and simmer for about 1 hour. Peel, chop and add the tomatoes. Add salt and pepper and, if you like, a little basil or oregano. Cover and cook until the mixture thickens. This dish can be served hot or cold and is delicious either way.

succotash in casserole

Use equal amounts of freshly cooked lima beans, corn kernels, and freshly cooked snap beans. Put them into a casserole or baking dish. Make a sauce Mornay. Pour this over the vegetables and sprinkle with buttered crumbs and grated Parmesan cheese. Bake in a hot oven, 400 F., until heated through.

curried peas and beans

Cook 1 package each of frozen string beans and peas until tender. Do not overcook. Drain and combine the vegetables in a casserole with minced and sautéed onion, 1 teaspoon curry, 2 cups of light cream and 3 eggs beaten together, and salt and pepper. Bake in a 350 F. oven for 25 to 30 minutes.

kadjemoula

2 pounds cubed chuck beef
2 pounds cubed lamb shoulder
3 tablespoons butter or olive oil
Flour
1 teaspoon salt
½ teaspoon freshly ground black pepper
¼ teaspoon cinnamon
¼ teaspoon ginger
2 medium onions, peeled and sliced
3 cloves garlic, peeled and chopped
4 carrots, peeled and quartered
2 small turnips, peeled and diced
⅔ cup dried apricots
⅔ cup dried, pitted prunes
2 cups meat broth
Quince preserve or quince paste

Cut the lamb and beef into 1½-inch cubes and flour very lightly. Heat the butter or oil in a large kettle and brown the meat cubes on all sides. Sprinkle the meat with the salt, pepper, cinnamon and ginger, and add the vegetables and dried fruits. Add meat broth to cover and bring to a boil. Lower the heat, cover the kettle, and simmer gently for about 2 hours. Remove the stew to a hot plate and surround it with steamed rice. Garnish, if you wish, with quince preserves or slices of quince paste. Serves 6 to 8. This is a favorite North African dish.

green onion tart

9-inch pastry shell
1 egg yolk, beaten
3 cups chopped green onions
¼ cup butter
2 cups light cream
4 eggs, slightly beaten
Basil
Salt and pepper

Make a rich pastry and line a 9-inch pie pan, being sure to make a fancy edge, and brush the entire crust with egg yolk. Bake this in a hot, 450 F. oven for no more than 5 minutes. Place another pie tin into the one containing the pastry, reduce the heat to 300 F. and bake until the pastry is slightly brown. Sauté the onions in butter until they are soft, being sure to include some of the green part. Put them on the bottom of the partially baked shell. Scald the cream and mix with the slightly beaten eggs, salt, pepper, and basil. Pour this over the onions and place in a 350 F. oven until the custard is set and beautifully browned. You may dot the top with bits of butter before putting it in the oven.

mushroom pie

Follow the directions for the green onion tart, substituting sliced mushrooms, which you sauté in butter until nicely colored. You may vary the herbs, if you wish—for instance, substituting tarragon for basil.

spinach and mushroom pie

Cook 1 pound of washed spinach in just the water clinging to it, with 2 tablespoons of olive oil, a crushed garlic clove, and salt and pepper. In another pan gently sauté sliced mushrooms. Follow the same procedure as for the green onion tart.

leek tart

Rich biscuit dough
2 cups sliced leeks
4 tablespoons butter
Salt and pepper
Oregano
5 eggs, slightly beaten
1 cup light cream

Use either a prepared biscuit mix and make according to the directions on the box, or use your favorite recipe. Press this into a well-greased, 9-inch pie pan and flute the edges. In a sauté pan, cook the leeks slowly in butter until they take on a golden hue. Sprinkle with salt and pepper, and a bit of oregano. Mix the eggs with the light cream and a bit more salt and pepper. Pour this over the leeks, which you have arranged in the pie shell, and bake in a 400 F. oven until the custard is set and the crust is brown.

baked onions

Use medium-sized Bermuda or Spanish onions, one for each person. Place them in a buttered casserole that you can cover tightly. Add salt and pepper to taste. Now pour in beef bouillon or stock to a depth of ¼ inch. Dot the tops of the onions with butter and cover the casserole tightly, using a sheet of aluminum foil if necessary. Place in a 350 F. oven and bake for about 1 hour, or until the onions are tender. Remove the cover and sprinkle the tops with grated cheese—American, Romano, Parmesan, or any other sharp variety. Place back in the oven or under the broiler until the cheese melts and becomes slightly brown.

baked onions #2

Select medium-sized, perfect onions, wash and dry them, put them unpeeled into a preheated 375 F. oven, and let them bake for a minimum of 1 hour. Longer is even better. They may go into an oven with a roast and be served with it. When they are finished, simply take off the outer skins and serve. This is a simple way to serve a lowly, but wonderful, vegetable.

broiled onions

These are exceptionally good with steaks and hamburger. Be sure to use the large, sweet Bermuda variety. Half of one onion usually suffices for each person. Cut off the ends to form a base, peel off the outer layer of dried skin, and cut the onion into ¼-inch slices. Place on a greased broiling rack. Season with salt and freshly ground pepper, and be sure to brush well with melted butter. Broil until golden. Do not overcook. They will be slightly crisp and have a wonderful crunchy quality.

casserole of yellow turnips and mushrooms

Melt about 4 tablespoons of butter in a pan and add a small, finely chopped onion, and a tablespoon of chopped parsley. Let this cook slowly for a few minutes to soften it and give it color. Add ½ pound of mushrooms very finely sliced and cook slowly until all the moisture has evaporated. Add salt and pepper to taste. Combine this with twice its volume of cooked and mashed yellow turnip. Sprinkle with breadcrumbs, dot with butter, and put into a 350 F. oven for about 20 minutes.

tomato casserole

Slice peeled ripe tomatoes and arrange them in layers in a well-buttered casserole. In between each layer sprinkle a mixture of bread crumbs, chopped parsley, and garlic and fresh basil. Reserve enough of this mixture to cover the last layer. Dot with butter and bake for 30 minutes in a 375 F. oven.

string beans

Be sure to buy fresh young beans, or don't bother to cook them at all. The older the beans the tougher and less flavorful they are and the less they are worth the effort of cooking them. Wash them briefly in cold water and snap off the ends. These days you will have to look far to find a variety that still has strings. However, remove them if they are present. Cut or snap the beans into 1-inch lengths, or, if they are really young beans, leave them whole. Cover with the barest amount of water and salt; cook them covered until they are done but still retain their crispness. Nothing is more horrible than mushy, falling-apart string beans. They can be served with melted butter, and salt and pepper. At the last moment add about 1 teaspoon of rosemary, mix well.

VARIATION:

Cook 1½ pounds of beans in salted water as above. Meanwhile, in a large skillet sauté ½ pound of sliced mushrooms in butter. When the beans are done, drain them, and add to the mushrooms. Add 3 or 4 tablespoons of chopped parsley, salt and pepper to taste, and 1 tablespoon of chopped chives. Combine and mix well, sprinkle with lemon juice, and serve.

string beans amandine

Melt 6 tablespoons of sweet butter in a saucepan. Add ½ cup slivered almonds and allow them to take on a golden color very slowly. Add 2 cups of cooked strings beans—fresh or canned —and toss well before serving.

broccoli amandine

Cook the broccoli until it can be just pierced— not until it is tender. Drain it and then return it to a skillet in which you have heated 4 tablespoons of butter and 2 tablespoons of very hot olive oil. Cook broccoli until it browns lightly, but be careful not to break the tender tips. Then add ⅔ cup of slivered almonds and allow them to brown lightly in the fat.

beets

Use young, small beets. The larger varieties are not generally used as a vegetable at the table. They have a strong flavor and a tendency to be woody. Always cook beets with the skin on and a few inches of the stems remaining. Otherwise, all the color and flavor will escape into the cooking water and you will have a wonderful base for borsch. Young beets usually require cooking from 30 to 45 minutes in salted water. When they are cooked, drain and cover them with cold water until they can be handled. The skins will slip right off. You may want to wear rubber gloves for this procedure as the juices are a powerful stain. Reheat the beets, whole if they are really tiny, or sliced if they are medium-sized. They may be served with butter, or can be sautéed with chopped green onion and sprinkled with finely chopped parsley. Or, add sour cream to taste.

VARIATIONS:

Herbed: Proceed as above, slice the beets, and sauté them in butter until heated through. Add 1 teaspoon chopped chives, 1 tablespoon chopped parsley, and ½ pint sour cream. Mix thoroughly and allow the cream to heat through, but do not allow it to boil.

With Egg: Sauté in butter in a large skillet 2 pounds of cooked, diced beets. Season with salt and pepper, and garnish with hard-cooked eggs and chopped parsley.

Marinated: This is a wonderful cold salad and simple to prepare. Combine: ½ pound sliced cold beets, ½ pound sliced sweet onions, ⅓ cup olive oil, ¼ cup wine vinegar, 1 clove, and salt and pepper. Let the flavors penetrate the beets and onions for several hours before serving.

carrots

Try to select tender, young carrots. Older ones are edible, but they require scraping and cutting into smaller pieces, whereas the young ones can be cooked in their skins and retain flavor and juiciness. Carrots should be cooked in a small amount of water, covered, with salt and perhaps a pinch of sugar.

Steamed Young Carrots: Melt 2 or 3 tablespoons of butter in a kettle or saucepan with a tight-fitting lid and cook the carrots over a low flame in the melted butter. Be sure the lid is tight or you will have fried carrots, not tender, sweet, steamed ones.

Glazed: Cook 1½ pounds of carrots, drain, and add 2 tablespoons of butter, 2 tablespoons of honey, and 1 tablespoon chopped parsley. Cook carefully over a low flame until the ingredients have melted and glazed the carrots. Sprinkle with a few drops of lemon juice and serve.

Carrots and Onions: The less said about the eternal and uninspired combination of carrots and peas, the better. However, here is a combination that will delight you: Boil tiny white onions until they are just tender and combine with cooked carrots. Add a good lump of sweet butter, a pinch of sugar, and chopped chives—and there you have a wonderful combination.

sauerkraut

If your sauerkraut is old, be sure to wash it well before cooking. If it is rather new, omit washing, as it will remove the flavor. (You can usually tell the age by the color. Newish kraut is still white or green; the older it gets, the more translucent and dark it becomes.) Line the bottom of a large, heavy pot with slices of salt pork and bacon—both of which have been cut at least ⅛ inch thick. Separate the kraut and place it in the pot in layers, being sure to grind lots of pepper betwen each layer. Bury a bouquet consisting of celery, parsley, thyme, bay leaf, and leek in the middle of the pot. Add 10 crushed juniper berries and cover with any one of the

CONTINUED ON PAGE 168

seasonings

A wealth of herbs is available for seasonings, but for best results one or two are all that should be attempted in any one dish. (Salt, pepper, and mustard are exceptions because they can be combined with other seasonings.) Be selective, prudent, and creative in your use of seasoning.

pork

ROASTED

anise, apricot, basil, caraway, cilantro, fennel, Italian parsley, juniper, parsley, prune, sage, thyme

BRAISED AND BROILED

anise, basil, caraway, chili, chive, curry, dill, fennel, garlic, onion, sage, Tabasco, thyme, tomato

veal

ROASTED

anchovy, dill, mustard, onion, parsley, prune, summer savory, tarragon, tomato

BROILED

chervil, chive, dill, onion, shallot, tarragon, tomato

BRAISED

chervil, chili, chive, cilantro, dill, lemon, lemon balm, mustard, olive, oregano, shallot, Tabasco, tarragon, thyme

beef

ROASTED

garlic, mustard, onion, oregano, parsley, pepper, rosemary, soy, thyme

BRAISED

anise, bay, caraway, cayenne, celery, cilantro, chili, clove, cumin, curry, dill, garlic, ginger, leek, lemon balm, onion, parsley, rosemary, sage, savory, summer savory, Tabasco, thyme, tomato

BROILED

chili, garlic, ginger, mustard, onion, rosemary, soy, tarragon

SKEWERED

ginger, mustard, onion, rosemary, soy, thyme, tomato

lamb

ROASTED

cinnamon, dill, garlic, onion, rose geranium, rosemary, tarragon, tomato

SKEWERED

bay, chili, curry, dill, garlic, oregano, rosemary, sage, tarragon, thyme, tomato

CHOPS

garlic, rosemary, tarragon

BRAISED

bay, chili, dill, garlic, green pepper, leek, lemon balm, onion, orange rind, rosemary, sage, savory, Tabasco, thyme, tomato

JUST DESSERT, BY WILLIAM HARNETT.
ART INSTITUTE OF CHICAGO, FRIENDS OF AMERICAN ART COLLECTION.

chicken

ROASTED
*basil, chervil, ginger,
onion, parsley,
rosemary, tarragon, thyme*

BROILED
*chili, chive, curry,
garlic, ginger, mustard,
onion, parsley,
rosemary, shallot,
soy, tarragon, thyme*

FRIED
*chili, garlic, ginger,
parsley, Tabasco*

BRAISED
*chili, cilantro, garlic,
marjoram, olive,
oregano, parsley,
rosemary, soy, tarragon*

vegetables

*basil, celery seed,
chervil, chili,
chive, curry, dill, fennel,
garlic, ginger, mustard,
nutmeg, paprika,
parsley, poppy seed,
tarragon, turmeric*

duck

ROASTED
*cherry, cinnamon, clove,
curry, garlic, ginger,
honey, olive, orange,
oregano, peach,
pineapple, plum, sage,
tarragon, thyme*

BROILED
*chili, curry, garlic,
ginger, honey, parsley,
soy, tarragon, thyme*

turkey

ROASTED
*mustard, onion,
oregano, parsley, sage,
tarragon, thyme*

BRAISED
*bay, chili, chocolate,
cilantro, cumin,
curry, garlic, onion,
oregano, Tabasco, thyme*

game

MARINADES
*bay, celery seed, clove,
garlic, ginger,
juniper berry, mustard,
onion, parsley,
peppercorn, rosemary,
shallot, thyme*

ROASTED
*celery top, garlic,
grape leaf, juniper berry,
onion, parsley, sage,
summer savory, tarragon, thyme*

BRAISED
*anise, bay, caraway,
cinnamon, clove, curry,
dill, fennel, garlic,
ginger, juniper berry,
mace, orange rind,
parsley, sage, thyme*

fish

*basil, chervil, chive,
curry, dill, fennel,
garlic, lemon balm,
mustard, onion, paprika,
parsley, rosemary, shallot,
sorrel, tarragon, thyme*

following: champagne, beer, white wine, or beef bouillon with 1 cup of gin added to it. Cook slowly for 6 hours or more.

choucroute garnie

3 pounds of loin of pork
Bacon or salt pork in thick slices
4 pounds of sauerkraut
6 pig's feet or knuckles
1 large piece of salt pork
3 cloves of garlic
2 teaspoons pepper
Juniper berries
White wine
Garlic sausage
6 knockwurst
9 to 12 potatoes

As you will discover when you try this, it is not only a hearty hot-buffet dish, but can be varied in many interesting ways. Another advantage is that it can be made a day ahead and reheated. As a matter of fact, it is better this way. Line a large kettle with strips of salt pork or bacon. If the sauerkraut is old, wash it in cold water and tear it apart. If it is fairly new it will not require this. Place in the kettle and cover with white wine. Cover kettle and steam for 2 hours. Then add the pork loin, pig's feet or knuckles, the large piece of salt pork, garlic, pepper, and juniper. Simmer gently for about 2 hours. Now add the garlic sausage and cook for another 15 minutes. Then add the knockwurst and cook for another 20 minutes. About 30 minutes before the dish has finished, cook your potatoes in their jackets, separately. When they are finished, remove the jackets and shake them over a flame to dry them out. Arrange the choucroute in the center of a large platter and surround it with the various meats.

VARIATIONS:

Substitute beer for the white wine. Or any good stock or bouillon to which you have added a good half-cup or more of dry gin and 7 or 8 crushed juniper berries. *You may* also make this dish with a smoked pork loin, or chicken and fresh pork, or a piece of feathered game, such as pheasant or duck.

broiled tomatoes

4 large tomatoes
Salt and pepper
Butter
Buttered crumbs

Be sure to select tomatoes that are not over-ripe. Wash and core them, but do not peel them. Cut them in half and place on a baking sheet with the cut side up. Season with salt and freshly ground pepper, sprinkle with fine buttered crumbs and a large piece of butter. Put under the broiler until the crumbs are nicely browned. Do not overbroil. They will get quite watery if you do.

VARIATIONS:

With onions: Mix grated onion with the crumbs. *With cheese:* Mix grated Parmesan cheese with the crumbs. *With chives and parsley:* Mix chopped chives and chopped parsley with the crumbs. *With basil:* Use fresh or dried chopped basil and mix it with the crumbs.

broiled eggplant

Peel and cut a medium-sized eggplant into slices about ½ inch thick. Dip these slices in seasoned flour and place on a well-oiled or greased baking sheet. Cover well with pieces of butter and broil over coals in basket grill. Turn and butter the other side of each slice, and broil until they are golden.

broiled zucchini

Cut young, tender zucchini in half. Dip the cut surface into melted butter and, if you like, sprinkle it with bread crumbs, chopped parsley, and a bit of garlic, all mixed together. Arrange zucchini on a greased baking sheet and broil over charcoal in a basket grill.

THE WHITE TABLECLOTH, BY JEAN-BAPTISTE CHARDIN.
ART INSTITUTE OF CHICAGO, MR. AND MRS. LEWIS L. COBURN COLLECTION.

celery

There are many ways to serve this vegetable other than the usual cold and unimaginative "raw" state. Wash the celery well, discarding the tough and stringy parts that occur at the base. Do not throw away the leaves and tops. They are usable in an endless number of ways in soups, flavorings, salads.

Boiled Celery: Cut the branches into 1- or 2-inch lengths and soak them in salted ice-water for about 30 minutes. Then cook in a small amount of boiling salted water for 15 to 18 minutes, or until the celery is tender, not over-cooked. The dish can be sauced in a number of ways: simple melted butter, a cream sauce, hollandaise. If you have any left over, marinate it in a vinaigrette, and serve it again as an hors d'oeuvre.

VARIATION:

Sauté 1 cup finely sliced mushrooms in butter (or the same type of fat you are using in the dish) and add to the celery just before serving.

foiled vegetables

Way back when, before the day of gas, electric, and other kinds of stoves, our ancestors would build a fire, and when it had burned down to coals, place on them the food they had collected that day. It would be wrapped for protection in wet leaves, husks, seaweed, or even wet clay. Today we do not have to resort to these materials to achieve the same succulent results. We now have aluminum foil available. It keeps in all the flavor and juiciness of the enclosed food and is a wonderful way to do vegetables. In particular, since pots are eliminated, you may cook a variety of vegetables or a mixture of all. Some of the possibilities are:

Tomatoes: Cut tomatoes in half, dot with butter, salt and pepper, and basil. Wrap in foil and bake for 20 minutes.

Stuffed Tomatoes: Cut the tops off and hollow out firm tomatoes. Sauté hamburger in butter, with onion, salt, pepper, and oregano. Fill the tomatoes with the mixture, heaping it over the top. Enclose in foil and bake for 20 to 30 minutes. Serve a packet to each guest.

Zucchini: If they are young and small, leave them whole, cutting off only the ends. If they are large, slice them lengthwise or in rounds. Dot with butter, salt, pepper, and oregano or marjoram, and wrap in foil and bake.

Eggplant: Cut peeled eggplant into finger-size pieces. Or, if they are very tiny you may simply cut them in half. Dot with butter or olive oil, salt and pepper, enclose in foil, and bake for about half an hour. You may vary this by sprinkling with bread crumbs and Parmesan cheese; or perhaps a combination of eggplant and tomato with basil; or eggplant, chopped green pepper, and pimiento.

french fried vegetables

Almost any of the vegetables you might encounter are delicious prepared this way. If they are too large for a bite-size snack, cut them to size. The Japanese have been doing vegetables this way for centuries. Wash and dry the vegetables, dip in flour and then into batter, drain for a second or so to let excess batter drip off, and put into hot fat. If you are using a deep fryer, be sure the basket is already in place when you do this or the morsels will be difficult to retrieve at the precise moment of doneness. Or you may fry them in a skillet which has at least an inch of fat in it. Do not crowd. The batter puffs up.

BASIC BATTER
2 eggs, slightly beaten
½ cup milk or beer
2 tablespoons melted butter
1 teaspoon baking powder
1 cup flour

Beat eggs slightly and add the milk (or beer) and melted butter. Sift together flour and baking powder. Stir the mixture into the liquid and combine thoroughly. Try the following:

Onions: Peel and slice large, sweet Bermuda variety. Proceed as above.

Celery Root: Peel and cut into shoestrings about 3 inches long and no more than ½ inch square. If you prefer, you may parboil them.

Eggplant: Treat the same as the celery root.

String Beans: Choose young and tender beans. Snap off the ends and proceed as above.

Zucchini: Cut young, tender zucchini into 1-inch cubes, dip into batter, and fry.

fettucine giacomo

1 pound noodles, narrow
6 tablespoons butter
⅓ cup grated Swiss cheese
⅓ cup grated Parmesan cheese
Salt, pepper, nutmeg
½ cup heavy cream, heated

Bring to a boil a large quantity of salted water. Put in the noodles and cook them until they are tender but not mushy. Drain them well, lifting with a fork so that all the steam escapes. Add the butter, which you have previously creamed with the grated cheeses. Toss this lightly and rapidly, adding salt, pepper, and a tiny bit of grated nutmeg. Add the hot cream and serve at once with additional grated cheese. If you work rapidly you will achieve one of the most heavenly dishes known.

spaghetti al pesto

Pound in a mortar 1 clove of garlic and 1 cup of basil leaves. Add to this ¼ cup each of melted butter and olive oil and ¼ cup of finely chopped parsley. Mix all together until very smooth. Boil 1 pound of spaghetti until it is *al dente*—that is, firm "to the tooth" but cooked through — drain, and cover with the "pesto" mixture. This is so good that you may completely revise your opinions about tomato sauces for pasta.

Note: This may be prepared in a blender.

rigatoni with four cheeses

Make a mixture of the following cheeses: Fontina, Gruyère Mozzarella, and Parmesan. You will have to make very small cubes of the first 3 and grate the last. Cook the pasta to the *al dente* stage, drain it and put into a large serving bowl. Add a lump of butter and the cheeses and mix thoroughly. Sprinkle additional Parmesan on top if you desire.

macaroni alla carbonara

While your macaroni is cooking, prepare the following sauce: Grate ½ cup of Parmesan cheese, ½ cup of Romano cheese. Mix in a bowl 2 raw eggs, the 2 cheeses, and ¼ cup white wine. In a skillet, gently fry 4 thin slices of bacon until they are very crisp. Drain them on paper and reserve about 3 or 4 tablespoons of the fat, discarding the rest. Drain the macaroni and put into a large serving bowl. Now work very quickly. Pour onto the hot pasta the cheese,

egg, and wine mixture. The heat from the macaroni will at once cook the egg and melt the cheese. Now add the fat, for a bit of lubrication as well as flavor, crumble the bacon over the top, and serve with additional grated cheese.

linguine with clam sauce

½ pound linguine
2 cans (7 oz. each) minced clams
3 cloves of garlic
⅓ cup olive oil
½ cup chopped parsley
Oregano

While your linguine is cooking, which should take no more than 9 minutes, you can prepare this quick and delicious clam sauce. First, peel and chop the garlic and sauté it in the olive oil until it takes on color. Add the juice from the clams. Bring it to a boil and reduce the heat so that it just simmers. Just before you are ready to serve, add the clams to heat through, since they are already cooked and will only toughen if cooked too long. Pour over the drained linguine. Sprinkle with the parsley and oregano.

spaghetti with oil and garlic

½ cup of olive oil
2 cloves of garlic
Salt and pepper

Peel the garlic. This becomes a simple task if you crush it slightly with the side of a knife blade. Put it into a skillet and add the oil. Heat it through, but do not let it boil or smoke, all the while pressing the garlic gently to extract the juices. Season with the salt and pepper and pour over drained spaghetti.

anchovy-garlic pasta

Sauté 6 finely chopped garlic cloves in ⅔ cup olive oil. Add 15 coarsely chopped anchovy fillets, ½ cup chopped Italian parsley, and ¼ cup each raisins and pine nuts. Pour on pasta.

sauces

basic brown sauce (espagnole)

3 pounds bones
¼ pound butter
½ pound each of veal and ham, diced
1 onion, sliced
4 sliced mushrooms
1 bay leaf
1 quart of stock or broth
¼ cup tomato purée
4 tablespoons of flour
Salt and pepper

Brown bones in 450 F. oven 35 or 40 minutes. In a saucepan, melt the butter and add the meat, onion, mushrooms, and bay leaf. Cook until thoroughly brown. While it is cooking, blend stock, tomato purée, and browned bones. Cook it until it is slightly reduced. Blend the flour into the meat-and-mushroom mixture, remove from the heat, and slowly add the stock, stirring all the time to keep it from lumping. Place back on the heat, cover the pan and simmer for about 30 or 40 minutes. Strain and correct the seasoning.

If you prefer a ready-made item, there is on the market a Franco-American canned beef gravy which is pretty much the same thing.

VARIATIONS:

Bordelaise: Chop finely 6 shallots or 8 green onions and cook briefly in 4 tablespoons of butter. Add 1 cup of red wine and simmer until it is reduced by half. Add 1 can of the gravy (or 1½ cups of the basic sauce), 2 tablespoons of lemon juice, the same of finely chopped parsley, and salt and cayenne to taste. Poach some beef marrow for 1 minute in hot water, slice, and add to the sauce. Superb on grilled steaks.

Charcutière: Brown ½ cup of finely chopped onion in 3 tablespoons of butter, add ¼ cup of dry white wine, 2 tablespoons wine vinegar, 1 can of beef gravy (or 1½ cups of the basic sauce),

1 teaspoon of dry mustard. Simmer for 5 minutes so that the flavors blend. Just before serving, chop ¼ cup of sour gherkins and add to the sauce. Goes well with roast or grilled pork.

madeira sauce

Reduce a sauce Espagnole (brown sauce) to about half the amount you started with. Cook until it acquires a stiff consistency. Add ¼ cup of good Madeira wine.

This sauce may also be made by combining 1½ cups of beef gravy with 2 bouillon cubes or 1 tablespoon of Bovril. Add ¼ cup Madeira wine.

Sauce Perigueux: Add 2 or 3 chopped truffles to Madeira sauce.

herb sauce

Combine 1 cup of white wine with 1 tablespoon of each of the following herbs: parsley, tarragon, chives, chervil. Bring to a boil and let steep for an hour. Combine with 1 cup of basic brown sauce (Espagnole) and let cook for 5 minutes. Strain through a fine cloth and add 2 tablespoons of the same mixture of fresh herbs. Add the juice of a lemon, and salt and pepper.

basic brown sauce for fish

1 quart fish essence
⅓ cup Madeira or sherry
¼ cup tomato purée
4 or 5 mushrooms
4 tablespoons butter
4 tablespoons flour

Make a fish essence by simmering together fish heads, bones, and skins to which you have added salt, pepper, parsley, onion, celery, ½ cup of white wine, and 3½ cups water, for about 1 hour. Now add the Madeira or sherry, the tomato purée, and the mushrooms, and cook slowly until it is reduced by half. Strain. Melt the butter in a skillet, blend in the flour, and cook slowly until it takes on a good color. Now add the reduced stock and stir until well-thickened. Season again and cook for another 15 minutes.

basic white sauce (bechamel)

2 tablespoons of butter
2 tablespoons flour
1 cup of milk
Salt and pepper

Blend the butter and flour over a low flame. Remove from the fire or place over hot water. Very slowly, add the milk, blending as you do so. Return to the heat and cook slowly, stirring all the time until the sauce thickens and is very smooth. Season it with salt and pepper. If you want thicker sauce use 3 or 4 tablespoons of flour.

VARIATIONS:

Rich Cream Sauce: Use heavy cream in place of half the milk. Or reduce the flour by ½ tablespoon. And when the sauce is finished, very carefully stir in an egg yolk.

With Vegetables: Reduce the liquid in which you have cooked the vegetables and use it with heavy cream in place of the milk.

With Meat or Fish: The same as above, reducing the liquid in which you have cooked the meat or fish, and using in place of the milk.

sauce mornay

To a basic white sauce, add ¼ cup of grated Switzerland Swiss or Parmesan cheese, or a combination of both, and 3 tablespoons of heavy cream.

velouté

To 1 cup of bechamel, made with milk or with 1 cup of meat, poultry, fish, or vegetable stock, add ½ cup heavy cream which has been blended with 2 egg yolks. Stir until thickened, but be careful that it does not boil or you will have scrambled eggs.

sauce supreme

First make a velouté by melting ⅓ cup butter and stirring in ⅓ cup flour and letting it cook for a few minutes. Add 3 cups chicken or veal stock (or its equivalent, made by using bouillon cubes and boiling water), ½ teaspoon salt, and a bit of pepper. Let it cook, stirring all the while until it thickens. Lower the flame and let it cook, stirring from time to time to prevent a crust from forming, until it has reduced to about 2½ cups. Now, cook 1 pint of chicken stock with about 3 sliced mushrooms until it has reduced to about ⅓ of its original quantity. Combine this with 1 cup of the velouté, and reduce this to 1 cup. When it has reached this stage, slowly add 1 cup of sweet cream that you have heated but not boiled, stirring all the time. Correct the seasoning.

quick sauce supreme

To velouté sauce, add 3 or 4 sliced, sautéed mushrooms and ¼ cup of sherry.

white wine sauce

To a basic bechamel sauce, add ½ cup white wine and 2 egg yolks. Heat thoroughly, stirring all the time, but do not let it boil.

oyster sauce

To 1 cup of a basic bechamel add ½ cup of oyster liquid and 2 egg yolks. Heat but do not let it boil. One minute before serving, add 4 chopped oysters. Let them cook in sauce.

shrimp sauce

Proceed as for oyster sauce, except that you substitute the liquid in which you have cooked the shrimp. Chop the cooked shrimp and add to the sauce just before serving.

egg sauce

To a basic bechamel add 2 or 3 thinly sliced, hard-cooked eggs.

parsley sauce

Chop ⅓ cup of parsley very finely. Add it to 1 cup of bechamel and flavor with 1 tablespoon of onion juice.

mustard sauce

1 cup bechamel sauce
2 teaspoons dry mustard
1 teaspoon prepared mustard

Add the 2 mustards to the bechamel sauce, blend it well, and let it stand for 30 minutes.

horseradish sauce

1 cup bechamel sauce
½ cup grated horseradish (fresh or reconstituted)
Lemon juice

Add the horseradish to the bechamel. If you are using bottled horseradish, be sure to drain it well. If you reconstitute the dehydrated variety, use only enough water to bring it back to its original state. Do not use too much liquid.

sauce marchands de vin

1 cup red wine
2 shallots, chopped fine
A pinch of thyme
½ bay leaf, crumbled
Salt and pepper

Combine the above ingredients in a saucepan and cook until the liquid is reduced by half. Remove from fire and stir in 3 tablespoons of sweet butter and 1 tablespoon of lemon juice.

marchands de vin sauce for fish

3 small shallots or white onions
3 to 4 mushrooms
3 tablespoons butter
1 cup white wine
1 cup basic brown sauce (Espagnole)

Peel and chop the shallots and slice the mushrooms very thin. Melt the butter in a saucepan, add the shallots and cook until they color lightly. Now add the mushrooms and the wine, and reduce liquid to half. Stir in the brown sauce, and continue stirring until thick and completely blended. Taste and correct the seasoning.

bread sauce

Put 1 cup of milk and 1 very small onion stuck with 2 cloves in a saucepan and bring to a boil. Add ¼ cup of freshly grated breadcrumbs and let cook gently for 20 minutes. Remove the onion. Add salt and pepper to taste, 2 tablespoons of butter, and 1 tablespoon of heavy cream, and serve. This is the most authentic version of a traditional English sauce.

sauce louis

Blend together 1 cup mayonnaise, 2 tablespoons finely grated onion, ¼ cup chili sauce, 2 tablespoons chopped parsley, a few grains of cayenne, and ⅓ cup of heavy cream, whipped. Let this stand for 1 or 2 hours.

sauce ravigote

To 1 cup of mayonnaise add a tablespoon of Dijon mustard, 1 chopped shallot, 1 tablespoon of chopped capers, and 1 teaspoon of chopped tarragon. This is a delicious cold sauce.

sauce piquant

Add to 1 cup of mayonnaise, 2 tablespoons of Dijon mustard, 1 tablespoon of dry English mustard, and a few specks of cayenne.

the boiling point. Turn the blender on high and pour the butter in a steady stream into the egg mixture until it is blended and thickened. Keep warm over tepid—not hot—water.

sauce mousseline

To the basic recipe for hollandaise, add ½ to 1 cup whipped cream.

sauce aurore

To a basic hollandaise, add 2 tablespoons of well-seasoned tomato purée.

béarnaise sauce

This is really a hollandaise sauce with certain flavoring added.

> *2 teaspoons chopped fresh tarragon*
> *or 1 teaspoon dried tarragon*
> *2 teaspoons finely chopped shallots*
> *or green onions*
> *Pinch of salt*
> *Pinch of pepper*
> *3 tablespoons wine vinegar*

Cook down the above until it is almost a glaze, and amounts to about ¾ of a tablespoon.

> *3 egg yolks*
> *1 or 2 teaspoons water*
> *¼ pound butter cut into small pieces*
> *Chopped tarragon and parsley*

Combine the egg yolks, the water, and the reduced glaze in the top of a double boiler. The secret of a successful Béarnaise is to never allow the water to really boil, and to remove the sauce from the heat the instant it has thickened, so that it does not curdle. It will continue to cook in its own heat, so this last is most important. Start by adding the butter, piece by piece as it melts and is combined, stirring all the while with either a wooden spoon or spatula, or a small whisk, until all the butter has been used. Now watch your sauce very carefully and as it

hollandaise sauce

Here are some "secrets" about making a good hollandaise: Be sure to use the freshest and finest butter obtainable. See that the water in which you set the bowl or pan when you actually make the sauce never boils. See that the upper pan never touches the water in the bowl below. Also, use a wooden spoon or a small wire whisk for stirring.

> *3 egg yolks*
> *1 or 2 teaspoons water*
> *¼ pound or ½ cup butter cut into*
> *small pieces*
> *A few grains of cayenne*
> *A few grains of salt*
> *Lemon juice or tarragon vinegar*

In the top of a double boiler combine the egg yolks and water and whisk them over very hot water until they are well mixed and very light. Piece by piece, add the butter, being sure never to stop whisking. The mixture will gradually begin to thicken. The moment it reaches the right consistency, remove it from the lower pan or it will curdle. If it should, add ½ teaspoon of boiling water and whisk furiously until it reconstitutes. Add the cayenne and salt, and lemon juice or vinegar to taste.

blender hollandaise sauce

In the bowl or a blender, place 3 egg yolks with 2 teaspoons of lemon juice, ½ teaspoon salt, and a few grains of cayenne. Very quickly, turn the blender on and off. Melt ¼ pound of sweet butter in a saucepan and let it get almost to

begins to thicken, remove it from the heat and keep stirring. To finish, you add chopped tarragon and parsley. Béarnaise may be served either hot or at room temperature.

duxelles

Chop 3 pounds of mushrooms very fine and cook very slowly with ½ to ¾ pound of butter. Add salt and, if you wish, a little chopped shallot. Let it cook, uncovered, until it is black. It will take about 3 hours of extremely slow cooking—the slowest—to finish this delectable sauce. Stir from time to time.

sauce poivrade

¼ cup minced onions
¼ cup grated carrot
3 tablespoons minced parsley
2 tablespoons olive oil
½ cup dry red wine
¼ cup cider vinegar
2 cups basic brown sauce
A pinch of ground cloves
1 teaspoon freshly ground pepper

Sauté the onions, carrots, and parsley in the oil for about 5 or 6 minutes. Add the wine and the vinegar. Cook until it has reduced by half. Add the brown sauce and cook over a low heat for 30 minutes. Strain and place into a clean saucepan. Stir in the cloves and the pepper. Continue cooking for another 4 or 5 minutes.

smitaine sauce

Add sour cream, paprika, and sometimes a little cognac, to the pan juices of any dish.

uncooked barbecue sauce

This sauce is so simple to do. No particular equipment is needed for its concoction. You may shake it up in a glass jar, or a cocktail shaker, or, if you have one, in an electric blender. Combine 2 cloves of crushed garlic, 1½ tea-

spoons of salt, 1 teaspoon of freshly ground black pepper, ¼ cup chopped scallions, 2 teaspoons of prepared mustard, 1 teaspoon of dry mustard, ¼ cup lemon juice, ⅓ cup beefsteak sauce (Heinz or A-1), and 2 cups of any of the following: tomato purée or sauce, or strained canned tomatoes. Shake very well and add a small dash of Tabasco. If you prefer a not-so-sharp sauce, add pinch of brown sugar.

california barbecue sauce

1 finely chopped onion
1 clove garlic, minced
1 teaspoon salt
⅛ teaspoon pepper
½ teaspoon chili powder
½ teaspoon celery salt
½ teaspoon dry mustard
1 tablespoon Worcestershire sauce
¼ cup brown sugar
¼ cup vinegar
1 can tomato sauce
1 can tomato purée
1 slice lemon
⅛ teaspoon Tabasco

Use a skillet or saucepan over a medium heat. Combine the above ingredients in the order listed. When the mixture begins to boil, lower heat and cover. Cook for about 30 minutes.

sauce niçoise

2 large onions
4 tablespoons olive oil
10 anchovy fillets
¼ cup chopped parsley
Thyme
Fresh or dried basil
1 cup tomato purée
¼ cup white wine

Peel and chop the onions. Sauté them in the oil only until they are colored, but not brown. Cut the anchovy fillets in half and add them to the onions. Add the parsley, a tiny pinch of thyme and basil. Mix the purée with the wine and add it to the mixture. Let simmer until well-blended and cooked down, but not too thick. Do not use salt, since the anchovies are quite salty.

sauce provençale

Peel, seed, and chop 6 tomatoes (or 2 cans of tomatoes). Put them into a saucepan in which you have heated ½ cup of olive oil. Season well with salt, pepper, and a pinch of sugar. Add a clove of garlic, crushed, and a teaspoon of finely chopped parsley. Cover and let it cook slowly for about 30 minutes. Do not let it get thick.

north italian spaghetti sauce

1 pound mushrooms
4 tablespoons olive oil
4 tablespoons butter
1 teaspoon salt
1 teaspoon freshly ground pepper
Juice of 2 lemons

Slice mushrooms very thin and sauté them in olive oil and butter. Add salt and pepper. Do not overcook. Remove from the fire and add the lemon juice. You will find this a nice change from the usual tomato-based spaghetti sauces.

neapolitan sauce

3 stalks celery
2 cloves garlic
2 medium onions
2 or 3 leeks
¼ cup pine nuts
4 or 5 sprigs parsley
4 tablespoons olive oil
1 thick pork chop
or Italian sausage, hot or sweet
2 teaspoons salt
Basil
2 cups thick tomato purée
Broth, or beef consommé,
or 2 bouillon cubes, dissolved

Put the celery, garlic, onions, leeks, parsley, and pine nuts through a meat grinder, using the fine blade. In a saucepan, heat the olive oil and quickly brown the pork chop or sausage. Lower the flame and add the chopped ingredients, and fry only until they take on a golden color. Add the purée and broth to cover, the salt and sweet basil, and let it simmer uncovered until the meat is quite tender. Add additional broth if it gets too thick.

meatless italian sauce

1 #2 can of tomatoes, solid pack
1 teaspoon dried basil or 2 teaspoons fresh
1 onion, chopped fine
1 bay leaf
½ teaspoon salt
½ teaspoon pepper
Olive oil

Sauté the onions in the olive oil only until they are softened and golden. Add the tomatoes, which you have sieved or put through a food mill; the basil, bay leaf, salt, and pepper. Simmer until it has reduced by about one-third.

garlic-and-tomato sauce

Sauté 1 clove garlic, 1 small onion, both chopped finely, in 2 tablespoons olive oil. Add 1½ cups or 1 can of solid-packed tomatoes, ½ teaspoon basil and simmer 30 to 40 minutes. Add 1 small can tomato paste and simmer for 15 minutes. Strain, and if the sauce is not thickened, let it reduce for several minutes over a brisk fire, but be careful not to scorch it. Stir frequently until it is done.

chinese sweet-and-sour sauce

3 tomatoes
2 green peppers
2 tablespoons cornstarch
¾ cup vinegar
¾ cup sugar
¾ cup water or tomato juice
½ teaspoon salt

Pour boiling water over tomatoes and let them stand for 2 minutes. Plunge into cold water and peel. Cut into sections, like a tangerine. Wash and cut green peppers. Mix the other ingredients in a saucepan and heat, stirring constantly until thick and clear. Now add the peppers and cook for another few minutes, or until they are bright green. At the last moment, add the tomatoes. Do not cook the tomatoes!

VARIATION:

With fruit: When you add the peppers, you might add drained, cubed pineapple, and/or sliced peaches, canned or fresh. Use your imagination. Cherries, plums, apricots are all fine.

italian sweet-and-sour sauce

Start with a brown sauce base. Reduce and add 1 tablespoon prepared mustard, ¼ cup chopped Italian fruits in mustard *(Mostarda Frutti),* and 2 tablespoons vinegar.

mexican chili sauce

Chop ½ cup beef-kidney suet finely and try it out in a skillet. Add 1 pound of beef cut into small cubes and fry until brown. Add 1 cup of chopped onions. When they color, add 3 tablespoons of chili powder and 1 cup tomato purée. Stir the mixture and let it fry for about 2 or 3 minutes. Add beef broth or bouillon to cover, and let it simmer for an hour, or until the sauce is cooked down and thick. Add more broth if necessary.

mexican mole sauce

Mole powder can be bought at specialty shops and comes in two varieties, mild and hot. It is basically a combination of spices, herbs, and grated bitter chocolate. Time was when if you wanted to do a mole dish, you spent hours combining all the ingredients. The tinned product simplifies life. All you do now is add the powder to 3 times its volume of broth, add tomato purée to your taste, and simmer. Chicken and turkey in a mole sauce are delicious.

salsa fria

2 pounds of peeled, chopped ripe tomatoes
1 cup chopped sweet onions
4 or 5 canned green chilis, chopped
1 can Mexican tomatillas
3 tablespoons olive oil
3 tablespoons wine vinegar
Salt, pepper, and coriander to taste

One of the popular sauces of the West and Southwest. It goes well on all grilled meats. Combine all ingredients, leave the mixture to blend and ripen in the refrigerator, and serve it very cold with grilled meats. Should you not be able to get fresh coriander, which resembles parsley but has a distinctive flavor of its own, you may substitute oregano.

sauce diable

1 medium-sized onion, finely chopped
2 cloves garlic, finely chopped
4 tablespoons butter
1 teaspoon salt
2 teaspoons freshly ground black pepper
1½ teaspoons dry mustard
½ cup red wine
1 can beef gravy
1 tablespoon Worcestershire sauce
Juice of ½ lemon

Sauté onions and garlic in butter, add wine, and simmer for 4 minutes. Add seasonings, beef gravy, Worcestershire sauce, and lemon juice. Bring to a boil and simmer for 5 minutes over a low flame.

salmi sauce

Add the juice and grated rind of an orange and 2 tablespoons of port wine to 1 cup of brown sauce (Espagnole). This should simmer for a few minutes to blend and reduce slightly. Admirable with game.

english curry sauce

5 tablespoons butter
1 large onion
1 apple
2 stalks of celery
Salt
Curry powder
1 to 1½ cups of broth,
stock, or tomato juice
2 teaspoons of chutney

Peel and chop the onion. Leave the skin on the apple, but core it and chop it. Chop the celery. Sauté these gently in the melted butter, not allowing them to brown. Sprinkle the curry powder over the vegetables. For a mild curry, about 3 tablespoons should suffice. Increase or decrease to your taste. Season with a bit of salt and allow to cook and blend for about 3 or 4 minutes. Add the liquid of your choice and allow it to heat through and cook for another few minutes. Just before you serve, add the chutney. This can be used with any leftover meat. Also excellent with canned tuna, lobster, crabmeat, shrimp.

hawaiian curry sauce

Proceed as for the English curry sauce, but add to it the juice and finely grated pulp of half a coconut; chopped mango, fresh or canned; and apricot pulp. Use your imagination and add shredded pineapple, guava pulp, or any tropical fruit that is obtainable. All of them blend nicely with the pungent curry flavor.

french curry sauce

This makes a very mild curry sauce and is extremely good if you are in a hurry. Make about 2 cups of sauce velouté. Add to it ½ cup of cream and curry to your own taste.

chinese curry sauce

To 1½ cups tomato sauce add 3 tablespoons (or more) of soy sauce and 2 of curry powder.

indian curry sauce

¼ cup of clarified butter
1 large or 2 medium onions, sliced very thin
1 clove of garlic
2 chili peppers, coarsely minced
3 teaspoons coriander seed, ground
1 tablespoon turmeric
½ teaspoon ground ginger (fresh, if possible)
½ teaspoon ground cumin
½ teaspoon ground black pepper
½ teaspoon ground chili pepper
1 teaspoon ground fenugreek
Lime juice
1½ cups chicken broth

Here we start from scratch and make a curry sauce which is native to the south of India. Melt the butter and fry the onions very gently until they color but do not brown. Add the chili peppers and sauté for 4 or 5 minutes longer. Mix the remaining ingredients to a paste with lime juice. Add this to the pan with 1½ cups of chicken broth and let it simmer slowly for about ¾ of an hour. Add more broth from time to time so that the sauce does not become too dry and burn. This is one of the more delicious sauces in the curry family. You may vary the degree of "hotness" by reducing or increasing the ground chili pepper.

avgalemeno

3 eggs, separated
Salt
Juice of 1 large lemon
2 cups chicken broth

This is a favorite Greek sauce and is used in hot chicken soup, with chicken, or with fish. The flavor is unusual. Beat the egg whites and yolks separately, then together until they are blended. Gradually beat in the lemon juice and 2 cups of boiling chicken broth. Be careful not to let it curdle. If you use this sauce in soup, heat the soup and add the sauce, stirring constantly. Very carefully bring it to a simmer, but do not allow it to boil.

sauce robert

Especially good with roast pork, goose, and turkey. Brown ¾ cup of chopped onion in ¼ cup of butter. Add a can of beef gravy, 1 tablespoon vinegar, ½ cup of white wine, 1 tablespoon prepared mustard, and salt and pepper.

shallot sauce (argentine sauce)

Heat ¼ cup of butter and add to it 1 cup of chopped shallots. This is a variety of French onion which looks and grows like garlic. Its flavor is sort of a cross between the two, although its origin is not. At any rate, sauté them in the butter until they practically melt into a thick sauce. Add a cup of white wine, 2 tablespoons of vinegar, a teaspoon of salt, and ½ teaspoon of freshly ground pepper, and cook for another 4 or 5 minutes. Add ¼ pound of cut-up sweet butter and cook until it is melted.

cumberland sauce

This sauce is delightful with venison or other game. Cut the zest—that is, the outside skin—of an orange and chop it finely. Cook with 1 cup of Madeira or port wine until it is reduced by one-third. Add juice of 1 orange, 1 tablespoon of lemon juice, ½ cup of currant jelly, and a small pinch of cayenne pepper or ground ginger. When the jelly is melted, the sauce is ready to be served.

italian sauce

Make a brown roux by putting 4 tablespoons of flour in a heavy skillet and browning, then adding 4 tablespoons of butter. Chop 12 mushrooms finely and cook them in butter until they are almost a paste. Heat 1 cup of tomato purée, or 1 can of condensed tomato soup, and ¾ cup of fish stock almost to the boiling point and stir in the mushrooms and roux. Keep stirring until it is thickened, but not a paste. Add 2 tablespoons of finely chopped herbs (parsley, tarragon, chervil) and correct the seasoning.

aïoli

4 cloves garlic
2 egg yolks
1 to 2 cups olive or peanut oil
Lemon juice
Salt

You may prepare this in the traditional way—in a mortar and pestle—or you may simplify things by using a blender. Chop the garlic very fine or put it into a blender with the egg yolks and salt. Whichever way you do it, be sure that you start with a thick paste. Very gradually, add the oil. The amount will depend on the absorption of the yolks. Stop pouring oil when the mixture reaches the consistency of a mayonnaise. Finish by adding lemon juice to taste. This is a famous "Friday Sauce" used on fish in Marseille.

court bouillon

1 cup mixed vegetables, chopped fine
Salt and pepper
1 bottle white wine
Fish bones and heads
1 quart of water
1 teaspoon thyme
2 onions stuck with cloves
2 cloves garlic
Bay leaf

Cook the fish bones and heads in the water for 30 minutes, strain through a fine cloth. Add all the other ingredients and let them simmer gently for 20 or 30 minutes.

This is used for poaching fish. A wonderful sauce may be made from it after you remove the poached fish. Turn up the heat and reduce the mixture until it is ½ its volume. Strain and thicken with beurre manié (butter and flour blended together and rolled into little balls).

marinades

Red Wine Marinade: For game, beef, mutton, and rabbit or hare, combine the following ingredients: 2 cups of red wine, ¼ cup vinegar or lemon juice, ¼ cup each of chopped onion and chopped carrot, 1 large onion sliced thinly, 5 or 6 peppercorns, and a bay leaf, parsley, thyme, and a stalk of celery tied together. If you are using an especially lean meat, such as hare or venison, add ½ cup of oil.

Soy Sauce Marinade: Mix together equal parts of soy sauce and sake. If this is not available you may use a dry sherry. Add ¼ cup of peanut oil —or sesame oil if you can obtain it—1 clove of crushed garlic, and some grated fresh ginger.

Curry Marinade: To ¾ cup of soy sauce add 1 crushed clove of garlic, 1 tablespoon of curry powder, and a touch of grated fresh ginger. (If this is not available, substitute the dried.) Superb with lamb or mutton steaks or chops.

Vermouth Marinade: Combine equal parts of dry French and sweet Italian vermouth and add to it ¼ cup of olive oil. A beautiful thing happens to dishes marinated in this, as all the herbs that are blended in the vermouths permeate the meat most delicately.

Piquant Barbecue Marinade: Mix together an 8-ounce can of tomato juice with ¼ cup each of olive oil, chopped green pepper, chopped pimiento, and chopped green onion. Crush 2 or 3 cloves of garlic into this and add a tablespoon or more of chili powder and a pinch of salt. This should be simmered for 10 minutes and allowed to cool before you place the meat in it to marinate.

anchovy butter

Chop 6 anchovy fillets very finely, almost to a paste. Cream ½ cup of sweet butter and combine with the anchovies. Add a very few drops of lemon or lime juice, or a mild vinegar, and a teaspoon of chopped parsley.

herb butters

This is simply butter that has been creamed

and softened, and had various flavorings of herbs added to it. You may use just one herb or any combination that pleases you: parsley, tarragon, chives, rosemary, marjoram, chervil. For example, a tarragon butter would go beautifully on broiled chicken, a sweet basil butter on grilled tomatoes, etc.

garlic butter

Cream ½ cup of butter and fold into it the cloves of 3 finely chopped garlic. Blend well.

lemon butter

Heat the amount of butter you will need for a sauce for your particular dish and stir into it lemon juice to your taste.

dessert sauces

Simple puddings, ice creams, and fresh fruits are immeasurably brightened by the addition of sweet sauces. Here are some tasty ones that are easy to make.

raspberry sauce

1 pint fresh raspberries
½ cup sugar

Strain the berries through a fine sieve or food mill. Add the sugar and mix well. Bring it to a boil over a medium heat and cook at a simmer until the syrup is thick and heavy. This can be done nicely with frozen berries, omitting the sugar. You may flavor this with a teaspoon or so of kirsch or framboise.

chocolate sauce

Again, simplicity itself. In the top of a double boiler melt 12 ounces of Nestlé's Semi-sweet Chocolate Morsels, 2 ounces of unsweetened chocolate, and a tiny pinch of salt. When thoroughly melted, add ½ pint of heavy cream and a tablespoon of cognac. The most luscious chocolate sauce you ever tasted.

butterscotch sauce

Over hot water, melt a package of Nestlé's Butterscotch Morsels and add a tablespoon or so of cream if it thickens too much.

foamy sauce

4 tablespoons brown sugar
1 egg yolk
1 egg white
1 cup whipped cream
Jamaica rum or cognac

Beat half of the sugar with the egg yolk until light and blended. Beat the egg white until it is foamy. Slowly add the remaining sugar to the white and continue beating until it is stiff. Combine with the yolk-and-sugar mixture and add the whipped cream. Add the rum or cognac to your taste.

cognac sauce

Cream 4 tablespoons of butter with ½ cup of sugar. Add 2 egg yolks, one at a time, and mix well. Dissolve ½ teaspoon of arrowroot in part of ⅔ cup of heavy cream. When dissolved, add it and the remaining cream to the egg mixture and cook over hot water, stirring it constantly until it coats a spoon. Remove from the heat and add a jigger of good cognac. (Or rum.)

whipped cream

As a change from the eternal bland and oversweet whipped cream, try adding a bit of sherry, or Jamaica rum, or cognac, or any liqueur of your choice.

sour cream

Exactly that . . . sour cream by itself is one of the most delightful and refreshing sauces for desserts. You may vary it by adding 6 ounces of semi-sweet chocolate morsels which have been melted and stirred in, or butterscotch and a dash of cognac.

basic white sauces

BECHAMEL AND RICH CREAM SAUCE
baked fish, chicken, game, seafood,
steamed fish, tongue, turkey, vegetables

BREAD SAUCE
chicken, partridge, pheasant, quail, turkey

EGG
fish, veal

HORSERADISH
boiled beef, grilled chicken,
grilled pork chops, roast beef, roast pork,
some grilled fish, tongue

MORNAY
chicken, fish, pasta, shellfish,
turkey, vegetables

MUSTARD
boiled beef, grilled chicken,
grilled fish, grilled quail, grilled veal,
spitted fresh ham, spitted ham,
spitted veal, tongue

OYSTER
fish, veal

PARSLEY
chicken, eggs, veal

SHRIMP
fish, veal

SUPREME
chicken, pheasant, quail, squab

VELOUTÉ
chicken, fish, rabbit, shellfish,
turkey, veal, vegetables

WHITE WINE SAUCE
fish, veal

basic brown sauces

BASIC BROWN SAUCE FOR FISH
salmon steak, some lobster dishes,
some shrimp dishes, swordfish steak

BORDELAISE
entrecôte, frogs' legs, lamb steak, lobster,
rump steak, saddle of lamb, salmon steak,
shrimp, sirloin roast, swordfish steak

CHARCUTIÈRE
grilled pork chops,
grilled pork steak, wild boar

DIABLE
broiled chicken, deviled broilers,
deviled kidneys, deviled lamb chops,
grilled pigs' feet, pork chops

HERB SAUCE
broiled chicken, broiled turkey,
fillet of beef, grilled kidneys, grilled
liver steak, lamb steak, tongue

MADEIRA
grilled duckling, ham steak, pork steak,
roast duck, spitted ham, spitted pheasant,
spitted squab, tournedos

MARCHANDS DE VIN
entrecôte, fillet, rump steak

MARCHANDS DE VIN FOR FISH
grilled sole, halibut steak, salmon steak,
striped bass, swordfish steak

PERIGUEUX
fillet of beef, porterhouse steak,
rack of lamb, roast sirloin, roast turkey,
spitted chicken, spitted duckling, spitted game,
spitted prime ribs, venison steak

POIVRADE
hare, pheasant, pork roast, venison

ROBERT
broiled pheasant, cold meats, ham, ham steak,
pork chops, roast duck, roast pork

SALMI
duckling, goose, squab

mayonnaise

cold fish, cold game,
cold meats, cold seafood, cold vegetables,
egg dishes, poultry, salads

SAUCE LOUIS
crabmeat, lobster, shrimp

SAUCE PIQUANT
cold chicken, cold duck,
cold fish, cold game, cold pork,
cold veal, cold vegetables

SAUCE RAVIGOTE
cold vegetables, crab, lobster,
mussels, scallops, shrimp

emulsified sauces

AÏOLI
chicken, fish; grilled, spitted,
or steamed vegetables; shellfish

AURORE
grilled fish, grilled lobster,
grilled veal, some vegetables

BÉARNAISE
broiled kidneys, fillets of beef, grilled chicken,
grilled duckling, grilled fish, hamburgers,
lamb chops, roast beef, steaks

HOLLANDAISE
eggs, spitted or broiled fish, vegetables

MOUSSELINE
asparagus, broccoli, leek, onion

barbecue sauces

CALIFORNIA
grilled chicken, grilled lamb,
hamburgers, lamburgers, pork steaks,
sausages, spitted turkey, steaks

UNCOOKED
frankfurters, grilled pork chops,
hamburgers, roast pork, sliced steak,
spareribs, steak sandwiches

mexican sauces

CHILI SAUCE
broiled chicken, frankfurters, grilled pork
chops, hamburgers, spareribs, spitted beef,
spitted pork, spitted turkey, spitted veal

MOLE
beef, chicken, pork, turkey

SALSA FRIA
cold meats, grilled fish

sweet-and-sour sauces

CHINESE
ham steaks, pork chops, pork steak,
shrimp, spareribs, spitted pork, whole fish

ITALIAN
broiled beef, broiled or spitted duckling,
hare, spitted lamb, spitted or grilled pork chops,
spitted pork loin

tomato sauces

GARLIC AND TOMATO
grilled fish, grilled pork steaks,
spitted veal, pizzaiola

ITALIAN
grilled kidneys, grilled
lamb steaks, grilled liver, grilled veal, pasta,
spitted pork, spitted veal

NIÇOISE
grilled chicken, grilled duckling,
grilled pork, grilled tournedos, grilled turkey,
grilled veal, spitted pork

PROVENÇALE
eggplant, fish steaks, frogs' legs,
grilled chicken, grilled kidneys, grilled lamb,
grilled liver, grilled pork, grilled small fish,
grilled veal, lobster, scallops, shrimp

curry sauces

CHINESE
frankfurters, grilled pork chops,
hamburgers, spareribs

ENGLISH
chicken, lamb, scallops, shrimp

FRENCH
grilled veal, spitted chicken, spitted veal

HAWAIIAN
grilled and spitted fish, pork chops,

INDIAN
duck, fruits, lamb,
lobster, shrimp, vegetables

other sauces

AVGALEMENO
chicken, chicken soup, lamb

CUMBERLAND
all game, cold meats, poultry

DUXELLES
canapés, omelets, pancakes, scrambled eggs,
stuffed eggs, stuffings, vegetables

SHALLOT SAUCE
deviled chicken, hamburgers, lamb steaks,
spitted lamb, spitted sirloin, steaks

SMITAINE SAUCE
chicken, frankfurters, some steak, veal

salads

The family of salads is so varied and so extensive that any complete discussion of it would be a book in itself. It can be one simple green with no dressing at all, or the most elaborate combination of vegetables, meats, fish, eggs, and dressing. Whatever variation you choose, remember that the principal function of the salad is to clear the palate of the flavors that have preceded it. It therefore should be slightly tart and crisp. This is not an absolute rule. The West Coast frequently serves salad ahead of the entrée, a practice that apparently does no damage to the palate, and, indeed, has much to recommend it. It does, however, ignore the salad's first *raison d'être*.

basic ingredients and equipment

Nothing is less appetizing than a wooden salad bowl that has had oil penetrating its pores for years and is not regularly or completely cleaned. In my opinion, a china, porcelain, or even better, a crystal or glass bowl is to be preferred. It can be washed and cleaned after use.

Shun the "prepared" salts, such as onion and garlic, because they depend for flavor on volatile oils that go rancid very quickly on exposure to air. Use freshly ground pepper from a little hand mill and, if you can obtain it, Malden salt from England. Failing this the closest thing to it is coarse Kosher salt. It is salt and nothing but salt. It does not have cornstarch to keep it flowing and is therefore "saltier." Fresh herbs, if obtainable, are wonderful. Out of season, well put-up dried herbs are almost as good. Again, beware of ancient herbs that have been sitting on the shelf for years, exposed to light and not too well bottled. They can ruin an otherwise superb dressing.

Greens should be fresh, clean, and not cut into pieces so huge that they require too much cutting on the plate. Do not add tomatoes until the very last, or you will have a watery salad. A good practice is to marinate them separately and drain them well just before adding them to the bowl.

basic salad dressings

Salad greens lend themselves to an almost endless number of dressings and offer the enterprising chef a fine opportunity to create a new conception. Still and all, probably 85 per cent of all salads wear a French, Russian, or Thousand Island dressing—and with reason. These are the premier salad tastes and every chef has them in his repertoire.

french

3 or 4 parts olive oil
1 part wine vinegar or lemon juice
Salt and pepper

Combine the ingredients and stir well. Of course, olive oil is by far the best of the edible oils for a salad dressing. There are some people, however, who prefer the blander taste of peanut, corn, or soybean oil. Your vinegar should be simple. It is not only less expensive than the tricked-up variety, but will give you better results. You can vary the flavor by adding herbs, garlic, or onion. Also, the same vinegar can be used in other dishes. Do not make up a batch of dressing. Mix it fresh each time. You may of course make it up an hour before you serve it, especially if you are using herbs. This will give them a chance to impart their flavor.

VARIATIONS:

Dry Mustard: This can be a pleasant addition to celery or fruit salads. Be very careful of quantity. You can very easily get the dressing too hot.

Vinaigrette: To a basic French dressing add chopped onions, chives, parsley, hard-cooked egg, and dill pickle. Chop all very fine.

mayonnaise

2 egg yolks
1 teaspoon salt
½ teaspoon dry mustard
1 pint of olive oil
Lemon juice

All ingredients should be at room temperature. In a shallow bowl place the egg yolks, salt, and mustard. Then start adding the oil, drop by drop at first, beating thoroughly each time you add it. Don't go too fast or it will curdle. If it should, start with another yolk and a little oil, and add this to the curdled mixture. Continue until you have added all the oil and the mixture is thick and stiff. Add lemon juice to taste.

VARIATIONS:

Remoulade: Add 1 minced clove of garlic, 1 teaspoon of dry or 1 tablespoon fresh-chopped tarragon, ½ teaspoon dry mustard, a finely chopped hard-boiled egg, 1 teaspoon of capers, 1 tablespoon chopped parsley, and a dab of anchovy paste to 1 cup of mayonnaise.

Thousand Island: To 1 cup of mayonnaise add 1 tablespoon finely chopped onion, 3 tablespoons of chili sauce, 1 chopped hard-boiled egg, and a pinch of dry mustard.

Green Goddess: To 1 cup mayonnaise add ½ cup mixed, chopped, green herbs — parsley, chives, tarragon—and 3 chopped anchovy fillets.

Russian: Blend together and allow to stand for 2 hours, 2 cups of mayonnaise, 1 teaspoon dry mustard, 2 tablespoons finely chopped onion, 1 tablespoon Worcestershire sauce, and 2 ounces of caviar.

Tartar: 2 cups of mayonnaise, 3 tablespoons finely chopped onion, 2 teaspoons finely chopped parsley, 2 teaspoons lemon juice, 2 tablespoons finely chopped dill pickle—or fresh dill, if you prefer.

blender mayonnaise

Put into the bowl of your blender 1 whole egg and 2 yolks, ½ teaspoon dry mustard, a pinch of salt, and a pinch of cayenne. Run the blender for about 30 seconds, then reduce the speed to low and begin pouring 1 cup of oil, a few drops at a time to begin with, then a very slow steady stream until all the oil has been used up.

Finish by adding 1 or 2 tablespoons of lemon juice or white wine vinegar.

boiled dressing

2 tablespoons of flour
1 teaspoon dry mustard
3 tablespoons sugar
2 egg yolks
1 cup white wine
½ cup wine vinegar or lemon juice
½ cup olive oil
Salt and pepper
¼ cup sour cream

Do not confuse this superb dressing with the commercial type masquerading as mayonnaise. Use a double boiler. Heat the water in the lower part but do not let it boil or you will curdle the dressing. Meanwhile, put the flour, mustard, sugar, wine, and vinegar or lemon juice into the upper section. Beat the yolks until they are light and add them to the mixture, along with the oil, salt, and pepper. Using a wooden spoon, stir carefully and constantly until thick. Remove from the heat at once and beat in the sour cream until it blends thoroughly.

green salads

Choose any single green or a combination of greens. Different lettuces, for instance, have different textures and degrees of crispness. Wash greens well and dry carefully on linen or paper towels. Many greens are very tender and bruise easily. Discard old or wilted leaves. Now spread the greens on a fresh towel, roll them up, and place in the refrigerator until you are ready to use them. Break the greens into bite-size pieces and put them in your salad bowl. Mix a good French dressing, pour it over the greens, and toss it lightly—using a fork and spoon—until each leaf is completely covered with the dressing. Never add dressing until the last second; it wilts greens rapidly.

VARIATIONS:

Add onion rings or coarsely chopped sweet onion. *Add* thin strips of green pepper, chopped green onion, and chopped celery. *Marinate* sliced raw mushrooms in dressing for several hours and add to the salad at the last minute. *Use* a single herb, or any combination that pleases your palate. *Rub* the bowl with fresh garlic, or if you really like garlic flavor, chop it fine and add. *Add* cubes of really ripe avocado. *Use* chopped chives. *Peel* and seed a cucumber and add slices or cubes. *Add* cooked shrimp, lobster, or crab chunks, and chives and capers.

caesar salad

Use romaine lettuce only, which should be crisped and cold. Crush 2 garlic cloves into 1½ teaspoons salt in the salad bowl. Add about 12 grinds of the pepper mill. Remove the garlic cloves, if you wish. Add the lettuce, broken in bite-size pieces, not cut. Add about ¾ cup good olive oil. Toss well. Add 1 to 1½ cups crisp croutons, which have been fried in butter or olive oil, 6 to 8 cut anchovy fillets, about ¼ cup wine vinegar, or vinegar and lemon juice mixed, or just lemon juice. Finally, add about ¼ cup freshly grated Parmesan cheese and a coddled egg, 1 minute coddling. Toss thoroughly and

sprinkle with a little more cheese, and bring to the table at once.

celery salad

Wash and dry crisp, fresh celery. Cut into 1-inch slices diagonally. Make a vinaigrette dressing and to it add French Dijon mustard and dry mustard to taste. It should be rather sharp. Toss the celery and let it stand for a while in the refrigerator to develop flavor.

mushroom salad

Choose white and very fresh mushrooms. See that the gills have not opened. Wash them briefly and dry well. Pluck the stems out and put the caps into a salad bowl. Cover with a French dressing to which you have added a bit of crushed garlic and a tablespoon of chopped fresh tarragon. If you are using the dried kind, use half that amount. Toss well and let the mushrooms marinate for at least an hour—longer is even better. Each time you pass the bowl in the course of your duties, give the mushrooms a light toss. When you are ready to serve, add Belgian endive—which you have previously rinsed and split into quarters, or stripped into long leaves and kept cold—to the salad and toss well. This salad seems to have a quality of great elegance and subtlety, and, oddly enough, if served outdoors it takes on a robust character. Try it!

chef salads

Arrange in a large salad bowl on a bed of greens any of the following combinations:

Beef: Sliced beef (boiled, corned, roasted, etc.), sliced hard-cooked eggs, onion rings, cubed boiled potatoes, tomato wedges. Do not toss, but have on hand a vinaigrette sauce, so that guests can help themselves to the amount they want.

Chicken: Chicken in slices or cubes (boiled, poached, roasted, etc.), sliced raw mushrooms on a bed of romaine or water cress. The dressing should have some dry mustard added to it.

Ham: Slices or cubes or strips of ham, cubes or strips of Swiss cheese, tomato wedges, sliced onions, hard-cooked egg quarters.

Tongue: Slices or strips of cooked tongue, mushrooms, hard-cooked egg wedges, crumbled Roquefort cheese.

cole slaw

2-pound head of cabbage
4 tablespoons of butter
1 tablespoon flour
½ cup water
2 eggs
6 tablespoons sugar
1 teaspoon dry mustard
Salt
½ cup vinegar

Make your dressing in advance so that when you are ready to blend it with the cabbage it will have cooled. Fill the lower half of a double boiler with water and bring almost to the boiling point. Insert top section and blend the flour and butter in it. Slowly add the ½ cup of water, stirring all the while. Cook the mixture until it is well blended and free of any lumps. In a bowl, beat together the eggs, sugar, mustard, and salt. Pour the hot sauce over this, stirring as you do so. Replace this mixture in the top of the double boiler and cook until it is thick. Stir constantly. Be careful not to overcook it. The moment it is thick remove it from the heat and add the vinegar. Let it cool completely. Shred the cabbage and soak in salted water for 1 hour. Drain well and add the cooled dressing.

quick cole slaw

2-pound head of cabbage
1 cup of mayonnaise
½ cup sour cream
Juice of 1 lemon

1 tablespoon sugar
1 teaspoon dry mustard
Salt and pepper

Shred the cabbage and soak it for an hour in salted water. Drain and dry it well. Mix together the other ingredients and pour over the shredded cabbage.

VARIATIONS:

Add 1 teaspoon of celery seed and ¼ cup of capers to the sauce. *Or add* 1 tablespoon or more of prepared horseradish to the sauce.

red and green cole slaw

½ head each of green and red cabbage
1 cup mayonnaise
1 cup sour cream
1 teaspoon chopped dill
¼ cup capers

Shred both kinds of cabbage, keeping them separate. Mix all the other ingredients together and blend with each kind of cabbage. Arrange in 2 halves on opposite sides of a bowl and let stand for at least an hour to allow the flavors to combine.

potato salad

3 pounds (6 to 8) potatoes
1 teaspoon salt
1 teaspoon freshly ground pepper
½ cup olive oil
3 tablespoons wine vinegar
1 cup chopped green onions
½ cup chopped parsley
Hard-boiled eggs, green peppers, olives

After washing the potatoes put them into boiling salted water. Cook only until they are done. Do not overcook. Drain and plunge into cold water for a few seconds and drain again. Do not let them stay in the cold water. Peel quickly and cut into slices or cubes. Put into a large deep bowl and add the salt, pepper, oil, and vinegar mixture. Cool and then place in the refrigerator. About 2 hours before you are ready to serve, add the chopped onion and parsley. Add more oil if needed. Taste for seasoning. Garnish with sliced hard-cooked eggs, strips of green pepper, and sliced olives.

Be sure to use new potatoes, as older ones are apt to be mushy when you put the dressing over them. Also, make the salad well in advance, so that it will have a chance to blend and ripen as well as to chill.

VARIATIONS:

Use a dry white wine in place of the vinegar and add blanched, sliced almonds, ½ cup of finely cut celery, ¼ cup finely grated carrot, and the juice of 1 lemon.

Leave out the vinegar and oil and use instead enough mayonnaise or boiled dressing to bind the ingredients together.

quick potato salad

1 package Pillsbury hashed-brown potatoes
1 package Lipton onion-soup mix
½ cup olive oil
⅓ cup wine vinegar
¼ cup chopped parsley
Hard-boiled eggs, tomato wedges,
ripe olives, greens
Mayonnaise

Follow directions on package for reconstituting the potatoes. Drain well. While still hot, add onion-soup mix, oil, and vinegar. Allow to stand until cool. Refrigerate for several hours. When ready to serve, add parsley and arrange on a bed of greens. Garnish with mayonnaise, hard-boiled egg quarters, tomato wedges, and black ripe olives.

VARIATIONS:

Add chunks of tuna fish (a 7-ounce can will do) to the salad just before arranging on a serving dish. *Or add* a small tin of anchovy fillets and 2 tablespoons of capers. *Or add* thin strips of cold boiled beef.

combination salads

A good way to serve a combination salad is to cook the vegetables separately in salted water, drain them, and marinate them in French dressing. Arrange on individual platters and let your guests help themselves to what they like. Serve additional dressing on the side. A large bowl of greens should accompany this. The following vegetables are only a few of the many that go well together: *Peas, little onions, leeks, celery, celery root, cauliflower, carrots, broccoli, beets, green beans, white beans, asparagus, artichoke hearts, tiny whole artichokes, zucchini.*

russe

This is nothing more than a mixed vegetable salad with mayonnaise to bind the ingredients together. Use a large platter or bowl, arrange your greens, and mound the vegetables on them.

other combinations

Combine cucumber cubes, bits of raw celery, diced cooked potatoes, raw carrots, peas, cubes of cooked chicken, duck, tongue, ham.

Combine cubed cooked carrots, beets, potatoes, peas, diced raw celery, chicken and ham cubes.

Combine cooked peas, diced carrots, diced potatoes, cooked beans, pimiento, together with cubes of ham and tongue.

Another way to serve any of the above is to mix the ingredients well, pack them into a ring mold of appropriate size and chill until ready to serve, then turn out on the bed of greens. Garnish with hard-cooked egg, pimiento, tomatoes, anchovies, capers.

lettuce and tomato plate

One of the simplest and best-known salad plates, it is all too often treated so badly. The tomatoes should be ripe and should be peeled. To do this, plunge them in boiling water for no more than a minute. Take them out and plunge into cold water at once. You will discover that the skin peels off easily. Slice them evenly and lay them on a few leaves of crisp lettuce, 3 or 4 slices per serving. Dress them with a vinaigrette sauce, mayonnaise, or a French dressing made with cognac instead of vinegar. This last is truly superb; your guests will be pleasantly puzzled by the elusive and delightful flavor.

waldorf

Again, one of the badly abused salads, and unnecessarily so. This can be a real treat if made properly. Combine 3 cups peeled and unpeeled diced apples with 1 cup finely chopped celery and ¾ cup broken walnut meats. Bind together with mayonnaise.

rice salad

Combine 4 cups of boiled, drained rice with 6 tablespoons olive oil, 3 tablespoons wine vinegar, 1 teaspoon of salt and the same of pepper, and ½ teaspoon of tarragon. Let it cool. Now mix with chopped green pepper, parsley, chives, cubes of cucumber, and chopped green onion. Add a vinaigrette to taste, mix it all well, and mound it on your greens.

fruit salads

French Pear: Peel and core ripe pears. Slice and marinate in a very tart French dressing.

India Salad: Combine grapefruit sections that have had all the membranes and pits removed from them with slices of ripe avocado. Use a French dressing to which you have added ¼ to ½ teaspoon curry powder.

Spiced Grapefruit: Combine grapefruit sections prepared as above with navel-orange slices or sections in a French dressing to which you have added fresh rosemary.

Melon-Peach: Thin slices of peeled cantaloupe combined with slices of peeled ripe peaches. Use a French dressing to which you have added ¼ teaspoon of dry mustard.

Fruit Market: Peeled, cored, and cubed apple, sliced pear, and grapes in a dressing made half-and-half of French dressing and sour cream.

tunafish niçoise

Make a dressing Niçoise by adding 2 mashed or finely cut anchovy fillets to a vinaigrette sauce. Open and drain 2 cans of white-meat tuna packed in olive oil. (You may use the drained oil for your dressing; it gives additional flavor.) Place the fish on a bed of greens. Surround it with ripe, quartered tomatoes, hard-cooked eggs, also quartered, and additional anchovy fillets. Garnish this with pimiento and olives and serve with your Niçoise dressing.

tuna aurore

Drain the oil from a can of tuna fish. Flake it and gently combine it with diced crisp apple, white seedless grapes, chopped celery, and chopped sweet red or white onion. Bind the salad with mayonnaise. Serve on a bed of greens.

two shrimp salads

One: Combine cooked shrimp with shredded cabbage. Make a dressing half-and-half of mayonnaise and sour cream. Bind with this dressing. Serve on greens.

Two: Marinate cooked shrimp and tangerine or orange sections in a mixture of soy sauce, salt and pepper, sugar or honey, a bit of ground ginger, crushed garlic, and chopped onion. Chill well and mound on greens. You may also add ½ to 1 teaspoon of curry powder, according to your taste.

avocado & shrimp

Serve half an avocado per person. Be sure you do not prepare it until just before serving.

BLINDMAN'S BUFF, BY JEAN-HONORÉ FRAGONARD.
NATIONAL GALLERY OF ART, WASHINGTON, D. C., SAMUEL H. KRESS COLLECTION, LOAN.

Once the flesh is exposed to air it oxidizes and takes on an unpleasant black appearance. Rubbing the exposed surfaces with lemon juice will assist in retarding the darkening. You may or may not peel the avocado. I prefer it unpeeled; it is easier to scoop out the ripe flesh, the stuffing does not go scooting all over the plate, and you have lessened the problem of darkening. Combine tiny cooked shrimp (they are now available in tins, jars, or even frozen, from such places as Denmark, Iceland, and Panama) with a good mustard-flavored mayonnaise. Or, if you cannot find the tiny shrimp, which incidentally most closely resemble the wonderful West Coast variety, use the standard-sized eastern or Gulf variety, and chop them coarsely.

VARIATIONS:

Use cubes of tomato and chopped green onion mixed with a vinaigrette sauce. *Or marinate* in a very sharp vinaigrette, chopped green pepper, chopped green onion, chopped cucumber, and chopped celery. *Or use* a chicken or turkey salad. *Or add* crabmeat as you would shrimp.

whole cold salmon

This is one of the "princely" dishes, spectacular to behold and not as difficult to make as you might think. Wrap the fish in cheesecloth and lower it carefully into a court bouillon. Cook the fish in it until it is done; about 8 minutes per pound is safe. Do not overcook or it will fall apart and be tasteless. After it has cooled a bit, remove from the liquid and peel away the skin. Leave the head and tail on. Arrange on a bed of greens and mask with a good mayonnaise. Decorate the platter with sliced cucumber, tiny tomatoes, or sliced tomatoes, parsley or water cress, and thin slices of lemon with scalloped edges. To be really "classic" you might reduce and clarify the court bouillon and make an aspic of it. Pour it into a pan to a height of about ½ inch and when it has set, cut it into fancy shapes and decorate with them. This is very, very elegant.

small fish

The same method for making a cold salmon dish can be utilized with great success with smaller fish, among them halibut, trout, and striped bass.

salmon/celery salad

2 cups of cold salmon (fresh or canned)
1 cup finely diced celery
Mayonnaise
Greens
¼ cup chopped parsley
Hard-cooked eggs

Bind the salmon and celery together with the mayonnaise. Heap it on the greens, sprinkle with chopped parsley and decorate with sliced hard-cooked eggs.

crabmeat

Arrange on a bed of either romaine or another lettuce, 1 pound of crabmeat—fresh, frozen, or canned—which has been carefully picked over. Pour over it a vinaigrette dressing and let it chill thoroughly.

VARIATIONS:

Use a good, not-too-spicy mayonnaise. *Or* use a remoulade dressing.

crab louis

To 1 cup of mayonnaise, add ⅓ cup of whipped, heavy cream, ¼ cup chili sauce, 2 tablespoons grated onion, 2 tablespoons chopped parsley, and a few grains of cayenne. Combine with 1 pound of crab meat.

avocado stuffed with crabmeat

Make Crab Louis and heap it lightly in halves of avocado. Serve on shredded greens with hard-boiled eggs and ripe olives.

cold lobster salad

One of the simplest and most delicious lobster dishes is cold lobster salad. How often do we find tired, rubbery hunks of lobster meat that have been overcooked and immersed in a so-called "mayonnaise"?

To make lobster correctly, prepare a court bouillon by boiling together a bottle of dry white wine, an equal amount of water, a carrot, an onion, bay leaf, thyme, salt, and 4 or 5 peppercorns. After half an hour of boiling, reduce to a simmer and plunge your live lobster into it. Let it barely bubble for about 15 minutes or so and turn it off. Allow the lobster to cool in the liquid. Remove, pick out the lobster meat, and let it chill. Serve on a bed of greens dressed with a mustard mayonnaise, remoulade, or Russian dressing. Surround it with any or all of these: sliced hard-cooked egg, ripe olives, sliced tomato, capers, strips of cucumber, small, cooked shrimp.

lobster oriental

Arrange cooked cold rice on a bed of greens, and top with cooked lobster chunks. Make a dressing of oil, vinegar, soy sauce, ginger, a pinch of curry, coarsely chopped water-chestnuts and chopped celery. Pour the dressing over all. Or the rice and the rest of the ingredients may be mixed together. Whichever way you serve it, it is a treat. Chopped or sliced almonds also are a pleasant addition.

beef salad

On a large platter make a bed of greens. Slice beef no thicker than ¼ inch. You may use boiled or roasted beef or leftover steak. Around the beef slices arrange in an attractive pattern potatoes that have been boiled, sliced, marinated in a French dressing, and dusted with chopped parsley; wedges of hard-cooked eggs, sliced or wedged tomatoes, sweet red or Bermuda onion slices, and olives. Dress with a vinaigrette.

chicken salad

2½ cups cubed cold chicken
Mayonnaise
1 cup chopped celery
Greens and garnishes

Be sure to remove all the fat, skin, and gristle from the chicken. Cut it into cubes. Combine with the celery and mayonnaise, add salt and pepper to taste, pile on a bed of greens, and garnish with any or all of the following: tomato quarters, wedges of hard-cooked eggs, capers, pimiento, stuffed olives.

VARIATIONS:

Add ½ cup of chopped green onions. *Or* ½ cup of chopped toasted nuts, almonds, walnuts, pecans, filberts, etc. *Add* 2 tablespoons of a not-too-hot chutney to the mayonnaise.

veal salad

Make exactly the same as chicken salad, substituting veal cubes or slices.

ham salad

2½ cups cubed ham
½ cup chopped green onion
Mustard mayonnaise
½ cup chopped celery
¼ cup chopped gherkins
Hard-cooked egg
Greens

Mix the ham (from which you have removed all fat, gristle, and skin) with the celery, onion, gherkins, and mustard mayonnaise. Pile on a bed of lettuce and garnish with hard-cooked egg.

pork salad

Use leftover roast pork cut into cubes. Mix with diced, unpeeled apple and with chopped celery, and blend with a mayonnaise.

canned-meat salads

Use canned corned beef, tongue, turkey, chicken, Vienna sausage, or frankfurters, and follow the directions on greens, dressing, and garnishes for any of the other meat salads.

cucumber salad

You might want to try this amusing but, at the same time, very logical way of doing cucumber salad. The French created this one, and very good it is, too. Be sure that you have a strong arm and, most of all, perseverance. Peel 2 or 3 cucumbers and slice very thin. Take 2 large, deep soup plates, place cucumber slices in one and add coarse salt. Now, cover with the other soup plate and shake vigorously for 15 minutes, or more. This bruises the cucumbers and gives you a limp salad, tender and delicious. Finally, drain off excess liquid and serve the cucumbers either with a French dressing or a good mustard mayonnaise. Have crusty French bread on hand as an accompaniment.

sweet-sour salad

For a crisp and sweet-sour salad, try this. Peel the cucumbers and slice them thin. Add 2 heaping tablespoons of sugar, and salt and pepper to taste. Now add ½ cup or more of vinegar—wine, cider, or any other of your choice. It should be a rather tart vinegar. Add ½ cup cold water and 5 or 6 ice cubes. Let stand in the refrigerator for 2 or 3 hours. Most refreshing—and an interesting change from the usual cucumber salads.

VARIATIONS:

Add chopped scallions. *Or* chopped chives and parsley. *Or* fresh or dried dill.

cucumbers in sour cream

Prepare cucumbers as for sweet-sour salad, adding any of the extra ingredients. Let marinate for 2 or 3 hours, drain well, and mix with commercial sour cream. Chill.

tomato and onion salad

Peel tomatoes. Slice and lay on a bed of greens on a platter. Over this put thinly sliced rings of sweet Italian or Bermuda onion. Salt and fresh ground pepper and a vinaigrette dressing complete this simple but wonderful dish.

tomato basilica

Basil is the perfect mate for tomato, just as tarragon seems to be the right one for chicken. Prepare the tomatoes, sprinkle with a good quantity of chopped basil, salt and pepper, and a vinaigrette dressing.

tomato charente

To sliced tomatoes add cognac, cognac with salt and pepper, or cognac in combination with a fine olive oil.

tomato and mushroom

This is great with grilled steak. Chop ½ pound of mushrooms coarsely and sauté them in olive oil with a touch of garlic. Slice tomatoes fairly thin and arrange the mushrooms on them.

stuffed tomato salad

Allow a medium-sized tomato for each person. Clean well, cut out the stem, and hollow them out. The list of stuffings is endless. Here are just a few: *Fill with* any kind of seafood salad, salmon, tuna, shrimp, lobster. *With avocado cubes* that have been marinated in a curried French dressing. *With meat or poultry salad*—chicken, ham, lamb, beef, tongue, turkey. *With poached*

eggs, trimmed neatly so they fit into the hollow, covered with jellied consommé; with a pastry tube, pipe a rosette of mayonnaise on top.

lentil salad

Prepare the lentils the same as for a lentil casserole. Drain and place them in the refrigerator to cool. Chop a bunch of green onions or chives with 1 cup of parsley. Make an oil and vinegar dressing and mix them all together.

white bean salad

Soak white picked-over beans overnight (or you may use the quick-cooking variety, following the directions on the box). Simmer in fresh water to which you have added a bay leaf, an onion stuck with 2 cloves, salt and pepper, and a clove of garlic. Drain the lentils when they are tender but not mushy, and chill them. Mix them with 3 tablespoons of chopped green pepper, 4 tablespoons of chopped parsley, 3 tablespoons of chopped chives, and French dressing. Serve them in a large salad bowl that has been lined with romaine or other lettuce.

hot bean salad

1 pound of green beans
Salt and pepper
4 strips of bacon
3 medium onions, sliced thin
2 tablespoons of mild vinegar
Lemon juice
1 teaspoon sugar

Prepare the beans as you usually would for boiling and, while they are cooking, cut up the bacon and slowly fry it until it is crisp. Remove the bacon and add the onion slices to the fat in the pan. Sauté these until they are just done. Add the vinegar, a dash of lemon juice, and sprinkle on the sugar. Taste for salt, add pepper, and when the beans are done, drain them and add the sauce and the pieces of crisp bacon, and mix thoroughly.

breads

Good fresh bread is so fundamental that it is easy to take for granted. Yet all your fine-quality meat and all your carefully prepared sauces and relishes will go for nought if the accompanying breads lack the texture and flavor that contribute so happily to good eating. Excellent bread may be prepared out of doors—one or two of the following recipes will show you how —but many, if not most, require an assist from your oven so that they may be brought to your open-air table at a peak of crusty perfection.

basic white bread

1 package or cake of yeast
2 cups of lukewarm milk
2 tablespoons of sugar
1 tablespoon of salt
6 cups of flour
4 tablespoons of melted butter

Use the largest mixing bowl you have or, failing this, a large pot. Put the lukewarm milk into it, and if you are using dry yeast, sprinkle it on and mix. If you are using a cake of yeast, crumble it into the liquid and mix well. Add the sugar and salt. Now add 1 cup of flour at a time and mix it well, using a wooden spoon. When you have a smooth, but not firm, dough, add the melted butter. Now add the rest of the flour and mix thoroughly until it is very smooth. Turn the dough out on a floured board and knead it until it is satiny and smooth. Let it rest, covered, while you wash the bowl or pot and grease it well with butter or shortening. Put the dough into it and set it in a warm place away from draughts so that it may rise until it is doubled in bulk. This usually takes about 1½ to 2 hours. Remove the cover and punch the dough down with your fist, and turn it out on a floured board and knead it again for a few minutes. You will find that it has an elastic quality it did not possess before. Divide it in 2 equal parts, shape into loaves, and put each loaf in a well-greased bread pan. Cover lightly with a clean towel and let it stand in a warm place to rise again. Place into a 375 F.

oven and bake for about 40 to 45 minutes. Remove from pans and allow to cool on a rack away from draughts.

cuban bread

1 package or 1 cake of yeast
2 cups of lukewarm water
1¼ tablespoons of salt
1 tablespoon of sugar
6 to 9 cups of flour

Dissolve the yeast in the warm water and add the salt and sugar. Using a wooden spoon, add the flour a cup at a time, beating it in well. We give you the variable amount of flour since all flour varies in the amount of liquid it will absorb. Use enough to make a smooth, firm dough. Cover with a towel and put in a warm place to rise until it is double in bulk. Turn it out on a table or board that is well-floured and knead for a few minutes, then shape into loaves in any of the following forms: long French, round Italian, or small individual loaves. Sprinkle corn meal liberally on a baking sheet and arrange the loaves on this. Allow to rise for 5 minutes. Cut a slash across the loaves 2 or 3 times or make a long slash down the middle, brush with cold water and place in a cold oven. Set the oven for 400 F. Place a pan of boiling water on the rack below the loaves and bake for about 40 to 45 minutes.

Note: The more you knead, the better your result will be.

camp breads

Bread on a Stick: Select a long branch that is green and will not burn when exposed to the heat. Strip it of all its leaves and twigs until it is quite smooth. Roll out your bread dough into a long "snake" and twist it in a spiral around the stick. Leave a good 8 or 9 inches of the stick as a handle so you can turn the bread over a campfire. Do so until it is brown on the outside.

Bread Baked in Foil: This is a good way to bake bread in the open when you have no oven and must improvise. Pull out a good length of heavy-duty aluminum foil and fold it double or triple, but be sure that it is long enough to accommodate your loaf. Shape the dough and place it on the foil, carefully folding the excess foil down and tucking the ends under. Place this on coals that have burned down, and bake. Remember that the dough will expand, so be sure to leave enough room.

basic biscuit mix

2 cups of flour
2½ teaspoons of double-action or
5 teaspoons of single-action baking powder
1 teaspoon of salt
2 teaspoons of sugar
5 tablespoons of fat
Approximately ¾ cup of milk

You may use any fat that is available: butter, margarine, vegetable, or lard. Whatever your choice, cut it into all the dry ingredients which you have sifted together, or rub it in with your fingertips. Add just enough milk to make a smooth, not-too-hard dough which can be handled without being too sticky. Turn it out on a floured board and knead lightly for no more than a minute. The things you can do with this basic mix are limitless, and you may want to double or even triple the recipe for large groups. Better yet, make up a really large batch of the dry ingredients only and keep it in a tightly covered tin can for use as needed.

VARIATIONS:

Square Biscuits: Pat lightly or roll out the dough to a thickness of about ½ inch if you like fluffy biscuits or thinner if you like crisper ones. Cut into long strips about 1 inch wide and then into squares. Arrange these on a buttered baking sheet and bake in a hot oven— 450 F.—for about 12 to 15 minutes.

Round Biscuits: Proceed as above and use a round cutter. Arrange on a buttered baking sheet and bake for approximately 12 to 15 minutes in a 450 F. oven.

Skillet Biscuits: You may use a skillet if you are really roughing it and do not have an oven. Grease the skillet well, cut or shape the biscuits, and arrange them in the skillet. Put them over the grill or coals only long enough to set them, then arrange them in front of the fire and finish them. You will hasten the matter considerably if you drape a long sheet of aluminum foil around the skillet to act as a reflector.

Cheese Biscuits: Use ½ cup of grated cheese—American, Gruyere, Switzerland Swiss—for each 2 cups of baking mix.

One Large Biscuit: Pat out the dough to a circle ¾ inch thick, place in a well-greased skillet and bake as you would basic biscuits. When the dough is brown on top, turn it very carefully, and bake until the other side is brown. Split the biscuit, or cut it into wedges.

Herb Biscuits: Chop parsley, tarragon, and chives not too finely and add to the basic mix; about 3 tablespoons to each 2 cups of mix.

Chili Biscuits: Add 1 teaspoon or more of chili powder to each 2 cups of basic mix, at the point at which you add milk.

Curry Biscuits: Same as above, but use curry powder to your taste.

Onion Biscuits: Sauté finely grated onion in butter until it just begins to color. Season with salt and pepper. When you prepare your dough be sure to roll it thinly and add some chopped parsley to it. Cut to any desired shape and top with a bit of the sautéed onion. Bake as usual.

Rich Biscuits: Prepare and roll the dough in the usual manner, cut into rounds or squares or diamonds, but dip each piece into melted butter before baking.

scones

Sift together 2 cups of flour, ½ teaspoon salt, 1 tablespoon of baking powder, and 2 tablespoons of sugar. Using a pastry blender, 2 knives, or your finger tips, cut in ¼ cup of sweet butter until the mixture resembles coarse corn meal. Add ½ cup of cream and a beaten egg. Roll or pat out the dough until it is about ¾ inch thick and cut it into wedges with a very sharp knife. Brush with egg white, shake granulated sugar on top, and bake in a fairly hot oven—400 F.—for about 15 minutes. The English serve these at tea with Devonshire cream.

VARIATION:

Chop coarsely ¼ cup of raisins and fold in just before you add liquid.

griddle cakes

Some of the best pancakes you ever tasted can be made with Basic Biscuit Mix. Just add enough milk to make a batter of pouring consistency with a bit of additional melted shortening. You may further enrich it by adding a beaten egg. Bake these on a griddle or a large skillet that has been lightly greased.

VARIATIONS:

With blueberries: To 3 cups of batter add 1 cup of blueberrries and 3 or 4 tablespoons of sugar. *With chocolate:* Use ¼ cup or more of Nestlé's Chocolate Morsels in the batter and bake as usual. *With butterscotch:* The same amount of Nestlé's Butterscotch Morsels. *With corn:* Drain a small can of whole-kernel corn, stir into the batter, and bake as usual. You might even add 2 or 3 tablespoons of ground corn meal to the batter for additional corn flavor. *With bacon:* Fry 6 strips of bacon until very crisp and dry. Crumble this into the batter and mix well. Use a tiny bit of the bacon fat when you grease the griddle or skillet. *With almonds:* Chop shelled almonds coarsely and add to the batter. *With cheese:* Add ¾ cup grated Cheddar cheese to the batter and bake as usual. *With herbs:* Add 3 or 4 tablespoons of chopped herbs—parsley, chives, tarragon, etc.—to the batter. *With coconut:* Add 1 cup shredded coconut to the batter.

french pancakes

1 cup flour
¼ cup sugar (if used as a dessert)
Pinch of salt
2 eggs
2 egg yolks
¾ cup milk
3 tablespoons of heavy cream
1 tablespoon of melted butter
1 teaspoon cognac

Sift together all the dry ingredients. Beat together the eggs and egg yolks and mix into the dry ingredients. Add the milk and heavy cream, stirring the mixture until it is very smooth. Now add the melted butter and cognac. Be sure there are no lumps. If there are, strain the mixture to eliminate them. Let the batter stand for 2 or 3 hours. Use a 6- or 7-inch heavy pan to make these pancakes. Melt a little bit of butter in the hot pan and pour in enough batter to cover the bottom. Pour back the excess. Bake each pancake until it is lightly browned, then turn and bake on the other side. Stack them in a folded napkin, so they keep warm and do not dry out. These pancakes can be used in all sorts of dishes, from hors d'oeuvres, through main courses, to delicious desserts. They can be rolled, folded, mounded, etc. Filled with jelly or jam or berries of any description, they make delicious sweets. Simmered in a sauce and flamed with a liqueur, they make the famed crepes suzette.

tortillas

As bread is the "staff of life" to the European and North American, so is the tortilla to the Mexican. Two varieties exist. Those made from corn and those made from wheat. Undoubtedly the corn is the better known and more widely used. To make tortillas is a long drawn-out process, and throughout Mexico you can hear the sound of tortillas being prepared. Corn is first leached, the skin removed, and the kernels ground on a slab of stone, using another piece of stone as a pestle. This flour is mixed with a

WOMAN WITH LOAVES, BY PABLO PICASSO.
PHILADELPHIA MUSEUM OF ART.

COURTESY OF RARE BOOK ROOM, NEW YORK PUBLIC LIBRARY.

bit of water and formed into small balls. Then comes the patting process, the sound of which is so familiar to travelers below the border. The dough is slapped and patted until it forms thin, round cakes, then baked on a griddle until done, but not brown. The tortillas are sold, and the purchaser reheats them at home on a griddle or even over a direct flame. They are used in innumerable ways: fried until crisp, filled with chili con carne, beans, bits of shredded lettuce, cheese, etc. Today in the Southwest there are factories that turn out tortillas by the thousands daily and pack them in pressure-sealed cans, so they remain fresh. They even come frozen.

Note: If you should want to make your own tortillas, but do not want to go through the arduous process of producing them "authentically," you can achieve a very near relation by using any commercial corn-meal mix that will make bread. Add water to make a stiff dough, pat and shape into tortillas, and bake on a griddle. You will be amazed at the results.

herbed bread

Cut a loaf of French bread in half the long way and spread both pieces with the following mixture: A bunch of parsley and a bunch of scallions chopped fine, with green parts included, and mixed with ¼ pound of soft butter. Add salt and pepper to taste and reform into a loaf. Bake in a 375 F. oven for about 15 minutes. Serve very hot, cut into thick slices.

fines herbes

Use the classic combination of fresh herbs—tarragon, chives, and parsley—chopped finely and mixed with butter, and spread on French bread that has been prepared as for Herbed Bread and heated in the oven.

rosemary butter

Cut bread lengthwise; spread with butter that has been combined with fresh rosemary and creamed. Sprinkle with chopped parsley and onion and place under the broiler until the butter is melted and edges are brown.

garlic loaf

Combine ¼ pound of butter with 3 cloves of mashed garlic, spread on bread cut in thick slices (but not quite through the loaf), place in the oven and heat for 15 minutes.

VARIATIONS:

With chopped parsley: Chop parsley finely and add to the garlic butter. *With green onion:* Chop a bunch of scallions, green and white parts, and add to the garlic butter. *With mustard:* Mix 3 or 4 tablespoons of French's prepared mustard with the garlic butter and spread on the bread before baking.

cheese bread

Combine ¼ pound of butter and grated sharp Cheddar. Spread on the bread before baking. You may vary it in any of the following ways:

VARIATIONS:

With cheese and parsley: Combine ½ cup chopped parsley with the cheese butter. *With poppy seed:* 4 tablespoons of poppy seed added to the cheese butter. *With sesame seed:* 4 or 5 tablespoons of sesame seed added to the butter. *With onion and cheese:* Add finely chopped onion to the cheese butter. *With cheese and herb:* Mixed herbs, finely chopped with the cheese butter. Of course, you may vary cheese: Parmesan, Gruyère, Jack are all satisfactory.

stuffed bread

This is the ancestor of the currently popular hero sandwich, which is nothing more than a Gargantuan sandwich, using a whole loaf of French or Italian bread stuffed with just about any combination of meats, cheeses, and condiments you choose. This version is a little more elegant, but certainly not "sissy," since it traces one of its origins to New Orleans, where dandies arriving home in the early hours of the morning after a night's carousing needed something substantial to stick to their ribs. First, take a loaf of French bread and carefully cut it lengthwise one-third of the way. In effect, cut a cover, because you now scoop out the insides and fill the loaf with a variety of ingredients. Only your imagination is the limit on what may go inside: Ham, cheese, salami, pickle, olive, bits of chopped cooked vegetable, etc. These should all be cut coarsely and bound together with some sour cream or mayonnaise. Replace the "cover," wrap in foil, and heat in the oven. Cut in thick slices and serve.

onion bread

Sauté in butter finely chopped or grated onion. Mix this with ¼ pound of butter, spread on a loaf of French bread cut in half the long way, and put into the oven to heat through.

corn bread

¾ cup corn meal
1 cup boiling water
2 tablespoons butter
Salt
2 eggs, well beaten
2 teaspoons baking powder
1 cup milk
1 tablespoon sugar

Pour the boiling water over the corn meal. Add the butter and ½ teaspoon salt. Beat the eggs until they are light and lemon-colored. To the eggs, add the baking powder, milk, and sugar. Add this to the corn meal and mix well. Pour into a well-buttered baking pan and bake in a moderately hot oven, 375 F., for about 25 minutes, or until it is nicely browned and thoroughly cooked.

cheese, fruit, dessert

devil's food tower

Prepare 2 packages of devil's food mix (I prefer the Duncan Hines brand), according to the directions on the package, and bake 4 nine-inch layers. For a fluffy white frosting, use:

1½ cups sugar
¾ cup light corn syrup
4 egg whites
4 tablespoons water
½ teaspoon salt
¼ teaspoon cream of tartar
2 teaspoons vanilla

Combine the sugar, corn syrup, egg whites, water, salt, and cream of tartar in the top of a double boiler. Cook over boiling water, beating constantly with a rotary or electric beater. The mixture is finished when it stands in peaks. Remove it from the heat and add vanilla. Ice the layers and place them one on top of the other. If you want to, you can pile it with freshly grated coconut or with chocolate morsels, or chocolate shot. Or, you may dribble melted semi-sweet chocolate over it.

cheese

Cheese, in its endless variety, is one of the more useful and versatile foods in existence. It is one of the better sources of protein in any diet—10 pounds of milk being concentrated in every single pound of cheese. It can be served at any meal and in many ways—as an appetizer, a garnish, in the preparation of innumerable dishes, and as an elegant, yet simple, dessert. In many parts of Europe, the natural finale to a lunch or dinner is a loaf of good, crusty bread, a bit of sweet butter, a cheese, and red wine. It is wise to remember when serving cheese that white wine does not go as well with it as red. A bottle of red wine enhances and complements the flavor of cheese, and the cheese will bring out the best in the wine.

Unless it is unobtainable, use natural cheese. Many large cheese producers have brought out so-called "processed" cheeses, but, at best, they are a poor substitute for the real thing. They are made from skim milk and the whey (or watery part of the milk) from natural cheeses, and other products. Try to avoid them in the preparation of your meals and treat yourself to the aroma and flavor of natural cheese.

A word about keeping cheese. In the past, when refrigeration was hit-or-miss, storage was a problem. Cheese dried out, became overripe, or just went bad. These days, it is far simpler to keep cheese properly. Heavy aluminum foil or Saran wrap are perfect for sealing in the natural moisture of the cheese.

Cheese varieties are as numerous as the people who produce them. If you are a country dweller, look for a small farm nearby that still makes its own cheese. If you are fortunate enough to know the farmer, you may be able to persuade him to part with some.

For General Cooking: Switzerland Swiss (Emmanthaler), Gruyère, Aged Cheddar.

For Grating: Italian Parmesan, Italian Romano; Dry, aged Swiss or Gruyère; Dry, aged Cheddar.

For Melting: Swiss Gruyère, California Jack, Mozzarella, Muenster, Coon.

For Appetizers: Roquefort, Gorgonzola, Blue, Stilton.

For Dessert: Brie, Camembert, Pont-l'Eveque, Bel Paese, Tallegio.

For General Eating: Gruyère, Swiss, Cheddar, Oka, Port Salut, Edam, Gouda. And so on.

coeur à la crème

1 pound cream cheese
1 pound cottage cheese
1 cup light cream
½ cup heavy cream
½ pint sour cream
2 heart-shaped baskets
Strawberry jam

Mix the cheeses together and slowly add the light cream. Line the baskets with cheesecloth that has been wrung out in cold water. Fill these molds to the top with the cheese mixture. Fold the excess cheesecloth over the top to cover the cheese. Place baskets in the refrigerator for 6 or 7 hours. Be sure to put them on something to catch the excess moisture that will drip through. Remove the baskets from the refrigerator when you are ready to serve and carefully turn them out on serving plates, removing the cheesecloth. Mix the sour cream and heavy cream together and pour over the tops. Surround with mounds of strawberry preserve and heated French bread.

welsh rarebit

2 tablespoons butter
½ pound sharp Cheddar cheese,
grated or shredded
2 egg yolks
2 egg whites
1 teaspoon dry mustard
1 tablespoon Worcestershire sauce
½ teaspoon salt
Grated horseradish
1 cup beer or ale

Melt butter in a heavy saucepan. Add **cheese** and allow it to melt until smooth and creamy. Mix egg yolks with the mustard, Worcestershire sauce, salt, and a little grated horseradish. Beat the egg whites very stiff. When the cheese is completely melted, add the yolks, stir well, and thin with beer or ale. When the ingredients are well blended and the rarebit is almost at the boiling point, fold in the beaten egg whites. Serve at once on toast.

fruits

Fruit is endlessly versatile. For a complete chart of ways to serve it, see pages 210-211.

tangerine sections pickled in rum

Carefully unzip the skin from 12 tangerines. Separate them and remove all the strings that cling to each section. Prepare a marinade made of Jamaica rum, grated onion, vinegar, honey, fresh or dried rosemary, salt and pepper. Let the sections marinate in the refrigerator for at least 24 hours before you plan to serve them.

baked bananas

Use firm, ripe bananas. Be sure that they are not too soft. Peel them and place them side by side in a well-buttered baking dish. Sprinkle with brown sugar and a little lime juice. Dot lavishly with butter and bake in a moderate oven for about 15 or 20 minutes. Remove from the oven and pour over them about 3 ounces of Jamaica rum and light it.

basic ice creams

If you ever sat on the back porch of a summer Sunday afternoon when you were little, and turned the crank of a freezer until you thought your arm would come off, anticipating the moment that the dasher would be yours, you know the cold lusciousness of honest-to-goodness ice cream and cannot be content with the pseudo mixtures that go by the name of ice cream today. It is sad that honest ice cream has gone by the boards, since it is simplicity itself to make. Of all the millions of gallons of "ice cream" frozen commercially today, I doubt that more than one-tenth of one per cent is true cream combined with eggs, flavorings, liqueurs, spices, etc. Usually, it is dried or condensed milk combined with stabilizers, cornstarch, and other "modern improvements" all whipped together and pumped full of air. If you would like to experience the texture and flavor of genuine ice cream, try the following recipes.

homemade, freezer ice cream

You may start with a number of different ice cream mixtures, listed below, but be sure to chill them in the refrigerator before putting them into the freezer. Freezers, incidentally, can be found at—or ordered from—good hardware stores, or the housewares section of a department store. They range widely in price—anywhere from $5 up. Scald the container, rinse it with ice water, and fill two-thirds full of the mixture. Do not overfill! Fit the dasher into place, cover, and place into the freezer tub. Fill the tub a little above the cream-mixture line with a combination of 3 parts ice to 1 part rock salt. Start turning the crank, slowly at first, adding ice and salt to the tub as it melts and forms a brine. After about 15 minutes the cream will have become mush and you may turn the crank a bit more rapidly. As the cream freezes it will be increasingly hard to turn the crank. When the ice cream is finished, carefully remove the freezer from the tub and wipe the top. Remove the dasher, scrape it clean, and pack the ice cream down into the container. Cover it very carefully, making sure that no salt seeps in when you return the container to the tub. Pack it with a mixture of 4 parts ice to 1 part rock salt, cover with a piece of burlap, and allow it to stand for 1 or 2 hours.

ice cream in a refrigerator freezer

First, set the temperature of your freezer or freezing compartment as high as it will go. Prepare a mixture, turn it into a refrigerator tray, and place on the freezing shelf. Let it freeze to the mushy stage. Spoon it into a mixing bowl that has been chilled and beat it with a rotary or electric beater until it is smooth. Return it to the tray and freeze for about 3 hours, or until it is solid. Cover the top of the tray with wax paper to prevent the formation of ice crystals.

frozen cream

Slit a 2-inch piece of vanilla bean in half and scrape the pulp into 1 quart of heavy cream. Scald the cream, add ¾ cup of sugar, and let it cool. Chill it, and then freeze as above.

french ice cream

½ cup sugar
¼ cup water
¼ teaspoon cream of tartar
4 egg yolks
1 one-inch piece of vanilla bean
3½ cups heavy cream

Combine the sugar, water, and cream of tartar in a saucepan and bring to a boil. Lower the flame slightly and let it cook until the syrup spins a light thread. Now, beat the egg yolks until they are light and fluffy. Very gradually, begin pouring the syrup on them, beating all the while until the mixture is thick and pale. Scrape the pulp from the vanilla bean and add it to the eggs with the cream. Stir until blended and freeze it in tub or refrigerator.

Chocolate Ice Cream: Instead of vanilla, use 6 ounces of semi-sweet chocolate morsels that have been melted together with 5 tablespoons of very strong black coffee.

Strawberry: Stir 1 cup cold strawberry purée into the basic mixture before freezing.

Various Fruit Ice Creams: You may use fruit purées, or small pieces (as in the case of peaches and apricots, etc.) in the proportion of 1 cup to the basic mixture as above.

mousse

This is perhaps the richest of all frozen creams, yet it is not at all difficult to make. You may freeze it in a refrigerator tray, in silver or crystal serving bowls, or even in little paper cups.

basic vanilla mousse

¾ cup sugar
½ cup water
4 egg yolks
1 one-inch piece of vanilla bean
2 cups heavy cream

Bring the sugar and water to a boil in a saucepan and let cook for 5 minutes. Let it cool. Meanwhile, beat 4 egg yolks in the top of a double boiler. Very gradually stir in the sugar syrup, add the pulp from the vanilla bean, and cook over hot water, stirring all the time until thick and creamy. Put it through a very fine hair-sieve to remove any lumps, or whip it in a blender for 1 or 2 minutes. Let it cool. Whip the heavy cream until it is stiff and combine with the blended mixture. Then allow to freeze.

VARIATIONS:

Chocolate: Use ½ cup melted semi-sweet chocolate morsels in place of the vanilla.

Fruit Mousse: In place of the vanilla, use 2 cups of sweetened fruit purée of your choice, and the juice of half a lemon.

sherbet

Extremely simple to prepare, just as simple to consume, and variable to unbelievable degrees are the sherbets. They are, in effect, fruit juices —plus a simple syrup and white of egg—which have been frozen to mush and served in a glass. You may top them with additional fruit, liqueur, etc. A beautiful finish to a rich dinner, since they fill the needed desire for something sweet, without additional richness.

lemon sherbet

Combine 2 cups sugar and 4 cups of water in a saucepan, and boil for 5 minutes. Cool. Stir in ¾ cup lemon juice, 1 tablespoon grated lemon rind, and the whites of 2 eggs. Freeze.

orange sherbet

Combine sugar and water as for lemon sherbet. Stir in 2 cups orange juice, ¼ cup lemon juice, grated rind of 2 oranges and whites of 2 eggs. Freeze. This is delicious with Cointreau or Triple Sec dribbled over it when served.

VARIATIONS:

Substitute peach, pineapple, blackberry, blueberry, or grape juice. Also the purée of apricots, plums, peaches, pineapples, etc.

baked alaska with a blowtorch

Sponge cake
⅓ cup Grand Marnier
6 egg whites
2 egg yolks
1 to 1½ quarts of ice cream, assorted flavors

Since this dish does not go into the oven it is unnecessary to use a wooden plank. Instead, arrange a layer of sponge cake on a platter or serving dish. It should be at least 1 inch thick, but not more than 2 inches. Sprinkle with the Grand Marnier. Beat the egg whites very stiff. Now beat the egg yolks and combine with the sugar. Fold in the beaten whites. Arrange the ice cream in spoonfuls on the cake, alternating the flavors. Cover the ice cream with the egg mixture and smooth with a spatula. You will have to work rather quickly so that· the ice cream does not melt. You can make it very festive and attractive by putting some of the mixture in a pastry tube and piping it over the top in rosettes and swirls. Now, start your blowtorch, being sure to use a tip that will give you broad coverage. The Bernz Co. makes a variety of tips that fit over their disposable butane tanks. Using the flame as though it were a paint brush, cover the entire surface of the Alaska— never stopping too long in one spot—until it is delicately browned and finished. Serve.

STILL LIFE WITH APPLES, BY PAUL CÉZANNE.
COLLECTION, THE MUSEUM OF MODERN ART,
LILLIE P. BLISS COLLECTION.

ways to

	as hors d'oeuvres	as desserts	with liquors	with entrees
apples *(eating: delicious, golden delicious, newtown pippin, northern spy.* *cooking: greening, gravenstein, rome beauty, macintosh.)*	WITH SAUSAGE, GRILLED BACON, OR PROSCIUTTO.	EATING: RAW, GRILLED OR BAKED. WITH CHEESE. AS APPLESAUCE. COOKING: SPICED OR GLAZED. IN PIE, TARTS, AND KUCHEN.	CALVADOS COGNAC KIRSCH BOURBON	PORK SMOKED PORK HAM CHICKEN DUCK
apricots	GRILLED WITH LAMB ON SKEWERS.	PURÉED, POACHED, OR BRANDIED. IN SOUFFLÉS, PIES, AND TARTS.	COGNAC KIRSCH BOURBON GRAND MARNIER	VEAL LAMB HAM
avocados	AVOCADO BALLS IN RUM. GUACAMOLE. POOR-MAN'S BUTTER.	PURÉED WITH SUGAR, RUM. WITH ICE CREAM.	RUM	CRAB LOBSTER SCALLOPS SHRIMP
bananas	GRILLED WITH PROSCIUTTO. MARINATED IN FRENCH DRESSING.	BAKED, BROILED, FLAMED, PURÉED.	RUM COGNAC	GRILLED WITH STEAK, FISH, AND DUCK
blackberries		IN TARTS, PIES. WITH CREAM, SOUR CREAM, OR MAPLE SYRUP.	KIRSCH RUM	PANCAKES
blueberries		IN TARTS, PIES. WITH CREAM, OR SOUR CREAM, OR MAPLE SYRUP.	KIRSCH RUM	PANCAKES
boysenberries		IN PIES.	KIRSCH	PANCAKES
cherries *(sweet or sour)*	STUFFED WITH CREAM CHEESE.	RAW, POACHED OR FLAMED. IN PIES, TARTS, AND STRUDEL.	COGNAC KIRSCH RUM CHERRY HEERING	DUCK PORK HAM CHICKEN GOOSE
currants		IN PIES. BAR LE DUC. POACHED. WITH CREAM CHEESE.	KIRSCH COGNAC	GAME LAMB TURKEY CHICKEN
dates	BROILED WITH BACON. STUFFED.	BRANDIED. WITH RUM.	COGNAC RUM BENEDICTINE	BRANDIED, WITH ROAST TURKEY
figs *(fresh or dried)*	WITH: HAM, BACON, AND PROSCIUTTO. IN ANCHOIADE.	BRANDIED OR POACHED. WITH CREAM, RUM, OR COGNAC.	COGNAC RUM	HAM PORK VEAL POACHED WITH PANCAKES
grapefruit	BROILED. SECTIONED.	BROILED AND GLAZED WITH COGNAC OR KIRSCH.	COGNAC SHERRY KIRSCH	
grapes *(seedless, muscat, ladyfinger, emperor, tokay)*	STUFFED WITH CREAM CHEESE.	GLAZED. IN TARTS, PIES. WITH CHEESE.	WINES COGNAC CHAMPAGNE	AS SAUCE FOR FISH, VEAL, AND GAME
mangoes	WITH BACON, CREAM CHEESE, PROSCIUTTO.	PRESERVED. WITH CHEESE.	COGNAC RUM KIRSCH FRAMBOISE	CURRIES DUCK

	as hors d'oeuvres	as desserts	with liquors	with entrees
elons *(antaloupe, cranshaw, oneydew, cassaba, anish, persian)*	WITH: HAM, BACON, PROSCIUTTO, PORT WINE, LIME JUICE, OR FRESH-GROUND PEPPER.	STUFFED. IN TARTS. WITH BRANDIED FRUITS, GINGER.	PORT SHERRY MADEIRA COGNAC KIRSCH FRAMBOISE RUM	COLD HAM. SALADS, WITH MUSTARD DRESSING
ectarines	WITH PROSCIUTTO.	POACHED. WITH CHEESE. IN PIES.	KIRSCH FRAMBOISE RUM BOURBON CHAMPAGNE	POACHED OR PRESERVED WITH DUCK
ranges *(ing, temple, vel, tangerine)*	WITH: ONIONS IN SALAD, TOMATOES, COLD DUCK. PICKLED TANGERINES.	POACHED. BAKED. IN: TARTS, CREPES, CAKES, CHIFFON PIES.	GRAND MARNIER KIRSCH FRAMBOISE	DUCK GOOSE HAM LAMB PORK
eaches *(ing, freestone)*	BROILED WITH BACON OR PROSCIUTTO.	BRANDIED, POACHED, FLAMED, OR STUFFED. IN TARTS, PIES.	BOURBON COGNAC KIRSCH RUM FRAMBOISE GRAND MARNIER PEACH BRANDY	BROILED OR PRESERVED WITH HAM, PORK, LAMB, TURKEY, DUCK
ears *(artlett, comice, anjou, seckel)*	WITH: BACON, PROSCIUTTO, HAM OR CHEESE.	STUFFED, BAKED, BRANDIED, OR POACHED. IN TARTS. WITH CHEESE.	COGNAC KIRSCH FRAMBOISE BOURBON	PICKLED WITH COLD MEAT, FOWL.
ersimmons		WITH CHEESE. IN PIES.		
ineapple	SPICED, CURRIED, OR GRILLED. WITH CHEESE, HAM.	STUFFED OR BROILED. IN TARTS, PIES, CAKES.	COGNAC FRAMBOISE	CURRIES HAM DUCK CHICKEN TURKEY PORK
lums *(ed, yellow, greengage)*		POACHED, BAKED, OR SPICED. IN TARTS, PIES, KUCHEN.	MIRABELLE COGNAC RUM QUETSCH	DUCK
runes	STUFFED OR BROILED. WITH HAM, BACON.	BAKED. POACHED. IN TARTS, PIES, SPICED PUDDINGS.	MIRABELLE COGNAC BOURBON QUETSCH	AS STUFFING FOR PORK WITH: BEEF OR LAMB STEW, HAM, FOWL, GAME.
aspberries		PUREED. IN TARTS, PIES. WITH PINEAPPLE.	FRAMBOISE	
hubarb		POACHED. BAKED. IN PIES OR TARTS. WITH ICE CREAM, PECANS, OR STRAWBERRIES.		GLAZED, WITH HAM, PORK, AND CHICKEN.
trawberries	EN BRANCHE WITH DRINKS.	WITH CREAM. IN PIES, TARTS, OR SHORTCAKE.	KIRSCH COGNAC CHAMPAGNE FRAMBOISE	
atermelon	WITH PROSCIUTTO	PLUGGED.	CHAMPAGNE KIRSCH FRAMBOISE BOURBON	PICKLED RIND WITH: TURKEY, CHICKEN, VEAL, HAM, PORK, CURRIES.

picnics and trips *section* 6

Watteau's paintings of the French court

at play establish very nicely, I think, the air of

carefree elegance that produces a memorable

picnic. Every outing, however small, should have one

or two luxurious touches, an echo of

the formal dining room in a pastoral setting.

Among the warm memories of my childhood are the beach breakfasts and picnic suppers we used to have in the West. Some were small family outings, but the memorable ones were the great repasts for 20 or more. The ladies brought salads, or desserts, or cuts of meat to be cooked. The men toted the hampers and buckets and camp chairs; they gathered the wood and built and tended the fire. Somehow my mother was always the cook—probably because she was acknowledged to be a great one. Her outdoor pancakes, with ham and sausage, were notable. Her clam fritters superb. Her hamburgers—I'm sure she used a half-pound of meat in each one—were pan-broiled to perfection in a huge iron skillet over the hot embers of a driftwood fire. The salt breeze freshened the appetite—or the cool pine forest held off the midday sun—or the scent of summer lay on the meadows, and in all these places and times the food and drink was beyond compare.

Today, of course, the same opportunities offer, although it may be harder to discover the private, untouched glade or stretch of beach than it used to be. The picnic may be a romantic *déjeuner sur l'herbe* for two, or a gathering of the clan; it may be simple as a sandwich in wax paper, or as elaborate as appetite, inclination, and purse will allow. In the Edwardian era, at the turn of the century, the landed gentry thought nothing of sending servants on ahead to the picnic site to establish an outdoor drawing room. By the time the picnickers arrived, rugs had been spread, tables set, flowers arranged in vases, the gramophone was playing, and the food was ready. And what food! Caviar, foie gras, quenelles, larks, grouse, pheasant, several salads, red and white wines, molded desserts, coffee, cognac, and champagne were the least the well-to-do picnicker could expect.

Surely, this was overdoing it, but the impulse was a gay one. Even today I feel strongly that picnics should have touches of luxury and elegance. For my own picnics I always take the largest linen dinner napkins I have. I prefer good china plates to paper ones. And if wine is to be served I take the Baccarat. Few things are more detestable than good wine in paper cups. Let the circumstances of your picnic be your guide, but include the quality touch wherever you can.

snack picnic

menu

THERMOS OF BLOODY MARYS

SLICED CORNED BEEF, ROAST BEEF, TURKEY

VIRGINIA HAM

SWITZERLAND SWISS OR BEL PAESE CHEESE

CHEDDAR CHEESE

TIN OF ANCHOVY FILLETS

BONELESS, SKINLESS SARDINES

HARD-COOKED EGGS • VARIETY OF MUSTARDS

SWEET BUTTER

RYE, FRENCH, PUMPERNICKEL BREAD

FRUIT • ANGEL FOOD CAKE

PICKLES • COFFEE

There is not much to say about this one. Naturally, the corned and roast beef and the turkey will be better if prepared at home ahead of time.

But if you cannot do it, rely upon the best delicatessen you can find. The cheeses should be picked with care and you may vary them according to your taste, naturally. The angel food cake may be bought, or prepared from a mix, or made from scratch.

en route to a weekend

menu

THERMOS OF CHILLED MARTINIS
OLIVES • NUTS • CELERY STICKS
COLD BROILED CHICKEN HALVES
BERMUDA-ONION SANDWICHES
ON HOMEMADE BREAD
CHILLED PEELED TOMATOES
SLICED CUCUMBERS
APPLES OR PEACHES
THERMOS OF ESPRESSO COFFEE

broiled chicken halves

Use small, tender, young broilers. Split them down the back and remove the backbone. Flatten them slightly, brush well with melted butter or oil, and salt and pepper lightly. You might also sprinkle them with some chopped tarragon during the broiling period. Place them, skin side down, in the broiler rack (which you have preheated) and broil gently on each side. Do not place too close to the flame or you will have charred chicken, a not-very-appetizing dish, but one that is frequently served. It should take

about 12 to 15 minutes on the first side. Turn the chickens over and brush again with butter or oil and broil for another 8 minutes, or until the skin is golden. Cool, but do not chill. For some reason, fowl that has been cooked and refrigerated never tastes the same again. It will not spoil if used within a reasonable time. The other components for this picnic are self-explanatory and the recipes for them may be found elsewhere in this book. Be sure to wrap everything well in aluminum foil. (How *did* our forebears ever get along without it?)

a luxury picnic for two

menu

CHAMPAGNE IN COOLER
BOX OF PATÉ IN COOLER
TIN OF PROSCIUTTO • COLD MELON
CONTAINER OF LOBSTER NEWBURGH
PATTY SHELLS • CRISP ROLLS
CAMEMBERT CHEESE
BASKET OF FRUIT
THERMOS OF ESPRESSO COFFEE

Use the Chemex cooler and take extra champagne to drink through lunch. Lovely china and linen and Baccarat crystal, your best silver, and good kitchen knives (for carving and peeling the melon) are a must. Transport the food—and keep it cold—in one of the new, portable ice chests that can be stowed in the trunk of the car. You will discover with a little poking about that many food-specialty shops now stock a fine prosciutto in flat tins that goes admirably with

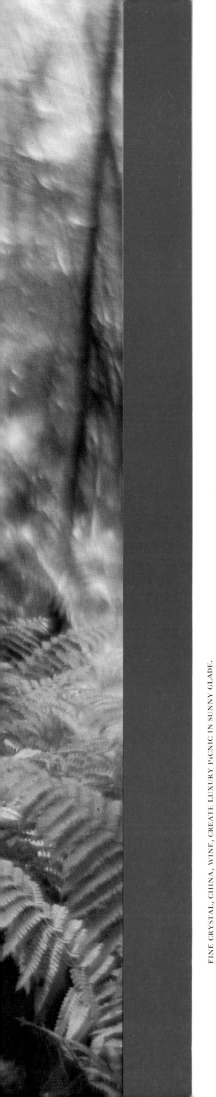

paté de foie gras—by which I do not mean a purée, but, rather, the entire goose liver with truffles down the center. Serve the prosciutto draped over wedges of cold peeled melon, along with salt and pepper.

lobster newburgh

2 two-pound lobsters
4 tablespoons of butter
4 tablespoons of olive oil
Salt and pepper
1 cup of dry white wine
⅓ cup of cognac
2 cups heavy cream
⅔ cup bouillon
Beurre manié

The quickest way to kill lobsters is to pierce them just behind the "eyes" with a sharp knife to sever the spinal cord. Then split and clean them, removing the alimentary cord and the gravel sac. Cut into pieces and crack the claws.

FINE CRYSTAL, CHINA, WINE, CREATE LUXURY PICNIC IN SUNNY GLADE.

LITHOGRAPH BY CURRIER AND IVES. MUSEUM OF THE CITY OF NEW YORK.

Heat the butter and oil in a large skillet. Sauté the pieces of lobster until they turn a bright red. Season with salt and pepper and remove to a hot platter. Add the wine and cognac to the skillet and boil rapidly until it is reduced by half. Add the cream and the bouillon. Now return the lobster to the pan, bring to a boil, then reduce the flame. Cover and simmer gently for 30 minutes. Now remove the lobster, take the meat out of the shell, and place it in a deep dish. Let the sauce cook down just a bit and thicken it with the beurre manié. Correct the seasoning and pour the sauce over the lobster meat.

a beach picnic

menu

GRILLED ITALIAN SAUSAGES
ITALIAN BREAD
CIOPPINO
TOSSED GREEN SALAD
ZUPPA INGLESE
RED WINE

You may carry a hibachi, a Skotch grill, or any table grill for this cookery, or you may build a fire on the beach and put up a big rack to accommodate the big pot you will need. You need bowls and spoons, plates and forks, and glasses. The red wine will be serving as an apéritif, as the dinner drink, as an ingredient of the cioppino, and as an aid to after-dinner conversation —so take plenty of it along. It seems to me that something like the Almaden Mountain Red in gallon containers would be an admirable choice. The sausages can be purchased in any Italian butcher shop and in many of the chain stores. They come both sweet and hot; if I were you I would take some of both along. Have plenty of Italian bread and, if you like hot things, some pickled peppers and mustard fruits, too. The sausages may be grilled in a basket grill or attached to sticks so that each person may grill his own. Or they could be cooked in a big skillet.

cioppino

No one is quite sure whether this is a Portuguese or an Italian dish. At any rate, the story is that after the fishermen brought in their catch, the wives would make cioppino on the beach, and then everyone would eat and relax, drink wine, and exchange news and banter. Like bouillabaisse, another famous coastal stew, cioppino has suffered all sorts of substitutions for the original combination. This one is not authentic, but very good. Serves 6.

1 sea bass or striped bass
1 pound shrimp
2 quarts of mussels
3 ounces dried Italian mushrooms
1 Dungeness crab
(or good-sized lobster)
3 or 4 tomatoes
½ cup olive oil
1 large onion, finely chopped
2 cloves of garlic, finely chopped
½ cup olive oil
1 teaspoon oregano
Red wine
Tomato purée (if needed)
Salt and pepper

Cut raw fish into serving pieces. Shell shrimp and devein them, leaving tails intact. Clean the mussels and steam them in a pot with a little celery, onion, and a little red wine. Soak the mushrooms in water. Break the crab apart (or kill the lobster, and cut it in pieces). Peel, seed, and chop the tomatoes. Heat the olive oil in a big pot, then add the onion and garlic, and let them cook for about 3 to 4 minutes. Add the tomatoes—and tomato purée, if needed—and let them cook for 4 minutes. Add the mushrooms and parsley, 1½ pints of red wine, and the liquid from the mussels. Let simmer for 10 to 15 minutes. Add the cut-up fish and cook for 12 to 15 minutes. Add the shrimp, the mussels, and the crab or lobster, and cook for just 5 minutes more. Pour in additional red wine if it is needed. Serve with plenty of garlic-scented French bread and glasses of red wine.

tossed green salad

Use any available seasonal greens for this salad. If you can get brugalo, chicory, and romaine, they lend themselves extremely well to this menu. You have plenty of garlic in your cioppino and your bread, so you do not need any in your salad. Substitute a few quarters of tomato and a little chopped basil. Make a dressing of 3 parts olive oil to 1 part vinegar. Add a splash or two of the red wine, and freshly ground pepper and salt. Pour the oil over the greens with the seasonings and toss well. Add the vinegar and wine and toss again. Sprinkle with a little grated Parmesan cheese.

zuppa inglese

Combine ½ cup sugar, ⅓ cup flour, and ¼ teaspoon salt. Gradually stir in 2 cups scalded milk and beat until smooth. Pour these ingredients over 4 slightly beaten egg yolks and cook over boiling water, stirring constantly until it thickens to custard. Be careful that it does not curdle. Cool, add ½ teaspoon vanilla, and set aside.

Soak 2 layers of sponge cake in rum. Make a stiff meringue with 4 egg whites, beating them until they are frothy, then adding a pinch of salt and continuing to beat them until they are stiff but not dry. Fold in ¼ cup sugar. Line the bottom of an oven-proof dish with one of the layers of sponge cake. Cover with ⅔ of the custard, then cover with the other layer. Spread the rest of the custard on top. When it is completely cold, spread meringue over all, right to the edges of the dish. Sprinkle with a bit of sugar and brown lightly in a slow oven. Chill thoroughly before serving. Sprinkle the top with candied fruits.

tailgate picnic for four

menu

CHICKEN AND RICE PAELLA
CRISP GREEN SALAD
BLUE CHEESE • FRENCH BREAD
BEER

For a tailgate picnic you need a station wagon, for this is simply a picnic that utilizes the spacious rear flap as a buffet table. Drive to the prettiest spot you can find, unload your grill and serve a delightful tailgate buffet.

chicken and rice paella

1 three-pound frying chicken
1 large onion, finely chopped
1 clove garlic
12 clams
12 shrimp
½ cup chopped tomatoes
1 or 2 Spanish or Italian sausages
1½ cups rice
Olive oil
Hot water or broth
Pinch of saffron
Salt and pepper

Cut the chicken in 8 pieces and brown in a skillet with olive oil. If possible, put in a few extra gizzards for added flavor. When the pieces are nicely brown, season with salt and pepper and set them aside. Leave the gizzards in the oil and sauté the onions and garlic with them; then add the rice. Toss it in the oil for several

minutes, or until it turns slightly yellow. Season with salt, pepper, and the saffron. Pour broth or water over to cover and let it cook down. Add the chicken, tomatoes, clams, shrimp, sausages, and more boiling water or broth. Continue cooking until the rice is tender and the chicken cooked through. Keep adding broth or water, if needed. Decorate with strips of pimiento.

crisp green salad

½ cup finely chopped green peppers
1 cup finely chopped onions
1 cup grated cucumber
⅔ cup olive oil
¼ cup wine vinegar
1½ teaspoons dry mustard
Salt and pepper

Combine the ingredients, toss, and marinate in the refrigerator. Just before serving, add the salad greens of your choice—chicory, water cress, endive, romaine. Toss well and serve.

the first picnic in spring

menu

CHILLED WHITE WINE
SHRIMP IN SHELLS
WITH MUSTARD MAYONNAISE
SCALLIONS AND RADISHES WITH SWEET BUTTER
OLD-COUNTRY MEAT LOAF
FRENCH BREAD AND BUTTER
ROQUEFORT-COGNAC SPREAD
STRAWBERRIES IN KIRSCH
ICED COFFEE WITH CREAM
KIRSCH

The chilled white wine should be a very dry Chablis or a Riesling and there should be enough of it to see you through the hors d'oeuvres. As a matter of fact, you can drink it all through lunch, or you may be very dressy and take a bottle of red wine for the cheese. Take your best crystal, your best dishes, and your large linen napkins.

shrimp in shells with mustard mayonnaise

The shrimp should be large ones. The shells should be split and the veins removed with a pair of sharp scissors. The shrimp should be cooked in a court bouillon for just 4 minutes and chilled before taking them on the road. The sauce is a good homemade mayonnaise, to each cup of which you add 1 teaspoon of French's mustard and a teaspoon of Dijon mustard. With the shrimp you will serve scallions and radishes with French bread and butter. If you are typically French or English, you will eat a little butter with your radishes.

old-country meat loaf

2 pounds ground veal
1 pound ground ham
1 pound ground pork
1 clove garlic, finely chopped
1 green pepper, finely chopped
2 medium onions, ground
½ cup breadcrumbs (soaked in broth)
½ teaspoon salt
2 eggs
1 teaspoon freshly ground black pepper
1 teaspoon thyme

Mix all the ingredients together until they are completely and smoothly blended. Form into a loaf and place on a bed of bacon strips in a flat pan. Cover with a few additional strips of bacon and bake at 350 F. for 1 to 2 hours. Baste frequently with the juices in the pan.

roquefort-cognac spread

1 pound Roquefort cheese
½ pound cream cheese
½ pound butter
1 teaspoon Worcestershire sauce
¼ cup cognac

Soften the Roquefort cheese with a fork and blend with the cream cheese and softened butter. Add the Worcestershire sauce and enough cognac to flavor and give it a spreading consistency. May be packed into crocks and kept refrigerated for several weeks.

strawberries in kirsch

Wash and hull fresh ripe strawberries (or raspberries). Sprinkle lightly with sugar and pour over them ¼ cup Kirsch. Chill for several hours to allow the flavors to blend. Put into container and store in portable ice box.

going to the game

menu

SCOTCH AND BOURBON • ICE AND WATER
QUICK CASSOULET
BEER • FRENCH BREAD AND BUTTER
APPLE TURNOVERS • CHEDDAR CHEESE WEDGES
FRUIT • COFFEE WITH CREAM

Take drinking mugs along and big bowls for the cassoulet. Paper napkins are indicated, plus spoons and fingers. Everything should be quick, easy, and hearty.

quick cassoulet

2 cans white cannelini beans
2 pounds (total) duck, lamb, pork
½ pound garlic sausage
1 teaspoon freshly ground pepper
1½ teaspoons salt
½ teaspoon thyme
1 bay leaf
½ cup consommé
½ cup red wine
½ cup finely chopped onion

Cut the meat into cubes and brown in a 450 F. oven. Add a little wine after 15 minutes. When the meat is well browned, reduce the heat to 350 F. and continue baking for 1 hour. Add the chopped onion, thyme, and bay leaf, and cook another 15 minutes. Add the beans, the garlic sausage, sliced, the broth and the rest of the wine. Mix well. Cook together for 30 minutes. You may sprinkle the top of the cassoulet with buttered crumbs for the last 30 minutes' baking time, if you wish.

apple turnovers

Peel and core 3 tart apples, then grate them coarsely. Melt 4 tablespoons butter in a sauté pan and cook the apples gently for about 10 minutes, or until they are just soft, but not mushy. Now add sugar to taste (white or brown), and about 3 or 4 tablespoons of cognac. At the last, 1 twist of the peppermill gives added zest to the mixture. Cut out 6-inch rounds of your favorite pastry, tart, or puff paste, and put some of the apple mixture on half of it. Fold the other half over, wet the edges, and seal, using a fork to press the halves together. Cut a small vent in the top and bake in a 375 F. oven for about 20 minutes, or until done.

picnic for the children

menu

TOMATO OR PINEAPPLE JUICE
HERO SANDWICHES WITH FRENCH BREAD
PEANUT BUTTER AND MAYONNAISE FINGER ROLLS
CREAM-CHEESE AND STRAWBERRY-JAM
SANDWICHES • ICE CREAM
OLD-FASHIONED CHOCOLATE CAKE
SLICED ORANGES WITH CINNAMON
MILK

No problem at all about the tomato and pineapple juices. I suggest you take along a separate Thermos for yourselves.

hero sandwiches

These have many names throughout the country—Heroes, Submarines, Grinders, and Po-Boy. My great fight with Heroes is the quality of meat that generally is put in them. Let us make ours very good. Try these combinations:

(1)
Switzerland Swiss cheese
Cold sliced turkey
Sliced baked ham
Cole slaw
Russian dressing

(2)
Ham
American cheese
Bologna
Shredded lettuce
Tomatoes

(3)
Anchovy fillets
Onions
Shreds of green pepper
Sliced tomatoes
Black olives
Sliced hard-boiled eggs
Olive Oil
Capers

(4)
Italian salami
Mortadella
Provolone cheese
Pepperoni
Black olives
Hot peppers

If you have room you might carry all these different fillings and let everyone vary the theme as inspiration dictates. Also carry along some peanut butter and homemade mayonnaise filling to spread on little finger rolls. Also some cream cheese and strawberry jam to spread on white bread. You can take a Thermos of milk and probably some chocolate syrup to add to it.

old-fashioned chocolate cake

3 cups sifted cake flour
3 teaspoons baking powder
½ teaspoon salt
1 cup butter
1 teaspoon vanilla extract
2 cups sugar
4 eggs
¾ cup milk

Measure all ingredients accurately, using standard measuring utensils. I cannot emphasize too strongly the need for accurate measuring if you want perfect cake. Start your oven at 375 F., or moderate. Next, grease heavily the bottoms and sides of 3 eight-inch cake pans or 2 nine-inch pans. Use shortening. *Don't* use butter, mar-

LE DÉJEUNER SUR L'HERBE, BY EDOUARD MANET. MUSÉE DU LOUVRE.

garine, bacon fat, or salted fat of any kind or your cake will stick to the pan. Sift a little flour into each pan and shake vigorously, so there is a film on bottom and sides. Dump out any surplus. Flouring makes it easier to remove the cake when it is done. Now, sift your 3 cups of flour. Spoon it lightly into a standard measuring cup and cut off excess to make a level cupful. Do not shake flour down into cup. Sift flour over again, this time adding the baking powder and salt.

With your hands, work or cream butter, margarine, or shortening with the flavoring until it looks like whipped cream. At this point, begin to work in the sugar a little at a time. Continue creaming until the mixture is very light and fluffy, and the grains of sugar have almost disappeared. Perfect creaming takes time and energy, but it's the trick that makes a beautifully textured cake. When sugar is all in, add the eggs, unbeaten, one at a time, and beat very hard after each addition.

From here on, work fast! Add about ¼ of the flour mixture to the batter. Stir only until smooth. Don't beat. Then add ⅓ of the milk, stirring only until it is mixed. Don't beat and overbeat; it makes a heavy cake. Repeat these last steps until all the flour and milk are in the batter. Divide batter evenly into greased pans. Then bang the pans sharply on your table top to distribute air through the cake. Bake for 25 to 30 minutes, or until cake edges leave the sides of the pans, or the cake tester (you can use a toothpick) comes out clean. Remove from oven, allow to cool about 5 minutes before turning out on a cake rack. Cool before frosting.

chocolate sour-cream frosting

For the icing, melt 1 six-ounce package of semi-sweet chocolate morsels, stir in 1 cup of commercial sour cream, cool slightly, and frost your cake.

sliced oranges with cinnamon

Just that. Keep the oranges chilled and do not peel and slice them until you are ready to serve. Sprinkle to taste with cinnamon. If you feel they won't be sweet enough, take some sugar along in an envelope.

rich, elegant picnic for 10

Magnificence in this degree cannot be constructed casually. Somebody should be sent on ahead in a station wagon (or station wagons) to set the stage properly. Further, you must choose a spot with a spectacular view. You will need folding tables and folding chairs, portable ice boxes, champagne coolers, good cloths and napkins, good silver, china and crystal, and the back of one or two of the station wagons for serving the buffets. Rigorous attention to these niceties will recreate the great Edwardian picnic with perfect service and perfect food—and discreet music from a good FM station in the background.

menu

FRENCH CHAMPAGNE

CAVIAR • TOAST

ONION • SOUR CREAM • CHOPPED EGG

DOUBLE CONSOMMÉ WITH CHOPPED PARSLEY

CHAUD-FROID CHICKEN

BAKED HAM IN CRUST

ASPARAGUS VINAIGRETTE

TINY FRENCH ROLLS

FROZEN RASPBERRY MOUSSE

SMALL CAKES • DEMITASSE

It is my feeling that if you are going to serve caviar you might as well go deeply into debt and have a lot of it—on ice. Serve it with toast or melba toast, or dark bread. I like mine with lemon juice only, but you had better have some chopped onion, chopped egg, and sour cream for those who think otherwise. Naturally, serve champagne or chilled vodka. *Do not rush.* Relax. Enjoy yourself. Take your time. When the caviar is cleared, small cups of hot, double-strength consommé with chopped parsley and more melba toast will give a pleasant contrast.

chaud-froid chicken

For 10 persons, cut 3 good-sized chickens into quarters and remove wing bones and backbones. Poach in enough water to cover with 1 sprig of parsley, 1 stalk of celery, 1 onion stuck with 2 cloves, 1 bay leaf, 1 teaspoon tarragon, and the giblets, necks, and backs. Poach until just tender, testing the white meat before the dark because it cooks more quickly. When the chicken is cooked, place it on a rack to cool and let the wings and backs cook down with the broth for 30 minutes, uncovered. Strain the broth through several thicknesses of cheesecloth. Chill and skim the fat. When the chicken is cold, remove the skin and chill it well.

In the meantime prepare a sauce velouté with 4 tablespoons butter blended with 5 tablespoons flour. Cook over a medium heat for several minutes so that the flour taste is cooked out. Add 1 teaspoon salt, ½ teaspoon white pepper, and a few grains of nutmeg. Gradually stir in 1½ cups of chicken broth and continue cooking until the mixture is well thickened. Add ¼ cup cognac and stir in ½ cup heavy cream which has been blended with 2 egg yolks. Cook, stirring constantly until the mixture has blended and thickened but does not boil. Add to this 1½ envelopes unflavored gelatin which have been dissolved in ¼ cup cold water. Allow to cool. When it begins to coagulate, dip the chicken pieces into it and place them on a rack over a baking pan. Spoon on additional sauce and decorate with truffle slices and leaves of fresh tarragon. Now dissolve another envelope of gelatin in ¼ cup of cold water, add 1 cup of boiling chicken broth, and cool until thick and syrupy. Brush it over the chicken pieces very carefully, so as not to disturb the decorations, and chill thoroughly. Serve with a well-flavored herbed mayonnaise.

baked ham in crust

For a picnic like this, a large, canned, precooked ham is probably the best idea. Trim away the excess fat and spread the top of it with a purée of foie gras. Make a double recipe of your favorite pastry and roll it out about ¼ inch thick to a large circle. Fit the pastry around the ham so that it fits snugly. You may have to cut and adjust. Roll additional pastry into a long strip, cut in thirds, and braid and fit it around the edge of the ham, sealing it on to the pastry with a mixture of egg and a little water. If you are in an adventurous mood, cut leaves and foliage from the pastry and attach them to the top of the crust. Brush it all with the egg wash, cut a little hole in the center and bake at 375 F. for about 40 to 45 minutes or until the crust is nicely browned. When cool, transfer gently to a platter and decorate.

frozen raspberry mousse

¾ cup sugar
½ cup water
4 egg yolks
2 cups pure, sweetened raspberry syrup
2 cups heavy cream

Combine sugar and water, bring to a boil and cook for 5 minutes. Then cool. Beat 4 egg yolks in the top of a double boiler, stir in the syrup gradually, stirring constantly, and cook over hot — not boiling — water, until it is thickened. Strain through a sieve and cool. Add the fruit purée and the juice of ½ lemon. Whip the cream until it is stiff and fold it into the custard mixture. Freeze in a mold.

cooking for campers

This section is not intended as a guide for those planning a safari into the wilds of Africa, or even for those who would like to take a pack trip through the Himalayas. It is merely an eating and cooking guide, designed to supply people who are doing what the French call *le camping* with ideas for their short trip into the mountains or woods. Since I always consider "le camping" and "cooking" synonymous, I feel the success of such a trip is as dependent on good campfire meals as on anything else. And I know that to be certain of achieving a flavorsome repast so far from the home larder, there are many different bits and pieces of equipment to consider; what you take along will depend on your destination, the distance you are going, the length of your stay, and the way you are traveling, as well as on what you expect to eat.

equipment

Grills: As far as kitchen equipment is concerned, you must decide whether you will be cooking over the crudest fire, or with a gasoline stove, a fireplace, and a propane (ceramic) grill, or a fireplace and a reflector oven. Each presents a different problem. The gasoline stove is similar to cooking with gas in your own kitchen. If one of these and a reflector oven are sufficient, you proceed in almost normal household fashion, occasionally cooking over the bonfire for a variation. If you decide to use the propane grill, you won't have to worry about searching for wood or carrying briquets, but you will have to allow enough room for fuel cylinders. Of course, you may wish to use one of the numerous folding grills, or carry an old-fashioned grilling rack which I think is perfect for this type of cookout. You surround your fire with rocks and bricks and balance the rack on top. It is just right for surface cooking, and for pancakes, scones, and corncakes. It also permits you to broil foil-wrapped foods in the coals, a most delectable form of cookery.

Reflector Oven: This is really an extra in many respects, because it has a limited use. But it's great for baking bread, biscuits, cakes, and pancakes, and it provides a handy device for warm-

ing already cooked foods. If you like the idea, but haven't room to carry a reflector oven, you may employ a Dutch oven for the same tasks.

Pits: The merits of using a simple hole in the ground for all sorts of fine and entertaining cookery are discussed in the section on pit roasting (see page 124), and camping trips are excellent opportunities to enjoy them. After you have removed the coals, place whatever you wish to cook into the Dutch oven, and before lowering it into the pit, place the cover on the pot and seal the crevice between lid and pot with a paste made of flour and water. This permits no steam to escape. Next, cover the pot with ashes and earth. It can rest this way for hours, cooking very slowly, and well. New Englanders made their famous "sweet beans" in this fashion, but I would choose to do beans with meat and chili or to cook a famous old French dish called *boeuf à la cuillère*. For this you need about 6 or 8 pounds of chuck rump or round. Stick it with garlic cloves and spice it with bay leaf, salt, pepper, and whatever other spices you have at hand and feel would add to the savor of the meat. Add a few strips of bacon and enough water to cover. If you can, add a good jigger of whiskey, too.

Then cover the pot and seal it with the flour-water paste so that no steam escapes. Heat over the fire for about 30 minutes before lowering the Dutch oven into the pit. Let it remain there for 6 or 8 hours. Serve with potatoes—and a spoon.

Dutch Oven: Aside from being a marvellous aid in pit roasting, the Dutch oven is invaluable for game—especially heavy game when you aren't sure of the tenderness of the meat. You simply add vegetables and seasonings to the meat in the pot and let it cook long and slowly. The Dutch oven is also fine for baking. To use it this way, you lower the pans in which you are baking into the pot, cover it, and surround it—on top and sides—with hot coals. Its galleried lid provides a level area on which to place the coals. You can buy these versatile pots in the traditional black iron or in copper.

Pressure Cooker: This is another boon to any type of outdoor living. It's fine for vegetables, tough meats, and for things such as beans, lentils, puddings, and cakes that may be steam-cooked to perfection.

Other Pots and Pans: You must carry along a skillet, and at least one or two large cooking vessels. If you happen to forget the pots, however, don't despair; large, empty juice cans are very handy for boiling and stewing.

Foil Utensils: The advent of foil has made the camper's burden much lighter. You can get skillet frames and foil filler and all sorts of foil utensils in varying sizes to add to your supplies.

Kits and Small Items: Tongs, large forks, and knives in several different types and sizes, a strainer, and, by all means, good can and bottle openers are indispensable. I think it's best when each person has his own eating kit, too, with knife, fork, spoon, plate, bowl, and cup. There are several of these kits on the market; you can judge for yourself which suits you best.

Containers for Liquids: Vacuum containers are essential for beverages that must be kept at certain temperatures, but the finest containers for carrying wines and spirits are the Spanish leather pouches. Sling a couple of them over your shoulder; they weigh very little.

Portable Iceboxes: These may or may not be necessities, but they are a great improvement over the boxes and buckets of the past. They can be used with regular ice or dry ice, and hold about enough fresh meat for three full meals.

Gadgets: I add this final note because I know that everyone has one or two pet gadgets which seem indispensable. By all means take them along if you feel they add enjoyment to your outdoor living, but don't be foolish and leave something important behind to make room for them.

food

Planning what foods to take requires even more care than choosing equipment. Things which hold for a few days without cooking, or some that will keep for several days if precooked, are best. I am convinced that it is wisest to carry a good supply of dehydrated foods and mixes. They're light, take up little space, and there is no worry of spoilage.

Meat: If you expect to bag game or will be able to catch fish, your problems are solved. Otherwise, depend on canned or smoked meats after the first day or two. Hams, bacon—slabs are best —corned beef in tins, or any other cured or canned meats you may prefer are excellent. Cured sausages are marvellous, too; they'll do for sandwiches for lunch, and go well with eggs and pancakes for hearty breakfasts. There are also certain new dry-frozen products slowly easing onto the market, but these will probably not be readily available for some time. However, if they work as planned, they will solve campers' meat problems for years to come.

Vegetables: A great selection of dehydrated vegetables is perfect for treks into the hinterland and can be purchased in almost any shop. Some of them are sensationally good, and all provide an opportunity to prepare dishes usually unavailable on camping trips.

Potatoes: In instant form, I like the hashed brown or cut potatoes best, but if the instant mashed potatoes are whipped well with a whisk, they can be good, too. Ordinarily, instant mashed just don't have the quality the others do.

Soups: Soup mixes—especially Lipton's onion, chicken, and mushroom; and some of the imported ones—add a versatility to meals. They're good as seasonings and for sauces. As soups, serve them with a little extra spice here and there for greater interest.

Sauces: Unlike the soups, packaged sauces are greatly overrated. The exceptions are salad-dressing mixes—the four-in-a-package ones, particularly. However, I prefer to use them as seasoners, rather than as salad dressings.

Tabasco: Always manage to include a bottle. It does much to help meats, salads, soups, and so forth. It can be almost as handy as a little wine or cognac—and if you have any space at all you should certainly not forget these.

Flour and Yeast: Indoors or out, there's nothing quite so tempting as hot rolls or freshly baked

bread and butter. To achieve this touch of luxury at the campsite, include a few packages of hot-roll mix, the kind with yeast packages inside. You can use the mix for a variety of things—pizza, turnovers, pies, rollups, as well as simple rolls or bread.

Cakes, Cookies, and Pies: On long trips, people always get a craving for sweets, and cake, cookie, and pie mixes are a tremendous help in satisfying it. Cornbread, biscuit, and pancake mixes help, too, by way of the syrups and jams that accompany them.

Candies: Hard candies, favorite candy bars, even store-bought cookies packed in tins, are also great high-energy foods, and they keep and carry well.

Sugar Substitutes: These are boons to both camper and calorie-counter. They certainly lighten the burden, and it is almost impossible to tell the substitutes from regular sugar.

Beverages: Of course, you will want to be prepared with some favorite wines or other alcoholic beverages in the leather bags, but you should also include powdered milk and, perhaps, the new buttermilk mix.

the luxury side of camping

The basics — canned meats, dehydrated vegetables, bread mixes, and sweets—offer few difficulties; they are readily available. But all campers, explorers, and voyagers lack fresh greens. Of course, if you know your herbs and plants, you can fare pretty well no matter where you happen to be, but if you do not, you will have to rely on a properly stocked larder. Pickles, relishes, and canned sauerkraut are perfect for adding tartness to your meals. A good vinegar and a little soy sauce, packed into the sack, provide all the needed ingredients for a sweet-and-sour sauce. Lemon crystals and orange crystals are good to have with you, too, because they combine well with so many things. Chili powder, curry powder, and a few envelopes of your favorite herbs will be useful. Also some fresh garlic. To add to the enjoyment of the occasion, I always feel you should carry a few absolutely silly items—anchovies, paté, sardines, lobster, and crab meat. These contrast so strongly with routine fare that they will be greeted with cheers.

cooking for mariners

Because the stowage space in a boat is cramped and the cooking facilities are extremely limited, the approach to food and drink and the techniques for their preparation must be special. A galley is the place for ingenuity, for testing good and efficient mixes, and for establishing comparative values between various canned foods. (Believe me, the differences can be tremendous.) Menus must be planned ahead, with gaps for stopovers, pick-ups, or a catch of fresh fish. Study the space on your boat and use your head about what to stock. It is wise to have a few things tucked away for special days. A celebration locker—on a bad day when you wish you had never set sail—may produce a touch of luxury to dispel the gray mood.

Stoves should not be a problem. There are propane-gas, oil, and gasoline stoves—one of which ought to suit your needs. Portable grills—hibachis and Bernz-o-matic grills—may be used on deck for grilling. These provide pleasant contrasts to other dishes prepared in the galley. Some craft are grand enough to have freezer space or a refrigerator; cooks on such boats can make all but the most elaborate dishes.

On calm days it is wonderful to prepare a long-cooking dish. It requires little effort. It can simmer until done with only an occasional check on its progress. By mealtime there is nothing to do but make a drink and a salad. Plan to have the ingredients for a hearty soup or casserole aboard for cool, brisk days.

invaluable items for the galley

Meats and Fish: Canned bacon, canned pork, canned corned beef are all efficient on trips. I find that S. S. Pierce roast beef hash is particularly good. Remember to add wine or curry or chili to canned beef stews. Tuna fish, both in oil and in brine, is a necessity. You can find kippered tuna in the West which offers a pleasant difference in flavor. Salmon—especially the best Columbia River pack—is excellent, as are some of the imported herrings. I find the canned shad roe good and I use it for soufflés.

Canned Vegetables: Drained and marinated with French dressing, or seasoned mayonnaise, they take the place of green salads when greens are out of the question. White whole-kernel corn, cut and whole string beans, peas, and asparagus are excellent salad choices.

Pastas: Good pastas make superb quick dishes. Use with clam sauce or with garlic and oil.

Packaged Soups: The dehydrated ones offer tremendous variety and also can be used in sauces, and for many different dishes.

Cheeses: There are good canned cheeses (from Denmark and Germany) useful for salads, or main dishes, or served alone.

Mixes: If your boat is big enough to have an oven, pie-crust mix, hot-roll mix, and Bisquick will vary your breads. The hot-roll mix makes pizza, Brioche, rolls, and so forth.

Meals can be planned with sandwiches and substantial salads, but at least one meal a day should feature more wholesome food, lavishly presented. Probably that meal will be dinner, assuming that all is calm. For example, you might like to try the following dish from Marseilles, which I find subtle and satisfying.

soupe de poisson

2 to 2½ pounds of fish—any variety at all
½ cup olive oil
Salt and pepper
2 large onions
1 #2½ can solid-pack tomatoes
3 tablespoons butter
¼ pound vermicelli
Pinch saffron
¼ pound grated Switzerland Swiss cheese

This dish is ideal if you have a surplus of fish. Clean and wash the fish—don't bother to scale it—and cook it in the olive oil. Stir often to break up the fish. Salt and pepper to taste, add enough water to cover, and continue to cook the pieces slowly for about 25 minutes. Chop or slice the onions very thin and sauté them in the butter. Then add the tomatoes and cook for 15 minutes. Strain the fish through a fine strainer, or squeeze it through a bag—the idea is to collect all the juices, but none of the pulp. Add the juice to the vegetables. Correct the seasoning, and add the vermicelli and the saffron. Simmer until the pasta is just tender. Serve with grated cheese. This will freeze beautifully.

fish chowder

This is simple and easy when you catch fish over the side—and you don't have to be particular about the type of fish you use. Clean and fillet the fish and cut it into strips. Try out ½ pound of bacon (or salt pork) and remove the crisp bits of meat when the fat is melted. Sauté 1½ cups of chopped onion in the fat. Add about 3 or 4 good-sized potatoes, thinly sliced, and let them brown slightly in the fat with the onions. Add enough water to barely cover, and cook the potatoes until they are tender. Add the fish, cover the pot, and steam for about 12 minutes. Salt and pepper to taste, and add a little thyme and a dash of cognac or whiskey, if you have it. Cover with milk—fresh, reconstituted, or evaporated—and simmer until the fish, potatoes, and onions have blended into good, hot stew. Sprinkle on the crispy bits of bacon (or salt pork) and serve in hot bowls with pilot crackers and paprika. Follow with some cheese, and you'll have a fine meal.

potato salad variations

3 pounds potatoes
or 3 cans potatoes
1 onion, or 1 package onion-soup mix
2 teaspoons dried parsley leaves
or 2 tablespoons chopped fresh parsley
½ cup olive oil
¼ cup wine vinegar

1. Combine with ½ pound sliced Bologna, or Bologna and summer sausage, and additional sliced onions. Decorate with hard-boiled eggs.
2. Add 1 small tin anchovies, coarsely chopped, and 1 can herring tidbits. Combine with sour cream, or mayonnaise.
3. Combine with 1 can white-meat tuna, a few pieces of crumbled bacon, and a little finely chopped garlic.
4. Add 1 or 2 cans chopped, canned chicken, ½ cup broken walnut halves, and a few chopped pimientos.
5. Add diced cold ham, or tongue and pimiento, a little sour cream, and some sliced gherkins.
6. Soak ½ to 1 pound salt codfish overnight. Bring to a boil and simmer until tender and flaky. Drain and add ¼ cup olive oil, 1 chopped garlic clove, and wine vinegar to taste. Chill and combine with basic salad mixture.

sautéed small fish

You will need a little less than 1 tablespoon of butter, or butter and olive oil mixed, for each small fish. Clean the fish. Melt the butter and oil in a heavy skillet. Dip each fish in milk, then in flour, and when the fat is very hot, cook the fish over a medium flame until it is well browned on the bottom. Turn carefully and brown the other side. Season with salt and pepper. Remove fish to a hot platter, add a little butter to the pan and about 4 tablespoons chopped parsley. Pour over the fish in the hot platter. Garnish with lemon wedges.

poached fish

This is one of the most delicate ways to prepare fish. Follow the directions for making a court bouillon (in the sauce section of "Outdoor Complements"). Poach the fish you have caught, either whole or fillet, in the court bouillon. Be very careful not to let the liquid boil. Simmer gently until the fish flakes when tested with a fork. Serve with a sauce made from the court bouillon or any sauce suggested for fish in the sauce chart (pages 184-185).

steamed clams

The clams you choose should be tightly closed in their shells. Clams are dead when the shell is damaged or open, and clams, like lobsters, must be alive when they are cooked. Wash and scrub the clams well. Rinse them until you get rid of the sand. Place them in a large kettle with ½ inch of salt water at the bottom. Cover tightly and steam until the clams open. This should take from 6 to 10 minutes. Discard any clams that do not open. Serve with large bowls of melted butter and cups of the broth.

steamed clams à la marinière

Scrub the clams well and put in a large kettle. For about 8 dozen clams, add 1 large chopped onion, 1 sprig of parsley, a little thyme, 1 bay leaf, 1 cup white wine, 4 tablespoons butter, a little freshly ground black pepper. Cover and steam until the clams open. Discard any which don't open. Remove the clams to a hot serving dish, put the sauce through a fine sieve, correct seasoning, and reheat, adding 2 tablespoons butter and a little more chopped parsley. Serve over the steamed clams.

steamed mussels à la marinière

Wash the mussels well and remove the beard—the vegetation on the shell. Follow the directions for Steamed Clams à la Marinière.

clam hash

6 tablespoons butter
1 tablespoon onion, finely minced
1½ cups finely diced, cooked potatoes
1½ to 2 cups minced clams
Salt and pepper
Nutmeg
4 egg yolks
4 tablespoons grated Parmesan cheese
Heavy cream

Melt the butter in a heavy skillet and cook the onions until they are transparent. Add the po-

tatoes and clams and press down with a spatula. Salt and pepper lightly and add a few flecks of nutmeg. Let the hash cook for about 10 minutes and stir from the bottom to mix in some of the crust. Press down again. Beat the egg yolks well, combine with the grated cheese and about 6 tablespoons heavy cream. Pour this over the hash very gently, and cover for a few minutes until the egg is set.

quick clam hash

Instant sliced or hashed-brown potatoes are invaluable. They reconstitute in no time at all, they're easy to pack, and they don't spoil. Reconstitute a package of potatoes according to the directions on the package and sauté in 4 tablespoons butter for 5 minutes. Add 1 finely chopped onion and 2 cans minced, drained clams (or 2 cups minced fresh clams). Blend well and add a little of the clam juice. Salt and pepper to taste and let cook, turning often as the mixture browns on the bottom. Add a little more of the clam liquid, or a little heavy cream or evaporated milk, and let it cook down.

clam pan roasts

This is really nothing more than a sauté, and it is particularly suited to clams. Melt ¼ pound butter in a skillet, add 2 cups clams; cook just long enough to heat through and plump up. Season to taste with salt, pepper, and paprika and serve on toast. Top with parsley. You may vary this by adding chives, parsley, or tarragon.

oyster pan roasts

Follow the directions for Clam Pan Roasts. The smaller oysters are particularly good served this way. Use plenty of butter.

fagioli al caviale

For the luxury meal, sauté 1 onion, finely chopped, in 4 tablespoons butter. Add 2 drained cans cannelini beans (or white cooked beans) and heat to the piping-hot stage. Serve in hot soup plates and pass chilled caviar from the luxury cabinet. If you have sour cream or chopped egg, it goes well, as does chopped raw onion.

sailor's delight

1 broiler-fryer chicken cut in serving pieces
1 teaspoon Accent
1½ teaspoons salt
¼ cup salad or olive oil
1 can (1 pound) tomatoes
1 cup beer
¼ teaspoon Tabasco
1 cup raw rice
1 cup artichoke hearts, drained
1 can (5 ounces) shrimp, drained

Sprinkle chicken with Accent and let stand for 15 minutes. Then, sprinkle with 1 teaspoon of salt. Brown slowly about 15 minutes on each side, in salad oil in skillet. Add tomatoes, beer, and Tabasco, and simmer for 20 minutes. Gradually stir in rice and add remaining ½ teaspoon salt. Bring to a boil, reduce heat, cover, and simmer for 20 to 25 minutes. Add hearts of artichokes and shrimp. If you prefer, you may substitute 1 can (1 pound) peas, drained, for the artichoke hearts. Heat to serving temperature. This will yield about 4 servings.

quick choucroute garnïe

2 cans sauerkraut
1 can beer
4 slices bacon, partly cooked
1 can luncheon meat, thickly sliced
2 cans Vienna sausage
8 to 10 slices summer sausage
2 garlic cloves
2 teaspoons freshly ground black pepper

Drain the sauerkraut and arrange in a Dutch oven with the partially cooked bacon. Top with the luncheon meat and chopped garlic and pepper. Add enough beer to barely cover (if you pre-fer, use white wine). Bring to a boil and simmer for 30 minutes. Add the Vienna sausage and the summer sausage and cover. Steam for 15 minutes. Serve with mustard, boiled or heated canned potatoes, and beer.

beans and frankfurters hel-sen

1 large jar beans
4 slices bacon
2 minced onions
1 or 2 cloves of garlic, finely chopped
½ teaspoon chili powder
1 teaspoon curry
2 tablespoons brown sugar

Cut bacon into small pieces and brown in skillet. When the bacon is brown, remove it and brown the onions and garlic in the bacon drippings. Add chili powder, curry, and brown sugar. Mix well and add this mixture, as well as the bacon, to the beans. Arrange frankfurters on top, cover, and simmer for about ½ hour on the burner, or if you have one, in the oven.

corn-cheese chili

3 slices bacon
1 can (1 pound) whole kernel corn
1 can (20 ounces) kidney beans
1 can (1 pound) tomatoes
1 medium onion, chopped
1 green pepper, diced
2 teaspoons chili powder
½ teaspoon salt
¼ pound American cheese, grated

Cut bacon in ½-inch pieces, fry crisp; drain on absorbent paper. Reserve 2 tablespoons bacon drippings. Drain corn, beans, and tomatoes. Add vegetable liquids with onion and pepper to bacon drippings in skillet. Cook until liquid is reduced to about one-half. Add bacon, corn, beans, tomatoes, chili powder, and salt. Heat to serving temperature. Reduce heat, stir in cheese. This will serve about 6 people.

A large party reflects the host's intention to restore his guests. If such is the goal, nothing short of perfection can be tolerated.

Entertaining a crowd is never easy, but it can be gracious and pleasant if you will utilize your lawn or patio instead of trying to squeeze everyone inside the house. Outdoor dining is less formal and restricted; the guests can dress more casually, and the party can spread out a bit, particularly if grounds permit croquet or other mild sports. Outdoor parties also have a gala, festive air that is difficult to duplicate inside.

In this chapter I have planned a number of large parties for various occasions and for guest lists ranging from 15 to 100. There is a beach breakfast, an old-fashioned chicken fry, a shoot-the-works cocktail party, among others. The number of guests indicated in each instance seems to me the maximum you can expect to handle comfortably without the help of a caterer. Where extra hands are needed—a bartender, or people to help serve—the fact is mentioned. Note, too, that the menus suggested are not inflexible. In some cases I have outlined a feast. You may eliminate some dishes along the way and still have a perfectly satisfactory party. Because I have tried to make the parties special, the menus also contain dishes not found elsewhere in this book. Feel free to take any of these specialties out of context and serve them on other occasions. Note, too, that any recipes *not* spelled out here are in other sections of the book. To locate them, simply use the index.

Each outing has its own special requirements, but there are a few general suggestions that apply to all outdoor festivities of considerable size. If you need extra help, for instance, don't depend upon friends. Hire as many people as you possibly can to avoid strain and confusion, and make sure they arrive well in advance of the scheduled party time. If you have never worked with them before, have them serve a small party first. You can see how they work, they will learn your requirements, and the large affair will run much more smoothly.

You will need plenty of tables and chairs. You are giving a barbecue, not a picnic, and there are many people who don't relish sitting on the grass while trying to balance a dinner plate and a drink.

Put a "weather permitting" note in your invitations. Also include your phone number for regrets, and, if guests live a considerable distance away, a map of the route to your house.

Be prompt; don't make guests wait endlessly for food. If the time specified in the invitation is an hour and a half before you plan to eat, serve on schedule.

summer lunch for 20

menu

HOT TURTLE SOUP WITH MADEIRA
TROUT IN ASPIC WITH HORSERADISH SAUCE
RICE • CHIFFONADE SALAD • CHEESES
PEAR HELENE
COFFEE • CHAMPAGNE

THE FEAST OF ACHELOÜS, BY PETER PAUL RUBENS
AND JAN BRUEGHEL, THE ELDER. METROPOLITAN MUSEUM
OF ART, GIFT OF ALVIN AND IRWIN UNTERMYER,
IN MEMORY OF THEIR PARENTS, 1945.

For the soup course, it would be best to purchase a fine, commercial canned variety, such as Fortnum & Mason, or Ancora, since it is a chore to prepare it at home. Just before serving, add to the canned soup a bit of fine old Madeira. Simple, elegant, delicious. Serve it in cups.

trout in aspic

You will need about 20 trout for this dish, each weighing about 1 pound. Prepare a court bouillon with 2 quarts of water, 1 quart white wine, ½ cup white vinegar, and a *bouquet garni* made with 1 onion stuck with cloves, a branch of celery, 2 or 3 sprigs of parsley, 10 to 12 peppercorns, 2 tablespoons salt, and 1 teaspoon thyme. Let it come to a boil and simmer for 20 minutes. Poach the trout very gently from 6 to 8 minutes, until they flake easily when tested with a fork. Remove the trout to a platter to cool and reduce broth to one-third its original amount. Add the whites of 2 eggs, lightly beaten, and the egg shells and simmer for 15 minutes. Strain through a cloth and measure the broth. For each 2 cups, dissolve 1 envelope of unflavored gelatin in ¼ cup of cold water. When the gelatin is dissolved, add it to the boiling broth, blend well, and chill. Remove the skin from the top part of the trout and make a design with tarragon leaves, parsley, sliced olives, or whatever you prefer to use to make a pleasant design. Brush with the gelatin mixture and chill well; brush again with gelatin after it has set in the refrigerator. Serve with a horseradish sour-cream sauce, made by combining 2 cups sour cream with ½ cup freshly made horseradish and the juice of a lemon. Salt and pepper to taste.

chiffonade salad

In a huge bowl, arrange on a bed of various greens little bundles of the following raw vegetables: tiny tomatoes, tender tips of asparagus, cauliflower, *mange-tout* peas (or, as the Chinese call them, "snow peas"), and any other tender, succulent vegetables that are in season. Have a dressing ready; do not use it until you are ready to serve the salad.

pear helene

Peel and halve 12 Bartlett pears. Make a syrup by adding 4 cups of sugar to 2 cups of water. Add 1-inch vanilla bean. Poach the pear halves very gently in syrup until soft but not mushy. Drain them on absorbent paper, and reduce the syrup to half. Reserve it in the icebox for use in another dish. Prepare a chocolate sauce with one 12-ounce package of semi-sweet chocolate morsels and 2 ounces unsweetened chocolate melted in the top part of a double boiler. Add 1 teaspoon powdered coffee. Stir in ½ pint heavy cream and ¼ cup cognac. Keep heated over warm water. To serve, arrange pears around a huge mound of vanilla ice cream in a large serving dish and top with chocolate sauce. For an extra touch, you may garnish with chopped nuts, if you wish.

ladies' lunch on a rainy day

MIXED GRILL
SAUTÉED ONIONS
SEASONAL FRUIT SALAD

If threatening clouds appear on the day you plan to entertain a group of ladies in your garden, you can use this simple yet attractive menu and rest assured that your luncheon will be equally pleasant, indoors or out. You'll need a propane grill for the meat. Sauté the onions and prepare the salad in the kitchen. Make a cream-cheese dressing, or, for a low-calorie meal, serve the fruit with cottage cheese. Have a good Dijon mustard on the table. If the rains come, you can easily rush indoors with the propane grill and serve the meal wherever you like. If you have to abandon the garden, I think it is gayer to use more elaborate china, linen, and silver than you might have outdoors.

beach breakfast for 20

equipment

PORTABLE GRILL AND RACKS FOR BONFIRE
OR 1 PROPANE GRILL
3 SKILLETS • 2 GRIDDLES
PAPER PLATES • PAPER OR PLASTIC CUPS
GLASSES • KNIVES AND FORKS
LARGE PAPER NAPKINS
LARGE PLASTIC CLOTHS AND FOLDING TABLES
CAMP CHAIRS • HAMPERS
PORTABLE ICE BOXES
CHARCOAL

menu

BLOODY MARYS AND SCREWDRIVERS
BASKET OF SEASONAL FRUITS
GRILLED SAUSAGE CAKES WRAPPED IN FOIL
BACON STRIPS • BUTTERMILK PANCAKES
MELTED BUTTER • HOT HONEY AND SYRUP

DANISH PASTRY HEATED IN FOIL
CREAM CHEESE AND STRAWBERRY PRESERVES
COFFEE

For the Bloody Marys and Screwdrivers you will need at least 2 bottles of vodka; take 4, just in case the cooking is slow. You will also need 2 or 3 containers each of frozen concentrated orange juice and tomato juice, a bottle of Worcestershire sauce, lemons, and Tabasco. Take a good shaker and good glasses for your drinks.

grilled sausage cakes

For 20 people you will need at least 10 pounds of sausage meat. You may not use it all, but be on the safe side. If possible, have the pork coarsely ground and season it with 3 tablespoons salt, 1 tablespoon freshly ground black pepper, 2 crumbled bay leaves, 1 tablespoon of finely chopped sweet basil, and 1 teaspoon of anise or fennel seed. Blend well. Wrap 5-ounce portions in aluminum foil and grill over the coals or over the propane grill, turning 2 or 3 times during the grilling period. They will take about 12 to 15 minutes over a fairly brisk fire. Split them in half and serve.

bacon strips

The bacon may be grilled directly over the coals, but I think a skillet is preferable. For 20 people you will need about 3 pounds of bacon.

buttermilk pancakes

These should be cooked on griddles over a wood or charcoal fire. Rub the griddles with a bag of coarse salt from time to time. This will help in the cooking. I have found that the Duncan Hines Buttermilk Pancake Mix does a magnificent job, so I suggest very strongly that you carry this along and mix it on the spot. You will need at least 2 packages. For best results, follow the directions on the package to the letter. Have a big pot of butter melting on the grill, and pots of honey or syrup keeping hot in Pyrex or metal containers. You can stagger the cooking process and give several people KP duty on the griddles.

danish pastry

If you feel that you want something to munch with your coffee, take some good Danish pastry along. Wrap it with foil before you leave, so that it can be heated over the coals. Take a jar of strawberry preserves and blocks of cream cheese. Make plenty of coffee.

sunday luncheon for 30

menu

Drinks

MINT JULEPS • TOM COLLINS • GIN AND TONIC
BEER • COCA-COLA

Wines

MUSCADET
LOUIS MARTINI OR ALMADEN MOUNTAIN WHITE
BEAUJOLAIS OR FLEURIE

Canapés

SEASONAL VEGETABLES IN ICED BOWLS: LETTUCE,
WATER CRESS, TINY TOMATOES, SLICED
TOMATOES, SLICED CUCUMBERS,
RADISHES, GREEN ONIONS,
RAW ASPARAGUS SPEARS, RAW CARROT STRIPS
SOUR-CREAM-CHIVE-AND-TARRAGON DIP
DILL-FLAVORED FRENCH DRESSING

A Table of Charcuterie

HAM WITH APRICOT GLAZE
SALAMI
SUMMER SAUSAGES
PLATTER OF THINLY SLICED PROSCIUTTO WITH
FRESH FIGS AND MELON
THINLY SLICED PUMPERNICKEL
FRENCH BREAD

The Beaujolais or Fleurie should be really good and is for those who prefer a light red wine

with their meal. Be sure to season the sour-cream dip with a great deal of salt and pepper and chopped parsley. Serve the salad dressing in a pitcher so that the guests can make their own salads later on, if they wish.

holiday cookout for 25

equipment

PORTABLE GRILL • SKOTCH GRILLS
PORTABLE ICE BOXES
GLASSES FOR DRINKS • PLASTIC CUPS
PAPER PLATES AND NAPKINS
KNIVES AND FORKS
CHARCOAL

menu

BEER FOR ADULTS • COKES FOR CHILDREN
RAW VEGETABLES: RADISHES, CARROTS,
CELERY, SCALLIONS, TOMATOES, CUCUMBERS
10 POUNDS HAMBURGER • 30 GRILLED KNOCKWURST
GRILLED ONION SLICES • FOIL-BAKED CORN
FRENCH POTATO SALAD • SALMON SALAD
GRILLED FRENCH BREAD
HERB DIP • MUSTARD SAUCE
BROILED PEACHES • ICE CREAM
COFFEE • MILK

Prepare the vegetables at home and take them along, packed in ice, in Skotch Koolers. Put your herb dip in a jar or plastic container and pack it in the Kooler with the vegetables to keep fresh. Foil-baked corn is simple and wonderful. Strip the corn of its husks and silk, wash well, discarding all bad parts. Do not dry it, as a bit of moisture is desirable. Wrap well in a double thickness of foil and twist the ends to seal. This can all be done at home the night before the journey and refrigerated. Roast on the grill and serve. Each person opens the ends and adds melted butter, salt, and pepper. It is a wonderful way to butter your corn without hav-

ing the butter slide all over the place! Peel onions and slice about ¼ inch thick, dip them into melted butter, and then place them on the grill. Don't cook them too long. They should retain some of their crispness.

french potato salad

8 pounds potatoes
2 pounds sliced onions
1½ cups chopped parsley
1½ quarts French dressing
Hard-boiled eggs for garnish

Let the potatoes cool, then peel them. Slice about ⅛ inch thick. Make the French dressing in a large bowl, using 3 parts oil to 1 part vinegar, and salt and pepper to taste. Add the other ingredients, and let mixture stand overnight to permit flavors to blend.

portable salmon salad

4 one-pound cans of salmon
3 cups finely chopped celery
6 finely chopped hard-boiled eggs
½ cup chopped onion
½ cup chopped parsley
½ cup whole seedless grapes
2 cups mayonnaise
2 tablespoons chopped dill
Salt and pepper

Mix all ingredients well and sprinkle with chopped dill.

herb dip

1 quart sour cream
1 tablespoon salt
2 tablespoons finely chopped garlic
½ cup chopped parsley
¼ cup chopped dill

Herb dips can, of course, be varied by using different herb combinations. Parsley, chives, and tarragon blend nicely with sour cream. Mayonnaise also can be added to the cream.

mustard sauce

Mix together 1 cup of sour cream and ½ cup of French's mustard. Add chopped chives, tarragon, and a bit of vinegar to taste. Keep cold.

broiled peaches

For 25 people, you will need from 12 to 15 peaches. Prepare them the day before, or, at the latest, in the morning of the day of your outing. Scald and skin fresh, ripe peaches and plunge them into acidulated water at once to prevent darkening. Drain and sprinkle with sugar and lemon juice and pack into glass or plastic jars. Keep cold until ready to use. Broil peaches until golden on both sides. Fine-quality canned peach halves, sprinkled with brown sugar, may also be grilled. Garnish with currant jelly.

fishing cookout

equipment

PORTABLE ICE BOXES • LARGE COOKING POT
SMALLER POT • FOIL • PLASTIC CLOTH
KNIVES AND FORKS • PLATES • GLASSWARE
PAPER NAPKINS • CUPS OR MUGS

menu

JUGS OF MARTINIS AND MANHATTANS
RAW VEGETABLES • CHEESE BISCUITS
TRUITE AU BLEU
POTATOES IN THEIR JACKETS
MELTED BUTTER • TOSSED GREEN SALAD
CHEESES • FRUIT • FRENCH BREAD
CHILLED CHABLIS • COFFEE

truite au bleu

The name of this dish is derived from the metallic-blue color the trout becomes when it is taken from the lake or stream and put directly into the pot. Prepare a court bouillon of 3 parts water to 1 part vinegar. Add 6 peppercorns, bay leaf, and 1 teaspoon salt to each quart of liquid. Bring this to a boil. Plunge the trout in just long enough to cook through. About 4 minutes should do nicely. The trout should be flaky and break away from the bone easily when tested with a fork. Serve at once with melted butter, lemons, and boiled potatoes. You will need 1 or 2 potatoes per person.

old-fashioned chicken fry

menu

MARTINIS IN PITCHERS
FRIED CHICKEN-IN-THE-ROUGH WITH BACON
FRIED POTATOES • ROASTED TOMATOES
EGG-AND-BEET SALAD
HOMEMADE BREAD AND BUTTER
STRAWBERRY PRESERVE
FRESH CHERRY PIE
BEER • COFFEE

Take along plenty of bread and be prepared with lots of sweet butter and strawberry preserves. You may bake the cherry pies at home according to a favorite recipe, or purchase them from a good bakery. For 20 people, you should have 3 or 4 pies.

fried chicken with bacon

To serve 20 people adequately you will need 10 chickens. And for 10 chickens you will need 3 or 4 skillets. Try out 8 strips of bacon in each skillet. Remove the bacon to absorbent paper and add the floured chicken to the pan. It is wise to put the dark meat in separate skillets because it takes a little longer to cook than white meat. Fry the chicken, skin side down, until nicely browned. Turn and brown on the bone side. Cover the skillets—with foil if you have no covers—adding just a little water or white wine to each skillet. Test for tenderness after about 10 or 12 minutes. Remove the covers and allow the chicken to finish cooking. Serve with bacon strips.

egg-and-beet salad

4 cans diced beets
10 coarsely chopped hard-boiled eggs
1 cup cut green onions
Mayonnaise to bind

Mix ingredients together and carry in your portable ice box, along with greens and extra mayonnaise.

buffet for 20 people

menu

CROWN OF ROAST PORK FILLED WITH
WALDORF SALAD
COLD BREAST OF DUCK, CUMBERLAND SAUCE
CHERRY-ALMOND SALAD
LOBSTER-AND-SHRIMP CURRY WITH CONDIMENTS
NOODLES
PÊCHES IMPÉRIALE
MERINGUES
ESPRESSO AND AMERICAN COFFEE

Drinks
MUSCADET • ALMADEN ROSÉ
BEAUJOLAIS • BEER

crown roast of pork

Have the butcher make 2 crown roasts for you. Be sure that you cover each bone with a piece of foil or a small piece of parchment paper to protect it while roasting. Season the pork with salt and pepper and a bit of thyme. Roast in the oven at 300 F. until crowns reach an internal temperature of about 170 F. They will take about 20 to 25 minutes a pound. Let the roasts cool. Place paper frills on each bone and fill the center of each crown with a mound of Waldorf salad. Make the salad by combining 1 quart each of peeled and unpeeled diced apples, 1 quart diced celery, and 2 cups of walnuts, cut coarsely. Blend with mayonnaise.

cold breast of duck

When roasting duck, you must forget the rules that apply to all other poultry, except goose. Duck and goose are insulated all over with a layer of fat and require long roasting at low temperatures to break down the tissues and drain off the excess fat. Basting at frequent intervals will assure a crisp skin. Clean the duck well and remove any bits of stray fat; salt and pepper it, and roast. You may spit-roast or roast in the oven; you'll need 6 to 8 ducklings for 20 people.

When the ducks have cooled, remove the breasts and save the rest of the meat for a salmi or a salad. Arrange on a platter with a mound of cherry-almond salad.

cherry-almond salad

1½ quarts pitted black cherries
2 cups blanched, toasted almonds
⅔ cup olive oil
¼ cup white vinegar
¼ cup sherry wine
1 teaspoon dry mustard
Salt

Combine the 1½ quarts of pitted black cherries with the 2 cups of blanched, toasted almonds. Use a dressing made with the olive oil, white vinegar, sherry, and dry mustard. Salt to taste.

lobster-and-shrimp curry

6 tablespoons butter
2 sliced onions
¼ teaspoon powdered cinnamon
¼ teaspoon powdered cloves
½ teaspoon cumin
¼ teaspoon chili powder
1 tablespoon coriander
1 tablespoon turmeric
2 sliced tomatoes
½ teaspoon salt
½ teaspoon sugar
1 tablespoon lime juice
4 cups coconut milk
or 2 cups evaporated milk
2 finely minced or crushed garlic cloves
3 pounds lobster meat
1 pound shelled shrimp
1 cucumber

Melt half the butter and fry the sliced onions with all the spices and tomatoes. Mix well and add salt, sugar, lime juice, and milk. Simmer on a very low heat for 15 minutes. In another pan, melt the remaining butter and lightly fry the garlic. Add the lobster meat and the shrimp. Be sure that they are liberally coated with butter. Cook for 5 minutes. Reduce the milk-and-spice mixture about ⅓ by cooking it over a brisk flame, stirring constantly. Add the thinly sliced cucumber to the liquid and cook for 5 more minutes. Add the lobster and shrimp and heat through. Serve with the following complements:

Raisins soaked in cognac.

Hard-cooked egg whites and yolks served chopped and separate.

Peanuts sautéed in clarified butter and served immediately.

Paper-thin slices of cucumber marinated in a very sharp vinegar with salt and pepper, drained, and served with chopped coriander.

Fresh coconut chutney made by grating coconut and adding enough cayenne pepper to make it quite hot.

A big bowl of noodles with butter, chopped chives, and poppy seeds added.

A bowl of sliced, ripe tomatoes with the following sauce: Pound in a mortar, garlic, grated Parmesan cheese, pine nuts, and parsley. Add olive oil, drop by drop, as though you were making a mayonnaise. This sauce should have a definite green color; the addition of basil leaves will accomplish this, as well as complement the tomato.

pêches impériale

You will need about 25 or 30 peaches. Prepare a syrup made with 4 cups of sugar and 2 cups of water flavored with a 1-inch piece of vanilla bean. Allow to come to a boil and simmer for 5 to 6 minutes. Add the peaches and poach them until they are just pierceable but not cooked through. Remove them from the syrup to cool and let the syrup cook down a little. Prepare a sauce by forcing 3 to 4 packages frozen raspberries through a fine sieve, or blending them in a blender. Add 1 cup sugar and bring to a boil. Let it boil for just 3 minutes. Cool, make a pyramid of peaches in a serving dish, spoon the raspberry purée over them, and chill very well. Serve with whipped cream which has been flavored with a little raspberry liqueur or framboise.

teen-age party

menu

HAMBURGERS • FRANKFURTERS
SAUERKRAUT • BAKED BEANS
ROLLS
MUSTARD • RELISHES
POTATO CHIPS
PEANUTS • PRETZELS
MILK • SOFT DRINKS

This is an all-day affair and the key words with hungry, restless teen-agers are quantity and variety. Young people need lots to eat and plenty to do, so provide them with such entertainment as records, radio, television, and home movies, and let them do a good share of the cooking. I find that kids like to show their skill with skillet and tongs. In addition to the basic menu, try to have as many assorted relishes, spreads, quickie drink mixes, and cold cuts as possible. Rolls should be of different sizes and shapes—and include some loaves of French bread for the hero-sandwich fanciers. Also some pizza mix for the do-it-yourselfers. Ice cream, cakes, and popcorn are wonderful extra treats. If you think you are serving too much, don't worry about it. If the initial guests don't take care of it, they have friends who will!

cocktail party for 100

Parties of this size are *tours de force*. Done properly they can be brilliant; done in a disorganized fashion, they can be tragic. You'll need help—lots of it. Press all able-bodied members of the family into service, and hire professional assistance for strategic jobs, such as bartending. Estimate at least 3 drinks per person and plan to get from 17 to 20 drinks from a quart bottle of liquor. Be certain that you have soft drinks, in addition to tomato juice, lemonade, beer, Coca-Cola, and so forth.

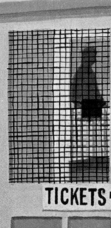

EASTWOOD ANNUAL

BAR-B
& BAZAAR

TICKETS ➤

A COURTLY FEAST, 13TH CENTURY FRENCH MANUSCRIPT.
PIERPONT MORGAN LIBRARY.

menu

Drinks

GIN • WHISKEY • RUM
SHERRY • CHILLED WHITE WINE CASSIS
CHAMPAGNE BOWL
WITH RASPBERRIES AND RASPBERRY SHERBET
TOMATO JUICE • LEMONADE

Hot Canapés

HOT SPITTED TURKEY • BARBECUE SAUCE
THIN-SLICED RYE BREAD
HOT PRIME RIBS OF BEEF
PUMPERNICKEL • MUSTARD BUTTER
SHASHLIK
SHRIMP BROCHETTES WITH GARLIC BUTTER
BROILED MARINATED GIZZARDS ON SKEWERS

Cold Dishes

TERRINE OF CANARD (A PATÉ OF DUCKLING)
VEGETABLES IN SEASON WITH MEXICAN HOT DIP

Desserts

BOWL OF FRUIT • TRAY OF CHEESES
BISCUITS • FRENCH BREAD

spitted meats — turkey and ribs of beef

2 turkeys
2 five-rib roasts of beef

Borrow one or two extra grills from your friends
and spit a turkey on one and a rib roast of beef
on the other, according to any of the recipes
given in the chapter on spitting that takes your
fancy. Start one turkey and one roast and have
them ready when guests arrive. Keep the remaining turkey and roast spitted for cooking
when the first ones are done.

shashlik

25 pounds of lamb
3 tablespoons garlic powder
3 tablespoons thyme
3 tablespoons salt
3 tablespoons pepper
Tomatoes
Green peppers

To serve 100 people, you will need at least 25 pounds of lamb. Marinate it for about 12 hours in enough red wine to cover. Add 3 tablespoons garlic powder, the thyme, and 3 tablespoons each salt and freshly ground black pepper. To skewer, use small-sized skewers and alternate pieces of lamb with tiny tomatoes and strips of green pepper.

broiled gizzards on skewers

Purchase about 5 pounds of gizzards, and clean and wash them thoroughly. Parboil them for about 1½ hours, then drain and cool them. Marinate gizzards for several hours in 1 cup soy sauce, 1 cup chopped onions, and several cloves of chopped garlic. Thread on skewers and broil over medium heat. Baste with marinade mixed with melted butter.

terrine of canard

1 Long Island duckling
1 one-inch strip of pork skin
1 leek
1 sprig thyme
1 stalk celery
1 bay leaf
4 cups bouillon or stock
1 pound chicken livers
1 pound lean pork
6 shallots
1 garlic clove
1 bunch chervil
5 eggs
1 tablespoon flour
1½ teaspoons salt
⅓ teaspoon pepper
¾ cup cognac
1 pound tongue
4 truffles
¼ pound larding pork
1 envelope plain gelatin
¼ cup cold water

Skin the duckling. To do this, cut duck skin along center of breast from neck to vent with a very sharp knife. Pull back skin, using tip of knife to cut connective tissue where necessary. Reserve skin. Cut the meat from the bones and reserve pieces of breast. Place bones, neck, and giblets in a large kettle, reserving the liver. Add pork skin, the leek, thyme, celery, and bay leaf to kettle. Then, add bouillon, or chicken bouillon cubes, and water. Cover, bring to a boil, and let simmer for 2 hours. Meanwhile, put duck meat, duck liver, chicken livers, and pork through food chopper, together with the shallots, garlic, and chervil. Add eggs to the chopped meats, one at a time, pounding well.

Use mortar and pestle or a heavy bowl and wooden spoon. Sprinkle in the flour, salt, and pepper, which you have previously mixed together. Add cognac, then mix well again.

With the duck skin, line the bottom of a large oval terrine, or 2½-quart casserole, or several smaller casseroles of equivalent size. To form paté carefully pour in half of the liver-egg mixture and arrange duck breast, fingers of tongue, and sliced truffles on top. Add remaining mixture. Top with thin strips of larding pork. Bake, uncovered, in slow oven, 300 F., for 2½ hours, or 1 hour per 1-quart casserole. When broth has been boiling slowly for about 2 hours, remove cover and turn up heat to let broth reduce to about 1½ cups, including fat. Strain broth and add gelatin which has been softened in cold water. Stir until gelatin is dissolved. When paté is removed from oven, pour broth into casserole over paté. Put a weight on paté to keep it submerged in the broth and let stand for 2 hours. Remove weight, cover casserole, and refrigerate. Chill thoroughly and serve paté as an hors d'oeuvre or as part of a cold meat platter; it can be sliced or spread, as desired.

hot dip

1 cup finely chopped onion
⅓ cup olive oil
2 cans red kidney beans
3 tablespoons chili powder
1½ teaspoons oregano
Tomato sauce

Sauté the onions in the olive oil until they are just limp. With a potato-masher, mash the 2 cans of red kidney beans, which have been drained, into the onions until you have almost a purée. Add 3 tablespoons chili powder, 1½ teaspoons oregano, and enough tomato sauce to moisten the beans well. Salt and pepper to taste and let simmer for 20 minutes. Correct the seasoning and force the mixture through a food mill or sieve. You may wish to add Worcestershire sauce or more chili, according to the degree of "hotness" you desire.

patio dinner for 15

menu

MARINATED EYE OF THE RIB, SPITTED
FOIL-ROASTED POTATOES
COLD STUFFED ZUCCHINI
CUCUMBERS AND TOMATOES
FRENCH BREAD WITH HERBED BUTTER
RYE BREAD WITH CARAWAY BUTTER
CHEESES
PINEAPPLES STUFFED WITH RASPBERRIES
CASSIS-FLAVORED WHIPPED CREAM
ICED AND HOT COFFEE
ICED TEA WITH JAMAICA RUM AND LEMON
LIGHTLY CHILLED BEAUJOLAIS

marinated eye of the rib

In the West, the eye of the rib is called the Spencer cut, and you'll need about 15 pounds of it to serve 15 people. Marinate it for several hours, brushing frequently with a mixture of ½ cup of soy sauce, 1 cup sherry, 3 tablespoons crushed, fresh ginger, 12 cloves chopped garlic. Be sure when you spit the roast that it is perfectly balanced; follow the procedure suggested in the spitting chapter. Roast over medium heat until it has reached an internal temperature of 120 F., for very rare. Remove meat from the spit to a carving board and let it stand about 10 minutes before carving.

cold stuffed zucchini

30 small zucchini
2 cups cooked rice
1 cup pine nuts
½ cup chopped, peeled, and seeded tomatoes
2 tablespoons chopped garlic
1 tablespoon sweet basil
1½ teaspoons salt
1 teaspoon freshly ground black pepper
½ cup olive oil

Cut the ends off zucchini and hollow out the centers with an apple corer. Blend the rice, tomatoes, pine nuts, and seasonings with ½ cup olive oil and stuff the zucchinis with the mixture. Arrange in a well-oiled baking dish. Bake at 350 F. for approximately 40 minutes, basting from time to time with the following baste: ½ cup each olive oil, white wine, and beef or chicken broth. Chill and serve cold.

cucumbers and tomatoes

Arrange thinly sliced tomatoes, cucumbers, and red onions on a large platter and serve with a dressing of 4 parts olive oil to 1 part cognac, seasoned with a little lemon juice, freshly ground pepper, salt, and a touch of fresh basil.

pineapples stuffed with raspberries

Cut 3 small pineapples lengthwise, keeping the leaves intact. Hollow out each half, remove the woody core, and dice the flesh. Combine it with 4 boxes of fresh raspberries that have been marinated in Eau de Vie de Framboise and a bit of sugar. Whip heavy cream and fold in a little cassis syrup to give it a nice pink color, as well as flavor. You may serve this 2 ways: Mix all together and pile lightly into the pineapple shells, or combine the fruits, pile into shells, and pipe the cream over it, garnishing with candied violets.

an evening party for 25

menu

WHITE WINE CASSIS OR CHAMPAGNE
SEAFOOD BROCHETTES PROVENÇALE
CUCUMBER SALAD
SPITTED SQUABS À LA RUSSE, FLAMBÉ
PISTACHIO-AND-PEPPER RICE
BOUQUET OF VEGETABLES
TOSSED GREENS WITH WHITE CORN KERNELS
HOMEMADE PEACH MOUSSE
FRENCH ROLLS, SWEET BUTTER

ESPRESSO AND AMERICAN COFFEE
TOASTED CHEESE SAVORIES

Drinks

POUILLY-FUISSÉ 1958 OR 1959
CHÂTEAU LÉOVILLE-LAS CASES 1952
FRAMBOISE • COGNAC

This is an ambitious party and you should plan to have four or five helpers in attendance. It is a special gathering and its success depends upon the ability of those assisting you to get things prepared, served, and quickly cleared away. Since this is a dressy occasion, the first course and the meat are the only outdoor-cooked dishes.

Toasted cheese savories are tiny sandwiches and should be served in the English tradition with the coffee.

seafood brochettes provençale

3 pounds scallops
3 pounds lobster meat
4 pounds large shrimp
3 pounds salmon cut in cubes

Marinate the seafood for several hours in 1 cup olive oil, 1 cup white wine, 1 cup chopped green onions, 1 cup chopped parsley, and 1 cup peeled, seeded, chopped tomatoes. Thread on skewers and grill over medium heat. Baste frequently with the marinade.

cucumber salad

Peel, seed, and slice 6 medium-sized cucumbers. Sprinkle with 1 tablespoon salt and cover with a well-seasoned mustard mayonnaise. Let the salad stand in the refrigerator for several hours before serving.

spitted squabs à la russe, flambé

Be sure to have a drip pan beneath the squabs to catch the juices which you will use later in the sauce. Roast the squabs, 1 per person. Baste with a mixture of white wine and butter, salt, and pepper. When they are finished, remove the juices from the drip pan and add 1 cup consommé and 2 cans of Franco-American brown gravy, which you have reduced to 1½ cups. Combine with 1 cup sour cream and season with salt, pepper, and ¼ cup cognac.

pistachio-and-pepper rice

Cook 4 cups rice according to your favorite method. Combine 1 cup melted butter, ½ cup chopped pistachio nuts, and ⅓ cup chopped green pepper. Add ¼ cup chopped parsley and toss with the rice.

bouquet of vegetables

Arrange every available young and tender sea- sonal vegetable in little groups or bundles. This is not too difficult; use tiny carrots, peas, pota- toes, artichoke hearts, beets, mushrooms, and tiny turnips. Cook in boiling water or in pres- sure cooker and serve with melted butter.

peach mousse

3 pounds ripe peaches, peeled and sliced
2 pounds sugar
2 quarts whipping cream
1 tablespoon vanilla

Peel and slice the peaches, then soak them with the sugar for an hour. Put them through a food mill or fine sieve to form a purée. Whip the cream and flavor it with the vanilla. Combine it with the peach purée. Pack it into a mold and put in the freezing compartment of the refrigerator, or in ice and salt, for several hours.

outdoor drinks *section* 8

DIAMOND CLARITY OF WINE LENDS ELEGANT NOTE TO OUTDOOR DINING.

COURTYARD SCENE OF FOREMAN AND LABORERS
WITH WINE CASKS, 15TH CENTURY
BURGUNDIAN TAPESTRY. TOLEDO MUSEUM OF ART.

Wine brings to light the hidden secrets of

the soul, gives being to our hopes, bids the coward

fight, drives dull care away, and teaches

new means for the accomplishment of our wishes.

HORACE

The first rule in serving good drinks is to be generous with the liquor. There is nothing worse than a weak drink. If you can't trust your eye, use a standard jigger, and remember that no matter what type of drink you are serving, it usually will require 1½ to 2 ounces of liquor to be made properly. When in doubt, stick to the rule that a little too much is better than not enough.

Be generous with the ice, too, and keep drinks refreshed by adding ice and liquor at intervals. If you are adding carbonated water or mixers, stir the drink just once or twice. Too much agitation dissipates the bubbles. Finally, serve drinks in glasses of good quality and spotlessly clean. It is amazing how the "feel" of a glass can affect the taste of a drink.

Drinks on the rocks and highballs are simplicity itself. You cannot go wrong if you are generous—but not overwhelming—with the liquor, and have plenty of ice and mixers on hand.

cocktails

Here are the correct proportions for some of the better-known cocktails you might like to serve before an outdoor-dining affair.

classic frozen daiquiri

2 ounces light rum
2 tablespoons lime juice
½ to 1 teaspoon sugar or sugar syrup
½ cup crushed ice

Combine in a blender and blend for 15 seconds. Pour into a wide-mouthed, stemmed glass.

VARIATIONS:

Mint Daiquiri: Add 4 to 5 mint leaves.

Banana Daiquiri: Add ½ banana in the blender.

Jamaica Daiquiri: Use dark Jamaica rum instead of light rum.

Pineapple Daiquiri: Add 1 slice ripe pineapple in the blender.

manhattan

A regular Manhattan consists of 3 parts rye to 1 part sweet vermouth. A dry Manhattan is 3 parts rye to 1 part dry vermouth. Pour over ice, stir, and pour into chilled glasses.

martini

Despite the living-room and cocktail-lounge battles that may rage over the proportion of vermouth to gin, I think what follows is the best martini going, unless, of course, you prefer to drink the gin straight. (But if you do, don't call it a martini!) Place 5 to 6 parts gin and 1 part dry vermouth in a pitcher half-filled with ice cubes, and stir until it is really cold. Strain into chilled glasses and twist lemon peel over each. Or, garnish with a small olive.

old fashioned

1 teaspoon sugar
Lemon peel
Dash of soda water
Dash of Angostura bitters

In an old-fashioned glass, crush the above ingredients with a muddler. Add cracked ice and 1½ to 2 ounces of any of the following: rye, Scotch, rum, bourbon, or cognac.

the perfect mint julep

Mint
1 teaspoon fine granulated sugar
3 ounces bourbon
Soda water

Crack enough ice, very fine, to fill a collins glass. Set the glass aside. Strip leaves from 2 springs of mint and muddle with sugar in another glass, then add a splash of soda water and the bourbon. Strain over the ice in the prepared glass and work a long-handled spoon up and down in the mixture until the outside begins to frost. Top with a splash of rum and decorate with a cherry and a sprig of mint. Shake some powdered sugar over the protruding mint sprig.

lillet

This delightful, aromatic French apéritif should become more popular in this country. It may be served right from the bottle, or on the rocks, or in a tall glass with ice cubes and plain water. It combines beautifully with gin in proportions of ⅓ gin to ⅔ Lillet. Serve with a twist of lemon peel.

gimlet

4 parts gin
2 parts Rose's Lime Juice
Cracked ice

Stir the gin and lime juice in a small pitcher as you would a martini. Pour the mixture into stemmed glasses filled with cracked ice.

suissesse

2 jiggers Pernod
5 dashes orgeat syrup
1 egg white

Shake ingredients together with ice until very frothy. Then strain into 2 old-fashioned glasses. (Orgeat—pronounced "or-zhat"—is a flavoring syrup prepared from almonds.)

collins

A collins made with gin is called a Tom Collins; otherwise, it gets its name from the kind of liquor used in it—Vodka Collins, Rum Collins, or Bourbon Collins. For each drink, combine in a cocktail shaker the juice of 1 freshly squeezed lemon or lime, ½ to 1 teaspoon sugar, and 3 ounces of the liquor of your choice. Add several ice cubes and shake vigorously. Pour

into a 12- to 14-ounce cocktail glass. Add more ice, if necessary, and fill glass with soda water. Decorate with a slice of lemon peel, cucumber, or a cherry.

sours

Place 1 part sugar syrup, 2 parts lime or lemon juice, and 8 parts of the spirit of your choice— bourbon, Scotch, rum, rye, cognac—in a container with cracked ice. Shake, and serve in sour glasses. Please omit the usual garnishes, such as cherries, lemon or orange slices.

rum daisy

1 part grenadine
2 parts lemon or lime juice
8 parts rum

Mix—do not shake—ingredients with cracked ice and pour into large goblets. Float a tablespoon of yellow chartreuse on top of each drink.

between the sheets

1 part Cointreau or Triple Sec
2 parts lime juice
3 parts brandy
3 parts Cuban rum

Shake well with crushed ice and serve with a twist of lemon peel.

bloody mary

1 jigger vodka
2 jiggers tomato juice
⅓ jigger lemon juice
1 dash Worcestershire sauce
Salt and pepper

Shake well with ice cubes; strain into glass.

pickled dilly

A variation on the Bloody Mary. Substitute dill-pickle juice for the lemon juice, and serve on the rocks with a spear of dill pickle.

MAN WITH THE WINE GLASS, BY VELASQUEZ.
TOLEDO MUSEUM OF ART, GIFT OF
EDWARD DRUMMOND LIBBEY, 1924

bull shot

Put ice cubes and a jigger of vodka in a double old-fashioned glass and fill with beef bouillon. Stir until chilled.

spritzers

These are light, delightful drinks for hot days. Put cracked ice in a tall glass and pour over it about 4 ounces of any wine you choose—claret, Rhine, Riesling, etc. For each drink cut a spiral of peel from a lemon or orange and place in the glass. Fill with soda water.

pimm's cups

These are mixed cups made with any one of three different liquor bases—No. 1 is gin, No. 2 Scotch, and No. 3 cognac. Place a small piece of cucumber rind or a slice of orange or lemon in a highball glass that has been filled with ice. Add 2 ounces of the Pimm's mixture of your choice, and fill with lemon soda, Seven-Up, or ginger beer. Stir and serve.

shandy gaff

This is half ale and half ginger ale. If you can find it, old, still ale is wonderful. Pour the ale first, then the ginger ale. Stir and serve.

punches

champagne punch

Peel, core, slice, and crush 3 ripe pineapples. Place in a large punch bowl and cover with 1 pound of powdered sugar. Let stand for about 2 hours. Then add 1 pint lemon juice, 4 ounces maraschino, 4 ounces Curaçao, 1 pint of cognac, and 1 pint of Jamaica rum. Mix thoroughly, cover, and allow to stand overnight to blend. When ready to serve, put a large cake of ice in the bowl and add 4 quarts of champagne. This recipe makes about 50 drinks.

strawberry champagne punch

2 boxes fresh strawberries
1 cup fine granulated sugar
1 bottle Moselle wine
2 bottles champagne
½ bottle claret

Hull the berries and put them into a large glass bowl that has been set in another larger bowl filled with cracked ice. Sprinkle the berries with sugar and pour the Moselle over them. Let it stand for 6 or 7 hours, then add chilled champagne, and the claret for color. Serve with a berry in each glass. About 25 cups.

fish-house punch

1 bottle Jamaica rum
1 bottle Cuban rum
1 bottle brandy
½ cup peach brandy
½ cup superfine sugar
3 cups lemon juice
2 quarts water

Combine ingredients in a large punch bowl, mix well, and let stand for 3 or 4 hours to blend. When ready to serve, place a block of ice in the bowl. About 60 cups.

artillery punch

1 quart strong tea
1 quart rye whiskey
1 bottle red wine
1 pint Jamaica rum
½ pint gin
½ pint brandy
1 jigger Benedictine
1 pint orange juice
½ pint lemon juice

Combine ingredients in a large punch bowl in which you have already placed a block of ice. If the blend is too dry for your taste, add a simple sugar syrup. About 45 cups.

claret cup

½ pint sugar syrup
½ pint lemon juice
4 ounces Curaçao
4 ounces pineapple juice
2 ounces maraschino
2 quarts claret
2 quarts soda water

Mix all ingredients except the soda water, which should be added when you are ready to serve. About 25 cups.

non-alcoholic drinks

50th state punch

Make a simple syrup by boiling together ½ cup sugar and 1 cup water. Let it cool. Combine 1 cup strong tea, 1 cup unsweetened pineapple juice, ¾ cup lemon juice, and ⅓ cup orange juice and chill this mixture. When you are ready to serve, pour all the ingredients into a large punch bowl containing a chunk of ice. Add 2 cups ginger ale and sweeten with the syrup to taste. Float orange slices, chunks of pineapple, and mint sprigs on top. This will serve 6.

cranberry punch

In a large punch bowl place ½ cup sugar and 1 cup boiling water. Stir until the sugar is dissolved. Add 4 cups cranberry juice (canned or bottled), 2 cups orange juice, and ½ cup lemon juice. Stir. When ready to serve, place a chunk of ice in the center of the bowl and add about 4 cups of chilled ginger ale. About 25 cups.

soft drinks and coolers

No outdoor function is complete without soft drinks. Served ice-cold in tall glasses, they are perfect refreshment for children and adults. I prefer those that are homemade—the lemonades and lime fizzes—but there are dozens of good commercial soft drinks available in about as many flavors as the imagination can contrive. Keep a variety on hand—and try mixing a couple of them for flavor variation.

lemonade

Make a simple sugar syrup (1 cup sugar and 1 cup water) in a saucepan. Heat, stirring constantly until the sugar dissolves; then bring to a full boil. For each serving, mix 3 or 4 tablespoons of syrup with 1½ tablespoons of lemon juice and 1 cup water. Pour into tall glasses filled with ice cubes, and garnish with mint sprigs and lemon slices.

lime fizz

For each fizz, combine in a shaker 1 tablespoon powdered sugar, the juice of 1 lime, and ice. Shake well, strain into a highball glass, and fill with soda water.

lime juice with bitters

Shake 3 dashes of bitters into a small glass and swirl the liquid around the bottom and sides. After coating the glass completely, pour off excess liquid. Add 2 ounces of lime juice and 2 or 3 ice cubes.

raspberry coolers

Use only pure, unadulterated raspberry syrup. There are some fine ones made in this country, but the best are imported from Germany, Switzerland, and France. Pour enough syrup into a tall glass to sweeten the mixture to your liking. Add cold water (carbonated if you prefer) and ice and stir.

grapefruit and apple mist

1 can (18 ounces) grapefruit juice
1½ cups apple juice or sweet cider
¼ cup lime juice
12 ounces ginger ale

Combine grapefruit, apple, and lime juice. Add sugar to taste, and chill. Add ginger ale just before serving. Pour over ice. Serves 6.

citrus party coolers

1 can (6 ounces) frozen
concentrated orange juice
1 can (6 ounces) frozen
concentrated grapefruit juice
4½ cups iced water
2 pints vanilla ice cream
1 pint chilled ginger ale or carbonated water

Combine concentrates with water in pitcher. Pour into 8 twelve-ounce glasses. Add large scoop ice cream to each glass and stir vigorously. Fill to top with ginger ale or carbonated water.

wines

Wine, like modern art, hi-fi, and growing a good lawn, can be as esoteric a specialty as you care to make it. Never forget, however, that it exists to be enjoyed and that the rituals of selection, serving, and tasting have evolved primarily to intensify this pleasure. Only incidentally are they ploys to disadvantage the vulgar, the hum-ble, and the innocent. Knowing what one likes is beginning enough with wine. After that, if the liking is truly keen, respect for wine will grow, and, with it, the impulse to savor wine fully by using it properly.

Much of what is somewhat pompously called "wine wisdom" is simple good sense. All wines are handled and uncorked gently, so that sediment in the bottle does not cloud the wine and impair its taste. The rigid prescription that wine should be drunk from a tulip-shaped, clear glass never filled more than half full, simply establishes the conditions for maximum enjoyment of two of wine's many sensuous delights: bouquet and color. Other rules are subtler and more esthetic, and worth heeding only if you feel subtle and esthetic. Only a purist will insist on white wine with chicken.

Here are some other cachets, all rooted in reason: Before-dinner wines should be dry; sweetness will cloy the taste for what's to come. Cocktails, unfortunately but invariably, detract from the taste of wine. White wines should be chilled. Red wines should be served at room temperature, which means uncorking an hour or so before serving to permit "breathing" and warming up from cellar temperature. Artificial warming of any sort will ruin wine. If you are serving several wines, serve the best one last. Red wine is better than white with cheese. Dessert wines are sweet. Champagne goes with anything.

the wines of france

Ungrudgingly, and with all due respect to the many superior and ever-improving American wines, it must be said that wine means French wine to most people. Actually, I think we should rejoice that such excellence survives and is so readily available. And we might also find modest pleasure in the fact that most of the great French wine today comes from the descendants of vines imported from the United States in the 1880's when Phylloxera, a plant louse, devastated the French wine industry.

Much has been written, most of it fascinating, about the patience, character, and finesse that is invested in the production of noble vintages. The significance of this for Americans lies principally in the guidance it affords for intelligent reading of French wine labels. For price is not an absolute criterion of value. Briefly, the label tells where the wine came from, who is responsible for it, and the year the grapes were grown. It may bear the name of a village, a château, or a particular vineyard. A Gevrey-Chambertin, for instance, may contain grapes from several vineyards in the little Burgundian village of that name. A Clos St. Jacques, however, can come only from certain acreage within Gevrey-Chambertin. And a Le Chambertin can come only from one specific parcel of land. This ascending scale of particularity guarantees the quality and refinement of the vintage. The inscription *mise en bouteille au château*—"château-bottled"—says further that the vintner bottled his wine on the premises. This not only assures that the wine was not diluted or stretched with baser product, but that the vintner's superlative judgment determined its readiness to be removed from the cask. A *négociant,* or wholesaler, on the other hand, will buy wine in bulk from many areas of a district and mix and bottle it under his own name. This may be excellent and honorable wine, but to the connoisseur it may suggest a grosser mingling of tastes and a less precise wine. (The reverse is true of champagne. Here all the great names are those, not of vintners, but of *négociants* whose sensitive blending of many white wines from the Champagne district northeast of Paris, and whose supervision of the process of effervescence, are the guarantee of quality wine.)

Only an expert taster can distinguish one vintage year from another, but it is important to know how vintages are rated because the uncertain climate of France can, on occasion, make even the greatest wines taste less than good. Vintage years have greatest meaning for red Burgundies and Bordeaux, which age, mature, and develop; less so for white wines, which are best drunk young, and no meaning for *vins ordinaire,* which have no future at all. It is an interesting game to buy several vintages of one wine and see whether you can discriminate among, say, 1952, 1953, and 1955. In addition to these great years, we also have 1959. For quality and quantity this will continue to be one of the fabulous vintages of the century. It will be wise to buy it and lay away. You will enjoy it for years to come.

a brief guide

If wines really interest you, find an enthusiastic wine merchant with a well-stocked store and gradually educate yourself with his help. What follows are simply a few of the known and respected landmarks among the many varieties of wine to spur your curiosity.

Bordeaux: Or claret. Instantly identifiable because of its high-shouldered, short-necked bottle. Bordeaux labels also carry an indication of the *crû,* or growth, of the wine, a scale of excellence established in 1855 and still a good guide, though not infallible. The Médoc district produces the greatest *premier crû* Bordeaux: Châteaux Margaux, Latour, Lafite-Rothschild, all of which are relatively scarce and perishingly expensive. Among second growths are Mouton-Rothschild, Léoville Las Cases, Cos d'Estournel. Among third growths: Château Palmer, Brane-Cantenac, occasionally Château d'Issan. All of these are brilliant, delicate, distinctive. Other good districts are St. Émilion, Pomerol, and Graves, which is the home of the famous Château Haut-Brion, whose vintages moved Dryden to song in the seventeenth century. South of Bordeaux is Sauternes, producer of great white wines, among them the fabulous, long-lived Château d'Yquem.

Burgundy: These bottles have a long, tapering neck and a fatter base than the Bordeaux. The best come from a painfully small strip of land running, roughly, between Beaune and Dijon and known as the Côte d'Or. Here, as in Bordeaux, the wines emerge from an elaborate

subdivision of regions, districts, villages, and acres, each flinty patch of soil, tilted gently to face the eastern sun, producing precious elixirs whose names are reverenced wherever wine is drunk. The majestic reds, the "big Burgundies," deeply colored, full-flavored, and richly fragrant, come from Vosne-Romanée, Gevrey-Chambertin, and Nuits-Saint-Georges. Lighter, more delicate, fruitier reds come from Volnay, Pommard, Beaune, and Chambolle-Musigny. Burgundy abounds in great whites, as well. Almost anything from the villages of Puligny-Montrachet and Chassagne-Montrachet are fine. The Meursaults are good; so are the Pouilly-Fuissés.

Other Wines: Once past the grand Burgundies and Bordeaux, high principles and exacting standards can be relaxed. Most of the other wines of France are for fun. *Beaujolais,* for instance. In terms of quantity drunk, this is the most popular wine in France. It is pleasant, clean-tasting, and inexpensive, a good, all-purpose red. It is the only red that takes chilling well, and it also "travels well," which simply means that it can jiggle and jounce in the back of your car en route to a picnic without ill effects. *Rosé* is, equally, a light, refreshing, informal wine with an even wider range than Beaujolais. It should be served cold and goes with almost everything. (It is not a mixture of white and red wines, incidentally, but gets its pink color from the fact that the grape skins are removed from the pressing before they have colored the juice too red.) The best rosés come from the village of Tavel; look for the name. The best Loire valley wines are light, carefree whites — *Pouilly-Fumé,* dry *Sancerre,* the soft and fruity *Vouvrays,* and the spirited *Muscadet,* for instance—again wines that should be chilled. The Rhone valley produces some very distinguished reds and whites, but these are not well-known in America. The reds, particularly, have a lusty, earthy quality and go well with red meats. The *Châteauneuf-du-Pape,* which dates back to the time of the Popes in Avignon, is a good starting point. Also try some of the white *Hermitage* wines. Alsatian wines are mostly white and flowery and somewhat similar to the German varieties produced across the Rhine. All are identified by the variety of grape used; *Riesling* is bone-dry and sharp, *Traminer* and *Gewurztraminer* are highly perfumed and go well as apéritifs or with fish, eggs, and light suppers; *Sylvaner* is mild, innocuous.

Champagne: Elegant, and expensive as elegance usually is. There are no bargains here. The top dozen names in champagne are all excellent. What you must look for, however, is the degree of dryness that suits your palate. *Brut* — also called English Market or English Cuvée—is the driest champagne made, which simply means that it contains the least amount of sugar necessary to produce effervescence in the bottle. *Extra Dry* actually is about two per

cent sweeter than Brut. *Sec,* which, of course, means "dry" in French, is six per cent sweeter than Brut. *Demi-sec* and *Doux* are both very sweet. Serve champagne cold—that is, around 45-50 degrees Fahrenheit. Warm champagne goes flat, too-cold champagne loses its flavor. Uncork champagne carefully. A popping cork and a spill-over waste wine. Wrapping the bottle in a napkin is an affectation which serves principally to conceal the label, of which you might well be proud. Remember, champagne comes in Magnums (2 bottles), Jeroboams (4 bottles), and so on up to Nebuchadnezzars, the equivalent of 20 bottles. These are wonderfully dramatic and impressive to display if you are planning a large party.

american wines

America today produces excellent wines. There is no reason to have any doubts about serving a good domestic wine at a grand occasion or with a fine meal. The two major areas of wine production are California and New York. The California vintners have long grown the same grape varieties that are used in France. The finest of the wines produced from these are known as varietal, or premium wines, and bear the imprint of the grape from which they are made. Although vintage years are indicated on the labels of several American vintners, they are generally not very meaningful. American wines are virtually uniform in quality from year to year. Here are some outstanding wines from the leading American vintners:

Almaden: Grenache Rosé — first among the rosés. Pinot Noir—resembles the French Burgundy. Cabernet Sauvignon — a full-bodied, aromatic red made from the Bordeaux grape. Pinot Chardonnay—a delightful white wine for summer drinking. Brut—an extremely good and very dry champagne.

Louis Martini: Zinfandel — a delightful red wine. Mountain Red—available in one-half and gallon jugs, this is a perfect wine for trips and tours; also Mountain White.

Charles Krug: Grey Riesling—a delicate, delicious white wine.

Beaulieu Vineyards: Beaumont and Beauclair —fine white and red from a fine vineyard.

Wente Brothers: Dry Semillon and Sauvignon Blanc are great favorites from this vineyard's renowned whites.

Inglenook: Produces a very fine cabernet.

Cresta Blanca: Produces excellent still wines and a particularly good sherry.

Souverain: Although production is limited, it has an extremely good rosé.

Paul Masson: Gamay Beaujolais and Pinot Noir are both very good.

Korbel: Well-known for fine champagne.

In New York State, most of the wines are from native vines, although many hybrids are being planted. The wines are delicious and very distinctive in flavor. Some of the best vintners are:

Widmer's: Isabella, Catawba, and several good wines of the Rhine and Moselle variety.

Taylor's: Best-known for champagne, but also produces very good Burgundy-type and claret.

Charles Fournier: Fournier Natur—an extraordinarily interesting American wine, similar to a still champagne of France.

Great Western: Famous for fine champagne.

italian wines

The Italians drink wine as we drink water. Many of the wines imported from Italy are delicious and especially pleasant for summer drinking. Among the white wines, I suggest *Soave, Verdicchio Di Jesi,* and *Orvieto.* These are light wines and should be served well-chilled. The reds most appropriate for summer are *Valpolicella,* sometimes served lightly chilled, *Barolo, Barbera,* and, of course, the famous *Chiantis.*

LE PETIT DÉJEUNER, BY JUAN GRIS.
GALERIE LOUISE LEIRIS (DROITS RÉSERVÉS A.D.A.G.P., 1960).

liqueurs

Liqueurs not only contribute a contrasting sweetness to the drinking of after-dinner coffee, but serve as intriguing sauces for fruit or ice-cream desserts. In fact, on occasion, a liqueur can itself be a satisfactory dessert. The principal liqueurs, most of them distillates of fruit essences, are: *Ananas* (pineapple), *Anisette* (licorice), *Apricotine* (one of several apricot liqueurs), *Banane, Benedictine, Blackberry, Chartreuse* (yellow type is mild, green considerably stronger), *Cherry Heering, Cointreau* (orange), *Crème de Cacao* (comes cocoa colored or as a clear liquor), *Crème de Cassis* (black currants), *Crème de Menthe* (mint; comes in green or as clear liquor), *Crème de Noyaux* (peaches and apricots), *Curaçao* (orange), *Drambuie* (scotch and honey), *Goldwasser* (contains flakes of 22-carat gold; heavy and sweet), *Grand Marnier* (orange-flavored, cognac base), *Kahlua* (coffee), *Kümmel* (caraway), *Southern Comfort* (bourbon base), *Strega* (similar to chartreuse), *Tia Maria* (rum base with coffee and cocoa added).

coffee

Coffee is the accepted finishing touch to any meal—simple or elegant, indoors or out, and no matter what time of the day it is served. Yet coffee-making is the Waterloo of all too many cooks. They find a palatable cup impossible to make, or think it simply a matter of luck. To me, there seems no reason to spoil an excellent repast with badly brewed coffee when, by following a few simple rules, you can make a delicious, satisfying cup. First, remember it is impossible to make anything but dreadful coffee in an unkempt pot. Coffee contains many oils which will collect on the sides and in the crevices of the coffee maker and turn rancid unless the pot is properly washed after each use. Secondly, use fresh coffee and the proper grind for your coffee maker. Rinse pot in hot water; if you are using a drip pot, heat it slightly on the stove before you pour in the water, so that the coffee hits a warm surface. Use fresh water and the proper-sized pot for the amount of coffee you need. Don't make 2 cups in an 8-cup coffee maker. Never brew less than three-quarters of the pot's capacity. And serve your brew steaming hot.

iced coffee

Good iced coffee may be made from regular-strength coffee cooled in the refrigerator, then poured over ice in a tall glass. Or, you may pour regular coffee into the freezing trays of your refrigerator, make coffee ice cubes, and pour regular hot coffee over them. My favorite way is to make hot coffee, double strength, then pour it over ice cubes.

old-fashioned boiled coffee

This is best made in a large, enameled coffee pot. Use 1 heaping tablespoon of coffee for each cup of water and 1 tablespoon for the pot. Break a whole egg into the coffee grounds and mix it up, then add the shell. Add cold water, stuff the spout of the pot with tissue paper, and bring water to a boil. Let it boil slowly for half a minute, add ½ cup ice-cold water and take the pot off the heat. Let it settle in a warm place for 4 to 5 minutes.

café royale

Place a lump of sugar in a spoon and set it across a cup of hot, black coffee. Pour cognac over the sugar. Let it warm for a few seconds, then ignite the cognac. Slide the flaming sugar into the coffee.

jamocha

This can be espresso or a very strong blend of regular coffee. Add 1 ounce Jamaica rum, whipped cream and sugar to taste. Serve in a cup or a glass with a holder.

irish coffee

Use a very strong blend. For each cup of coffee, use 2 teaspoons sugar and about 2 tablespoons Irish whiskey. Top with whipped cream.

viennese coffee

Use a large cup and fill it ¾ full with very hot coffee, sweeten to taste, and float a huge dollop of sweetened whipped cream on top.

espresso

The Italian term "espresso" really signifies two things: a particular roast and a method of brewing. In Italy, coffee is roasted to an oily blackness, producing an extremely rich and colorful brew. To be properly prepared, this coffee must be finely ground, and live steam should be passed through it. The droplets produced by the steaming process are caught in demitasses. The procedure can be as elaborate as the brewing machine, which resembles an enormous boiler and costs a small fortune. Today, however, hundreds of variations on the steam method exist, and many have been adapted for home use. One that is quite simple and inexpensive is the little Neapolitan *macchinetta,* which looks like a drip pot and operates on much the same principle. If you like espresso coffee, I suggest you investigate this.

cappucino

Make Italian or strong roast coffee. Combine with the same quantity of steaming milk. Pour into tall cups and sprinkle cinnamon or nutmeg over the top.

iced cinnamon coffee

Pour 4 cups of hot, strong coffee over 3 sticks of cinnamon and let stand for about 1 hour. Remove the cinnamon sticks and sweeten coffee to taste. Add about ½ cup heavy cream and chill. Pour over cracked ice in tall glasses and use the cinnamon sticks as stirrers. Try this either with regular strong coffee or with espresso.

coffee mocha

To 2 cups hot Italian coffee add an equal amount of hot chocolate. Top with sweetened whipped cream and sprinkle with grated orange peel. This is also wonderful iced.

tea

The rules for making good tea are practically the same as those for coffee. The teapot—preferably earthenware, china, or glass—should be scrupulously clean. (If you use a sterling silver pot, be sure it is free of silver-polish deposits.) Rinse your pot after each use in clear, scalding water. Don't use soap; it leaves a film and a taste. Use fresh, cold water to start and allow it to boil furiously. Rinse the pot with some boiling water before you add the tea. For most people, 1 heaping teaspoon per cup and "1 for the pot" is about right. Pour boiling water over the tea, cover the pot, and let steep—stirring occasionally—for 4 to 6 minutes. Serve tea very hot.

the larder *section* 9

Our cellar in the month of October was a picture

to behold: newly smoked hams and sausages, Gravenstein

apples filling the air with fragrance, root

vegetables, wheels of cheese—all these bespoke the

glories that would be ours in the coming winter.

A properly functioning kitchen requires a well-stocked larder, and both need planning. I will not attempt to list everything you should stock in your larder, but the following suggestions may be useful to you in implementing meals—or improvising when the chicken burns. I have listed the food I like to find in my larder when I plan a meal, and I have given, in most cases, brief comments on how to use them.

canned vegetables

Asparagus Spears: Make superb salads. Sprinkled with grated Parmesan cheese or with bacon crumbles, they serve as a good hot vegetable.

Baked Beans: Combined with bacon, garlic, and sausages, and a touch of vinegar to drown the sweetness, they are constantly useful.

Beets: May be used wherever fresh beets are called for. Also try them with a little vinegar, onion, and sour cream, served cold.

Celery Hearts: Marinate in your favorite French dressing and serve as a salad with strips of pimiento and you will find you have a superbly good appetizer. Heated in their juices and served with hollandaise, they are excellent.

Corn: Try the whole kernel corn marinated with French dressing and served with thin-sliced onion rings.

Kidney Beans: They make good salads and hot dishes, as various recipes elsewhere indicate.

Green Beans: Try heating them with parsley, cooked bacon, a little soy sauce, and a touch of chopped garlic.

Mushrooms: Chop very fine, sauté in butter, a dash of onion, and plenty of freshly ground pepper. Heap on pieces of toast for a quick snack while you wait for the steak to broil.

Peas: These have a tremendously wide range of uses. The tiny French ones, some of which are canned in this country, are considered to be the classic vegetable for formal entertaining. The big ones come in varying degrees of sweetness and may be used plain, or mashed with potatoes, or whole, mixed with rice.

Potatoes: Canned potatoes heated with some brown butter and a little curry powder are sensationally good. Or, they may be sliced, marinated with a basic French dressing, combined with chopped green onions, shredded cucumber, and parsley for an unusually good salad.

Tomatoes: Solid-pack tomatoes may be chopped and cooked down with butter and basil for a basic tomato sauce. Use your seasoning sense for a variety of ways to use tomatoes in sauces. Also, put solid-pack tomatoes through a blender and season well with Tabasco, Worcestershire, lemon juice, and fresh basil. Chill well for the best tomato juice you ever drank.

Tomato Purée: Many people confuse purée and paste. Purée merely means strained tomato pulp. Paste means concentrated, thick, flavored tomato meat.

Tomato Juice: There are so many different brands and grades that it behooves the good cook to taste-test several kinds before deciding on the best one for her. In making Bloody Marys you will find that if you combine a little tomato paste with tomato juice, your cocktail will not separate.

Sauerkraut: An ever-ready addition to many, many dishes. Cook with beer, with champagne, with white wine, or with broth. It may be combined with meats or served as a vegetable. It is also often served cooked, cooled, and mixed with a French dressing or a mayonnaise as a salad.

Wax Beans: They have a fascinating color when they are of good quality, and combined with fresh dill and a good French dressing, they make an excellent addition to any vegetable salad. Heated, with toasted almonds and plenty of butter and chopped parsley, they make a delicious dish.

soups

Asparagus: Combine with tomato soup and cream; it is most unusual. Or serve by itself with heated cream and grated Parmesan cheese.

Borsch: Combine with sour cream, serve chilled with a hot, boiled potato.

Bouillon: This is used in sauces, as an additive to marinades, and is combined with vegetables or meat leftovers—finely chopped or blended—to make soups. Try heating it with finely chopped boiled beef, onion, and hard-boiled eggs as a garnish.

Celery Soup: Add pea soup, cream, and grated onion, and serve with chopped parsley. Celery soup with bacon and a good dash of sherry is equally good.

Chicken Gumbo: Heat according to directions and serve with a large dollop of sour cream.

Clam Chowder: Serve with a little sprinkling of thyme, heavy cream, and crisp bacon crumbled on top.

Consommé: Combine with claret. Given a healthy infusion of chopped chives and slices of marrow, it is even better. Combine a can of consommé with a can of peas, add some onions and put through the blender. Heat, add a little sherry and serve with salted, whipped cream. A sensational beginning to an outdoor meal on a cool evening.

Cream of Chicken: Serve with curry and cream, and accompany with crisp, toasted noodles.

Cream of Mushroom: With chopped, hard-boiled eggs, curry and sour cream, this makes a very exciting soup.

Lobster Bisque: Add Madeira or sherry and 1 tablespoon of chopped lobster meat on top of each cup; a good soup and a substantial one.

Onion-soup Mix: Chicken broth with a white wine added to it instead of water makes a truly Epicurean soup. Or, try it with beef broth instead of water and place it in a casserole with grated Gruyère cheese and a jigger of port wine. Bake in the oven for 20 minutes at 375 F. Serve with garlicked French bread.

Pea Soup: Combine with cream, chopped fresh mint, and some chicken broth. Chill and serve with chopped parsley.

Tomato Soup: Combine tomato soup with chopped, fresh basil, chopped chives and parsley, and sour cream. Shake in a cocktail shaker with ice for a quick, easily chilled soup.

Vichysoisse: Combine frozen or fresh-cooked potato soup with cooked leeks and chicken broth put through a blender or food mill. Serve fresh or sour cream and chopped chives. Add a touch of nutmeg.

pastas

Macaroni: Try it with your favorite tomato sauce combined with garlic and tuna fish. Quick and easy and substantial.

Noodles: Excellent combined with a sauce

made of curry, tomato sauce, and browned, chopped beef.

Ravioli: Should be coated, rather than drowned, with sauce. If you wish, additional sauce can be served on the side. It is also very good served with butter and cheese only.

Rice: Cooked for a few minutes in olive oil or sesame oil, and steamed over boiling water, it is extremely good.

Spaghetti: Cook the way you like it, drain, drench with butter, and garnish with grated white truffles. Elegant.

canned fish

Anchovies: I always keep a half-dozen cans around. Fillets arranged on pieces of buttered toast make a superb bed for scrambled eggs. They come in handy for giving a fillip to sauces, to salads, and snacks.

Crabmeat: Add to celery soup with heavy cream and a dash of scotch whiskey.

Herring: I use it out of the tin for hors d'oeuvres. I often combine it with cold veal, apples, beets, potatoes, dill, and mayonnaise to bind, for an excellent salad.

Minced Clams: Cream, blend with corn, and combine with eggs; makes a fine soufflé.

Sardines: The boneless, skinless variety from Spain or France is the best by far. With hard-boiled eggs, thinly-sliced potatoes and onion rings, and romaine lettuce, sardines make a substantial salad. They are also delicious grilled or heated with a little curry. Serve on toast.

Shrimp: Canned shrimp blended or pressed with some heavy cream and mace to a paste-like consistency, seasoned with a little chive and parsley, make a quick and delicious dip or cocktail spread.

Tuna: Flaked and placed in a pie shell with a little onion, chopped parsley, and a cream-and-egg custard mixture, it makes an extremely good hot hors d'oeuvre.

Lobster: Combine with mushroom soup, curry, and a dash of sherry.

Smoked Oysters: Try folding them into scrambled eggs or an omelet.

meats

Beef Stew: Mix 1 can of potatoes, 1 can of onions, 2 cans of stew, and 1 cup red wine and you have a campers' Beef Bourguignonne.

Corned Beef: Chopped and combined with canned potatoes, it makes a hash superior to the canned ones. Add a chopped onion, and nutmeg for flavor.

Roast Beef Hash: For an unusual casserole, combine with onion-soup mix and sour cream, and bake for 20 minutes.

Tongue: Cut in shreds, combine with sliced, canned potatoes, onion slices, and sliced canned beets; mix with French dressing or mayonnaise.

Turkey: Sliced, canned turkey placed on a bed of canned, whole-kernel corn, with a sauce of cream of mushroom soup, topped with grated Parmesan cheese, gives you a sensational main dish in a hurry. Flavor it with a little sherry.

miscellaneous

I find the following items indispensable. *Foie gras:* Always a treat for cocktails or for a snack. I keep 6 or 8 cans on hand. *Green chilis:* Invaluable accent for many dishes. Not available everywhere, so when I find the California chilis I prefer, I get about a dozen cans. *Mole powder:* Essential if you are partial to Mexican food, as I am. Also *tortillas:* I buy them canned and serve them steamed, as bread. *Italian cannelini beans:* Canned variety is available in many supermarkets, otherwise in Italian groceries. They are excellent when drained, washed, and covered with a good French dressing; mix in some chopped raw onion, a little garlic, and a generous amount of chopped parsley. Or they may be used for a bean purée with meat sauce. Or they are fine in a cassoulet.

index

THE BREAKFAST ROOM, BY PIERRE BONNARD.
COLLECTION, THE MUSEUM OF MODERN ART, N. Y., GIVEN ANONYMOUSLY.

credits

"The Treasury of Outdoor Cooking" was fortunate in being able to use a number of private homes and grounds for its location photography. For this privilege the editors wish to thank: MISS CHERYL CRAWFORD, MRS. JOSHUA LOGAN, MRS. KENNETH MacLEISH, MME. HELENA RUBINSTEIN, MRS. SLOAN WILSON.